Longmans' business studies

Edited by D. C. Hague

THE MODERN ECONOMY

INDUSTRIAL EVOLUTION OF UK
Reasons for development of industry
Why the eighteenth century?
Why Britain first?

NINETEENTH CENTURY
Loss of self-sufficiency
Control of Capital
Trade Unions
British supremacy
Free trade
Growth of USA and Germany
Control of banking
Laissez-fair
Factory Acts-social legislation
Trade cycle
Expansion of Empire

TWENTIETH CENTURY
Interwar Depression
Decline of traditional industries
Growth of new industries
Unemployment
Exchange control
Cheap money

Postwar affluence
New major industries
The big firm
Automation
Growth of service industries
Mixed economy
International economic cooperation

Balance of payments
Industrial relations
Need to modernize
Overseas competition
International economic cooperation
Government control
Inflation
Stop-go economics
Commonwealth-imperial preference
Export problems
Growth areas
Population drift
Full employment
Sterling area – value of £
Capital investment
Bank rate, monetary policy
Export incentive
Increased productivity
Mobility of labour
Control of incomes and prices
Budget and fiscal policy
Common Market

MODERN UK INDUSTRY
Fuel and Power
Coal modernization and the future
Oil expansion since 1945
Electricity – conventional and nuclear
Gas – from oil, natural gas

Iron and steel
Changing location and size of plant
New techniques in steelmaking
Sources of ore
Control of investment

Engineering
Electrical engineering – fast growing products
– traditional products
Machine tools

Motor vehicles
Rapid growth since 1945
Contribution to exports
Problems of motor vehicle production
Trade unions and the industry

Shipbuilding
Fluctuations since 1945
Modernization of yards
Growth in size of ships
Container concept
World competition in 1960's

Chemicals and manmade fibres
Growth of the big firm
Petrochemicals and plastics
Dyes, paints, agricultural chemicals
Pharmaceuticals
Rayons and synthetic fibres v natural fibres

The modern British economy in historical perspective

K. S. Reader BA

Director of Liberal Studies
Rugby College of Engineering Technology

Longmans

Longmans, Green and Co Ltd

London and Harlow

Associated companies, branches and representatives
throughout the world

© Longmans, Green and Co Ltd 1969
First published 1969

SBN: 582 41029 0

Set in 10 on 13 pt Times New Roman
and printed in Great Britain by
Spottiswoode, Ballantyne and Co Ltd
London and Colchester

Contents

List of tables

List of tables

List of charts and diagrams

Acknowledgements

This volume spans such a wide field that it must draw upon work more highly specialized and detailed than mine.

Economic evolution

There are many excellent published works on economic evolution and where I have drawn upon these consciously I have made a note in the text. I am aware, however, that I must have subconsciously included a wealth of ideas and facts which I have accumulated from authors, teachers, and others, who have instructed me in one way or another in the past; their ideas must be liberally sprinkled throughout the text. I hope that they will understand if they are not acknowledged here. At the end of this volume there is a list of recommended reading which includes those titles that I have used in writing this book. Where a particular publication has been useful for the subject matter of a chapter I have mentioned it either in the text or in the references at the end of the book.

Modern industry

In general I have, over a long period of time, plundered the *Financial Times*, the *Financial Times Review of Industry*, *The Economist*, *The Times Review of Industry and Technology* (now, alas defunct) and the articles of the Industrial Editor of the *Sunday Times*. Without the splendid work that these publications do in constantly reporting the changing industrial scene, it would be well nigh impossible to keep up with the overall development of the economy. I acknowledge a very considerable debt to these publications and, where possible, I have attributed facts to them in the text.

The Chemical Industries Association Ltd, the Information Office of the Shipbuilders Conference and the British Electrical & Allied Manufacturers' Association Ltd, have all been especially helpful; I acknowledge the use of information that they kindly supplied.

Of those individuals who have helped me with the twofold task of eliminating foolish errors and suggesting additions and amendments, I would like to acknowledge in particular the assistance of Professor Hague, A. F. Stobart, B.Sc., C.Eng., A.M.I.Chem.E., who very kindly read the manuscript chapter on steel and made several constructive suggestions thereon, and L. S. A. Smith, M.A., A.R.I.C., A.M.B.I.M., who contributed helpful comments on the chapter on chemicals. These gentlemen are, of course, in no way responsible for any errors that remain.

Finally, I am greatly indebted to my wife for her ever cheerful assistance in typing the manuscript (all too often amended after the original draft had been typed!) and in preparing the book for publication.

Introduction

Britain has an advanced economy. The standard of living of her people is higher than that of the majority of other nations in the world and the capital she has amassed is sufficient to place her in the top league of the wealthy nations. It may appear to the casual eye that Britain, because she seems to move from one crisis to another and is constantly preoccupied with the problem of the balance of payments, is not a wealthy country. This is just not true. Expenditure may occasionally run too far ahead of income and there may be recurring currency problems but these do not indicate either poverty or stagnation but temporary imbalance. By almost any economic measurement Britain is well off. The problem of overcoming scarcities, the fundamental purpose of economic activity, has been overcome in Britain to a much higher degree than in most countries, if the British Economy is considered in the perspective of all the nations of the world.

If, on the other hand, the British Economy is considered in the context of the advanced economies of the world, then it must be said that Britain is not doing as well as might be expected. Some of her rivals, Germany, Japan and France in particular, appear to be achieving a steadily superior pace of economic growth, though certainly not in every respect of the economy. Generalizations such as these are liable to give dangerously wrong impressions unless they are backed by fuller information on how the British economy has reached its present stage of growth, and what the special factors are that present Britain with problems that are different from her economic competitors and which, accordingly, make comparisons with other economies difficult.

The purpose of this book is to outline the growth and present condition of the British economy so as to bring out these special factors which present problems that are peculiar to Britain in many ways. It is an attempt to draw together selected features of economic evolution and modern industry in order to give a background to the current economic scene in Britain. The apparent contradiction of our times, that Britain secures a dwindling share of world markets, and has a diminishing influence in world economic affairs while at the same time her standard of living rises steadily, has it is hoped, been put into some perspective.

The first part of the book attempts to illustrate those aspects of Britain's economic evolution which have been important in creating the present economic scene. It is not so much economic history as a selection of economic factors in Britain's evolution that have had such a lasting influence that their effect is still present in modern times. In the succeeding chapters those industries are surveyed that can be regarded as the staple industries of the modern British economy. The whole of British industry cannot be surveyed in a book of this kind, but in any case the intention is not to do this but to single out those industries which, for one reason or another, are of greatest significance to the economy. Because of the importance of the export trade to Britain, the major exporting industries have been included but so also have those industries which are basic to economic growth. The intention has been to demonstrate that British industry, while greatly affected by economic evolution, is undergoing change induced by rapid advances in technology and world industrial and trading patterns. The particular problems British industry has to face at the present times have been illustrated industry by industry, but it becomes clear that the problems of one have, in many instances, become the problem of all.

Finally the threads of economic evolution and presentday British industry are drawn together to illustrate the problems fundamental to the overall control of the modern British economy.

This book has arisen from a series of lectures given in the last few years to students of engineering and science who have, in conjunction with their main disciplines, studied the social and economic background of the society of which we are all a part. It is hoped that in addition to being useful to all such students, this book will be of value to general readers who are interested in relating the economic past to the economic problems of our times.

1

Britain's economic lead

Two hundred years ago the whole world was, to use the term in its modern sense, underdeveloped. There were disparities it is true, between one country and another, and it could be said that Western Europe was wealthier than any other world region, but the great difference that exists between the advanced and underdeveloped countries of today had not yet emerged. The first country to increase the pace of economic growth and hence set in motion this drawing apart of some nations from others was Britain. It was here that the industrial revolution started in the late eighteenth century, initiating the impetus for change which has subsequently profoundly influenced social, economic and political policies in practically every part of the world. The realization of a very high standard of living in countries which have undergone this process of change has provided an example which most people of the world are striving to emulate or to surpass. The methods Britain has used have been copied, altered and greatly changed; her mistakes have been avoided, and the long evolutionary process has been so successfully distilled that what took Britain two hundred years now need take a mere forty years, starting from scratch. The lead has been largely taken over by others, but the fact remains that the original 'take-off' (Rostow's now well-known terminology[1]) was in Britain.

Several questions pose themselves automatically. Why should development of this kind have taken place in the Western world, and why should the change, when it came, have taken place in Britain? Why, for that matter, should the change have come at the particular juncture of man's development? Was there something special about the latter part of the eighteenth century and was there something particular about the condition of Britain?

The answers to these questions warrant a book on their own and, indeed, much has already been written on this score. So many widely varying and interlocking factors are involved that for the purpose of this book fundamental reasons only can be considered, but they are very important.

Growth of Western Europe
The wide issue of the growth of Western Europe cannot be explained without reference to climate. The change to an industrialized society took place first of all in

3

the temperate zones, where the angle of the sun's rays varies considerably but it is never directly overhead. The weather particularly in the coastal regions is not given to extremes and for much of the year the temperature is conducive to an active life if man is to keep warm. Natural vegetation does not inhibit communication as it does in the zones nearer to the equator, nor do the snow and ice of the northerly regions make the pursuit of agriculture and the exploitation of raw materials very difficult. The peoples of Western Europe burst out of their own continent with the great voyages of discovery but, significantly, settled in appreciable numbers only where they found the climate to be equable; they used the other territories they acquired for economic exploitation only.

The climate of Western Europe is not sufficient on its own to explain economic advance. Religion, particularly the growth of Protestantism and the Dissenting movement, geography and the importance of the Atlantic seaboard in East-West trade, the social structure of the state and the disappearance of the slave society, psychology and the impact on the mind of the discovery of the New World, politics and the invasion of the cradle of early civilization by the Turks with the consequent disruption of the trade route to the East, all these have a bearing. One clear fact emerges, that the development of trade with the new markets overseas set Europeans on the trail for more goods with which to trade, thereby increasing a demand that led ultimately to new techniques of production.

Britain's lead

The voyages of discovery took place about the beginning of the sixteenth century. The development of the colonies and the building up of the overseas markets proceeded steadily from that time over a period of 250 years. The countries blessed with an Atlantic coastline, now so favourably placed between East and West, possessed the greater potential for expansion. Spain and Portugal, the two countries responsible for the greater part of the geographical discoveries, were sidetracked into a quest for gold and silver in South America, which territory they duly exploited for its precious metals. They did not give the priority to trade that the countries without the gold and silver deemed so important to progress. In consequence, the three countries that successfully entered the phase of overseas trade expansion and economic nationalism were France, Holland and Britain. These three developed economic empires which lasted well into the twentieth century and fought each other for the control of the seas and the trading routes. France and Holland both had land frontiers to protect and were involved to a greater degree than Britain in the wars on the mainland of Europe. Holland was held back too by her lack of population to police and administer an empire. Britain, protected by the Channel from military invasion, enjoyed an internal security and stability (save for the interruptions of the Civil War) which gave her the advantage in the long run. This advantage proved itself in the late eighteenth century and by the nineteenth century

Britain had developed into the wealthiest and hence most powerful nation the world had yet known.

During the long period of growth of overseas trade after the voyages of discovery the many preconditions for rapid economic growth evolved. Historians in analysing the causes of this rapid growth have successively laid emphasis on a number of contributory factors. Population growth went hand in hand with improved techniques in agriculture and the bringing of more land under arable cultivation, while medical science made advances which affected mortality rates. Turnpike roads were well developed by 1760 and significant improvements had been made to river navigation and dock facilities thus providing improved communications. Capital became readily available at low interest rates and the money and banking system, though far from perfect, was sophisticated enough and sufficiently flexible to cope with expansion when the time came. There were changes in education which provided the training for the middle class sons who wished to pursue a life in industry and commerce. Socioreligious changes helped to create a climate favourable to industry and trade. All these, taken in conjunction with the favourable geographical situation which Britain enjoyed, go a long way to explain why the emphasis on an industrial economy started in the last part of the eighteenth century and in Britain.*

The period of industrial change

The increased pace of economic growth in Britain permanently affected the economy. The period of transition to a predominantly industrial society took seventy or eighty years. The preceding paragraph demonstrates that the requisite conditions had been introduced over a long period. The work of the modern historian has emphasized that what was at one time looked upon as a fairly swift transformation was in fact a more gradual change, the result of evolution rather than revolution. The changes of this century have been more startling. The changes in living and working conditions, the way of life and the variety of goods available for mass consumption in the period 1900 to the 1960s have been much greater than the changes in the period 1760 to the 1830s. It is possible to say, however, that the basis of the economy was changed in that by the 1830s industry played a much more important part in the process of increasing the country's wealth.

This is not to say that Britain was a country devoid of industry before the end of the eighteenth century. The steady growth of trade had led to the development of widely varying industry which had already shown a marked tendency to specialization and localization. Wool, for example, the staple commodity of English trade and industry from the earliest days of commerce, was manufactured in East Anglia from packs of yarn that were brought in from as far afield as Yorkshire and

* For a comprehensive, up-to-date review of modern thinking on this subject see M. W. Flinn, *The Origins of the Industrial Revolution* (Longmans, 1966).

Westmorland. Woollen cloth was made in many parts of the country but certain areas had specialized. The West of England was famous for cloth of high quality, serges and fine flannels. Yorkshire was famous for its kersies. Leicester and Nottingham had developed a speciality of manufacture of stockings on frames. Glass was made in the Midlands, Bristol, the North-East, and the London area. Iron-making had been centred upon the regions where a plentiful supply of timber was available. As the timber was consumed, so the industry moved. Stafford was the major centre for iron in the early eighteenth century although with the growing shortage of timber the industry was declining. Birmingham had already developed a reputation for the manufacture of metal goods, and Sheffield had long been famous for its production of steel.

The demand for new techniques in production led to major advances in already existing industries and created new ones. Production under the existing domestic system organized on an outwork principle, was no longer an economic proposition. The factory system was necessary in order to take advantage of the new source of power (the steam powered machine was hardly suitable for the weaver's cottage!) and to reap the benefit of the economies of scale.

The industries which emerged as those of the greatest significance to the economy once the new techniques had been introduced, were the cotton textile industry, coal (now an industry in its own right), the chemical industry, the new industry of engineering, and the iron industry. All these were interdependent. Advance in one produced advances in the others. Demand for metal machinery (the early machines were wood, leather, and only part metal) stimulated the iron industry, and this in turn increased demand for coal. Demand for coal increased the need for efficient pumps to avoid flooding in the mines.

Engineering

Overall there was a need for engineers. One of the great difficulties of the earlier part of the period was a shortage of men capable of making the new machines and understanding their function.

Once the inventor had made the first working model of a machine, he had next to make the machine in quantity if it was to have a commercial application. James Watt was one of those who early encountered this problem. Roebuck's Carron Ironworks, on which he relied for his steam engine, was unable to provide craftsmanship of the required new standards. Watt's partnership with Boulton was more successful in bringing together a labour force which was trained and sufficiently specialized to make the steam engine work satisfactorily. But steam engines were not used in significant numbers until after 1815, and even in the 1830s about half the cotton textile factories still relied on water power. Gradually an engineering industry evolved that could make and repair steam engines, textile machines, colliery equipment, machine tools and locomotives. The advanced nature of the

British economy now depends vitally upon the engineering industry that has its origins as recently as the late eighteenth century.

Coal

Coal was needed in quantity for four different purposes. Two of these, domestic heating and coal for export, were already well established. The other two were new. As a source of power coal became increasingly important first for machinery in the new factories and subsequently for the railways. Fourthly, coal was now used in the manufacture of iron. The discovery that coal could replace charcoal as the source of heat in the smelting process is usually attributed to Abraham Darby; although the new technique was developed in the early eighteenth century its application did not spread rapidly until the later part of the century, when it considerably increased the demand for coal. As the nineteenth century developed so the coal industry grew into one of Britain's major industries. The second half of the nineteenth century is sometimes described as the age of coal.

Iron

The new smelting process introduced by Abraham Darby made possible the production of pig iron in large quantities. The Napoleonic Wars would in any case have given the iron industry considerable stimulus, but added to this were the increasing demands of the new engineering industry and subsequently a whole new market created by the even newer railway industry. The techniques of rolling and puddling introduced by Henry Cort finally freed the industry from charcoal and introduced cheap wrought iron, which could be made in quantity and used for many purposes in an age when industry was becoming mechanized. Whereas the iron industry had declined in the early eighteenth century because of an acute shortage of timber for charcoal, and Britain was actually importing two-thirds of her iron supply (the metal not the ore) from Sweden and Russia, by the middle of the nineteenth century Britain was making $2\frac{1}{2}$ million tons of pig-iron, representing half the world supply. A thriving iron and steel industry has been shown to be an integral part of an industrial economy ever since. No developing country can consider economic growth without an early major investment in capital plant for iron and steel. In Britain this major step forward had taken place as far as iron is concerned by the middle of the nineteenth century.

Cotton textiles

One of the anomalous facts of this period of economic growth is that the great increase in production of textiles was not in the manufacture of woollen textiles but in cotton goods. So much of the early history of the growing wealth of Britain is the history first of the production of wool and then of the manufacture and export of woollen cloth. Wool was the foundation on which Britain's economy had been built. Yet the famous inventions of the eighteenth century, the spinning jenny, the

7

water frames, the mule, the machines that are so well known through school history lessons, were all applied in the first instance to cotton. Wool, it appears, took second place.

The reason for this lies partly in the very age of the woollen industry. Over a long period of development it had become regulated by guilds which aimed to preserve traditional methods and exclude new entrants. One aspect of guild control was the effort made to stop individuals with business initiative from getting ahead of their rivals. The climate in the woollen industry was thus not one to encourage innovation and drive. The cotton industry which sprang up in the northern part of England expanded in those towns which were outside the area of guild control. Manchester, which dominated the Lancashire textile area, was a non-corporate town.

The other reason why the cotton textile industry ran ahead of the woollen industry was that the woollen fibre was softer than that of cotton and hence could not withstand the same degree of strain to which the primitive machines subjected it. Only when the machines were more sophisticated and more smooth running was it possible to apply them to wool. The cotton industry was virtually fully mechanized by the 1830s, but the woollen industry had to wait until the middle of the century before it reached the same stage.

The advantages of cotton textiles were many. The most enterprising of merchants had always found it difficult to trade English woollens overseas, except in Europe and the North American markets, because the climate in India, the Far East and many other areas where Britain had so many commercial interests did not call for warm wear. Cotton textiles, on the other hand, offered a sizeable overseas market as well as an enormous market at home. Also cotton textiles could provide hygienic underwear–a fact which the British public discovered in large numbers as the eighteenth century progressed, and one which through its effect on public health has some bearing on the decrease in mortality rates which is characteristic of the times. The cotton textile industry thus became one of Britain's staple industries. By 1840 50 per cent of the total value of British exports consisted of cotton goods; if the value of woollen and worsted goods were added, the textile industry was responsible for more than two-thirds of Britain's exports.

Chemicals

Before the nineteenth century there was little that could be described as a chemical industry; apart from the production of gunpowder and a few acids and drugs there was nothing. The growth of the textile industry changed this. The manufacture of textiles called for acids, alkalis, soaps and chemicals of many kinds. The discovery of bleaching powder in 1785 and the Leblanc soda process, invented in France during the Napoleonic Wars because of shortage of soda, led to the manufacture of bleaching powder in many parts of Britain. The basic material for the manufacture of soda was salt, so that the chemical industry centred itself eventually on the salt field in Cheshire. It was not a big industry but it was new. Much of its valuable byproducts it wasted. The great expansion in the chemical industry did not come until the twentieth century but the foundations were laid in the early part of the nineteenth.

Table 1.1

Expansion in major industries, 1760–1830

Consumption of raw cotton	
1760	8,000 tons
1800	25,000 tons
1830	100,000 tons
Iron Output	
1800	250,000 tons
1835	1,000,000 tons
Coal Production	
1770	6,000,000 tons
1830	23,000,000 tons

The social changes: state control

The advance in economic growth, characterized by the emergence and growth of major industries, was accompanied by the gradual migration of the population to the towns, increase in the size of the population itself, and unemployment in agriculture brought about by the rationalization of that industry associated with the Enclosure movement. There was no precedent for the social changes that this development involved, nor was there any authority in a position to control the upheaval that was bound to take place in a society which was so altering its way of life. By tradition the action of government in Britain was remedial; something had to go wrong before it could be put right. Social changes take place over a period of many years, and their permanency is only gradually accepted. This is as true today as it was in the nineteenth century, the difference in modern times being that the state is expected to take a keen interest in social change and to legislate wherever the social conscience dictates.

In the nineteenth century the role of state was not so clearly defined. Legislation with regard to overseas trade (and this was the main source of wealth at the time) had been well defined in what was known as the Mercantilist System. There was active interference by the state to protect existing industries from overseas competition, to encourage exports and discourage imports, to confine as far as possible to British ships the carrying of goods to and from Britain, and to control absolutely the trade with the colonies; but there was no effective control of industrial development at home. There had been the Statute of Artificers introduced in the sixteenth century, during an earlier period of economic and social change, which had dealt with mobility and training of labour, and the regulation of wages, but it had long since become a dead letter. The regulation of the various crafts by the guilds had become ineffectual, so that change in the early nineteenth century took place with no effective legislation to curb excesses.

The concept of laissez-faire is associated with this period, but the belief that the nineteenth century saw the blossoming of a wholesale rejection of regulations on industry and trade does not accord with the facts. In the area of overseas trade it is true that laissez-faire (that is, free trade) as recommended by Adam Smith was systematically applied, but even this took time. Gladstone's famous budget incorporating the removal of the final protective duties from the tariff was as late as 1853, and the commercial treaty with France abolishing all duties on manufactured goods was not until 1860.

In contrast legislation on industrial development at home was, as we have seen, almost non-existent at the beginning of the nineteenth century, but as the century progressed so the state intervened gradually to control the worst aspects of capitalism. Parallel with the Free Trade movement was the introduction of legislation such as the Factory Acts, the Ten Hour Bill and the Trade Union Acts, which established two basic tenets that have been carried into the twentieth century, that governments may interfere with the free forces of the market in the interests of social justice, and that employees have a legal right to bargain collectively with employers. These tenets are quite contrary to the idea of laissez-faire.

This having been said, it must be admitted that the change to an industrial economy did bring living and working conditions in both town and country that by modern standards were appalling. The evils of the unrestrained use of capital are very well known and documented. The awakening of the social conscience in Victorian times led to the wide advertisement of the exploitation of child labour, the miserably low wages, the back-to-back houses, the overcrowding, the high mortality rate . . . it is a long recital. Although there is much evidence to support the evils that this recital describes, it must be remembered that much of the evidence comes from special reports and commissions of enquiry which naturally highlighted the worst cases of brutal treatment or poor living or working conditions, much as a modern newspaper will print only the unusual incidents as news. The judgment on these times must be tempered too with the knowledge that before the first Factory Act in 1833 there had been the slow uneasy recovery period after a long war (traditionally a difficult socio-economic experience), and that the earlier rural conditions, particularly the conditions of workers under the domestic system, were frequently worse than those in the towns.

Britain had no precedent for guidance. Capital was available in increasing quantities but was in the hands of comparatively few. Only when the results of the application of capital in this quantity and in these circumstances came to be observed did the movement for control begin. Even then a look at the individuals and reform bodies that pressed for control indicates that there was no concerted movement, no determined party political action, no strong movement from the people who were themselves most affected. Leading politicians of both sides supported factory legislation as vociferously as others decried it. Some humane manufacturers took action themselves by providing good working conditions and housing for their workers, while others argued that only by imposing long hours and by driving workers hard did they make business profitable. There were churchmen who were motivated by religious sentiments in their demand for better conditions for the working classes, while men like John Bright, ardent workers for the abolition of Negro slavery, opposed factory reform. This confusion of support and opposition reflects the fact that society at the time was unsure what was the right policy in a period of transition.

The working classes were ultimately driven to the gradual building up of the trade union movement in an effort to control the way in which capital was used, but before they succeeded in establishing their legal right to existence there had already developed a deep division between worker and employer which lasted throughout the nineteenth century and lingers in modern times. This was the consequence of the creation of a large permanent wage-earning class which emerged in the nineteenth century with the growth of the major industries. It is this division, coming as it did before any satisfactory method of controlling capital had been devised, that militated against good industrial relations in Britain and has done so ever since.

Loss of self-sufficiency

As Britain made the change from an agrarian to an industrial nation so she lost her self-sufficiency. Foreign trade became more and more important as she specialized in the production of manufactured goods and required an increasing quantity of raw materials and food. For nearly 150 years now Britain has had a uniformly unfavourable balance of trade, has imported year by year more goods than she has exported. In the nineteenth century the gap between imports and exports was more than covered by invisible items like shipping and financial services, and the income from foreign investments. The surplus was reinvested overseas to increase future income. The failure to achieve a balance of payments is a twentieth-century phenomenon but it has its roots in the changed pattern of trade during Victorian times.

The trade cycle

Another new feature of the industrialized economy of Britain in the nineteenth century was the appearance of the trade cycle (a peculiarity of a capitalist economy). The greater the specialization in manufactured goods and the greater the volume of trade, so the greater the tendency for the economy to experience a regular pattern of prosperity and depression. The time taken for the trade cycle to turn one revolution was about ten years as the table shows below. The depressions increased in severity as the volume of trade increased. The downswing of the trade cycle in the 1880s was known as the Great Depression, an epithet that would have been better reserved for the 1930s. The trade cycle came to be looked upon almost as an act of God until

Years of the lowest point of the trade cycle

1825	1866	1900
1837	1873	1907
1847	1882	1921
1857	1890	1931

the comparatively new science of Economics came to grips with the problems involved. Since 1945 the problem to be overcome has been not so much the control of boom and slump but how best to manipulate the economy to ensure the maximum rate of economic growth; the technique for doing this has been called stop/go.

Past and present

The modern British economy has thus inherited problems arising from the industrial revolution which are still having repercussions upon the task of achieving economic growth. The gradual emphasis on a select few major industries contributing largely to the country's prosperity has created a situation where the loss of self-sufficiency on the one hand promises greatly increased prosperity from specialization but on the other hand threatens insecurity should the major industries fail. Britain is irrevocably committed to overseas trade and is thus caught up in the complexities of the world trade cycle. The best way to control the economy in these circumstances is still to be determined, but the way in which it is controlled at present is influenced very much by the way in which the industrial economy has evolved.

The nineteenth century is with us still in many ways, and not just in the many buildings of the Victorian industries that still survive; the basis of the presentday relationship between labour and capital still reflects the early days of capital growth, while attitudes of mind adopted in the circumstances of social and economic change have been handed down and are still there in part. Any interpretation of the modern economic scene in Britain must take this into account.

2

Britain's lead challenged

By the middle of the nineteenth century Britain had secured an economic lead over potential rivals that placed her for a period of twenty years or so in a position of genuine supremacy. The wealth that economic leadership had brought was matched by political power, thus making Britain the dominant nation of the times. The hundred years between the end of the Napoleonic Wars and the outbreak of war in 1914 are sometimes referred to as the century of Pax Britannica, in recognition of the fact that Britain was the most important world power for a century of comparative peace. Until the latter part of the century there was not one country that could challenge Britain's authority. France, the traditional rival, had been defeated at Waterloo. Germany was not a political entity until well past the mid-century and the United States of America did not settle down to uninterrupted political and economic development until after the civil war in the 1860s. Italy was not united until 1870, while Japan did not emerge from her feudal cocoon until the 1850s and Russia was economically undeveloped. Britain's position of supremacy was eloquent testimony that economic leadership meant a similar political domination.

The markets of the world were wide open, with Britain in a position to flood them with manufactured goods in quantities that no other country could challenge. The benefits of the change to an industrial economy were now accruing rapidly.

The railways had been built from the 1830s onwards and were now functioning with the appropriate benefits. They provided employment not only in the basic industries of coal and iron but also in the maintenance and running of the railways themselves. It has been estimated that by 1848 about 300,000 people had found employment directly or indirectly through the railways; if their dependants are taken into account this means that about one million people were relying upon the railways for their livelihood. The railway industry was an excellent example of the multiplier effect following investment on a large scale. The benefit to society was a major contribution to political stability at a time when there was political upheaval in so much of Europe.

As the benefits of the railways in Britain became apparent other countries developed an interest in railways of their own. Britain was the only country with the skill and the experience necessary to help and (what was just as important) the only country with the capital in the large quantity that was necessary for railway development. There was thus a great outflow of British capital, technical skill and even labour (the hardworking English navvy was much admired on the Continent) that produced both a welcome increase in income from overseas and also an added stimulus to the basic industries at home that supplied the needs of the railway workshops. Thomas Brassey, the great railway contractor of the time, illustrates the magnitude of the British contribution to railway building overseas. Between 1850 and 1870 he was concerned with the building of thirty foreign railway lines in countries as far apart as Poland, Mauritius and the Argentine.

Railways were not the only industry that the British exported at this time. The benefits of the technological advances in Britain were made available to many foreign countries while at the same time British capital was used to exploit the raw materials in foreign regions for the benefit of the manufacturing industry at home. Gasworks, docks and harbours were constructed all over the world with the help of British capital. By 1870 at least £700 million was invested abroad. The significance of this was that Britain was not only reinvesting her interest and dividends in further projects overseas, but she was also exporting a surplus of capital. This situation lasted as we shall see, only until the 1870s, but until then Britain's balance of payments problems were virtually non-existent.

Supply of capital

During this period the necessary legislation was passed to facilitate the supply of capital. This great expansion of economic activity called for the application of capital from as many sources as possible, but ever since the fiasco of the South Sea Bubble Parliament had been chary of making the formation of joint stock companies easy or of granting limited liability to shareholders. As the nineteenth century progressed it became evident that joint stock organization was the one method that could cope with the enormously increased demand for capital. In 1844 incorporation became possible through registration rather than an Act of Parliament, and by 1862 the principle of limited liability was conceded by Parliament. The number of companies thereafter steadily increased. In 1844 there were less than 1,000 but by 1900 the number of companies had increased to 30,000.

Attempts to stabilize the supply of circulating capital were made also in the middle of the century. The Bank Charter Act of 1844 sought to emphasize the role of the Bank of England by limiting the issue of paper money by the joint stock banks, and by fixing the size of the Fiduciary Issue. This did not prove to be very successful and crises still occurred. Banknote inflation had been stopped, but credit inflation was still possible. There were runs on the Bank in 1847, 1857 and 1866. After that improvements in banking practice and technique steadily built up confidence in the Bank of England.

Sterling Area

The level of investment overseas and Britain's devotion to Free Trade meant that Britain accepted goods of many kinds in payment of debt or interest. Much of what she imported she did not require herself but re-exported at a profit. England became one enormous market place. Many countries accordingly in their commercial transactions with Britain were anxious to convert their currencies to sterling, which developed into a major trading currency. The fixed sterling rate became so important that a group of countries adopted the £ sterling as the external standard of their currencies' value. They deposited their reserve in Britain so that the gold in the Bank of England now had to serve as backing for the sterling reserves of these countries. The countries so involved came to be known (but not until the 1930s) as the Sterling Area. The complications that survive to the present time of £ sterling being an international currency we shall meet again later on.

Even in agriculture the prosperity of the mid-Victorian period was reflected. There was a better balance between arable and pasture farming, new machines were introduced for threshing, ploughing, mowing and haymaking while artificial fertilizers were used in quantity for the first time. There was a succession of good harvests, as if to illustrate the validity of the new methods. The landowners prospered in a period when the ownership of land became concentrated more and more in the hands of a few. It was estimated that in 1874 about one-quarter of the land of England had passed into the ownership of about 1,200 people.[2] The peasant population, so much a feature of European agriculture, did not exist in Britain. All this made for greater efficiency, improved productivity and higher profits that matched the achievements of industry.

Table 2.1

British trading figures

	Exports	*Imports*
1850	£71,000,000	£100,000,000
1870	£200,000,000	£300,000,000
	British capital overseas	
1854–1874	Annual Average Surplus of capital exported £15,000,000	
	Total of British capital assets overseas	
By 1850	£300,000,000	
By 1870	£700,000,000	

The British supremacy of mid-Victorian times inevitably had a psychological impact. Britain led the world in almost every economic activity but the causes tended to be overlooked in the euphoria that developed. The real reasons why

Britain's trading position was dominant at that point of time were, unfortunately, neglected; the Victorian emphasis on the virtue of 'self-help' and the principle of free trade was sufficient to persuade many people that Britain had become wealthy and powerful solely as a result of an innate British ability. The feeling of national superiority that was engendered is difficult to measure; its chief drawback can perhaps be best understood if we compare it with the pride of a commercial concern that has secured a commanding position for itself in the market for a particular commodity and in doing so has made its trade-mark a household word. There is a danger that a point will be reached when the assumption is made that because a commodity bears the well-known trademark it must be the best of its kind. There is then a temptation for the firm to rest on its laurels and assume that the trademark is a guarantee against any potential rivals. In just this way Britain built up a conviction that British goods were best because they were British. The Victorians had the national pride that comes naturally to a country that finds itself for the first time well ahead of all others. The role has now been passed on to the USA but it was relinquished very gradually and unwillingly. The recognition that leadership had been lost did not come until long after supremacy had in fact gone, and meanwhile a conservatism that dwelt upon the period of supremacy started to have a hindering effect on economic change.

The period of prosperity lasted until the early 1870s. By then the economic pattern of world trade had started to change and the self-confidence of the Victorian period received its first setbacks. This is best demonstrated by the very significant change in the balance of payments situation in Britain, hitherto so comfortably secure. As the figures in Table 2.1 show, up to the 1870s Britain had been exporting capital regularly and at the same time she had been reinvesting abroad the interest received from existing foreign investments. From the late 1870s onwards the gap between imports and exports was so big as to absorb all the surplus capital and, further, Britain was compelled to use income from foreign investments to help cover this widening gap. Thus the period of exporting surplus capital came to an end and Britain found herself living on the proceeds of earlier investment abroad. This was the second step (loss of self-sufficiency was the first) towards the balance of payments problems that have become so important in the twentieth century.

Professor Ashworth has pointed out that this way of looking at Britain's export of capital can be misleading.[3] He demonstrates that Britain's export of capital continued at a rate of expansion that was greater than ever before to give a figure of total British assets abroad by 1913 of £4,000 million. This disappearance of a surplus of exported capital he attributes to the fact that dividends and interest by this time constituted a much bigger proportion of the total income from abroad. The fact that visible exports enjoyed a smaller share of the total income from trade thus meant that more of the dividends and interests were used to cover the gap. This being so it serves to emphasize that Britain's balance of payments was now dependent more than ever on the volume of capital invested overseas. Any major disturbance to trade that compelled Britain either to sell capital assets overseas or to lower the rate of capital outflow, was bound to have serious repercussions. The two world wars in the twentieth century were both major disturbances of this kind.

By the 1870s two countries, the USA and Germany, had arrived on the economic scene; these by their sheer size and supply of natural resources were both capable of outstripping British manufacturing production. Their economic development had been held back partly because of political factors but mainly because of the lack of a good communications system; the building of railways in both countries had made rapid political development possible. Germany had become a powerful political and economic entity for the first time in the history of Europe. A series of successful short wars had established her as a dominant power on the continent of Europe. Her war with France in 1870–71, which culminated in the establishment of the first German Reich, had provided her with the iron ore fields of Lorraine, but, more important, she now had a desire to consolidate her power in Europe and take her place on the international political scene as a power of considerable stature. The most effective way in which Britain could be challenged was in the development of overseas trade, and this in turn meant the development of an efficient manufacturing industry in Germany itself.

The USA having settled her internal dissensions was also poised for rapid economic expansion. Her potential was measurably greater than that of Germany. She had natural resources in abundance which could be exploited rapidly now that the railways had opened up the West. The building of an East-West communication system marked the beginning of remarkable economic growth. The USA too was a young nation which was just realizing its capabilities. There was none of the restriction and inflexibility of the old world, and there was much of the original pioneering spirit still present in the USA.

Both the new rivals to Britain were territorially much larger, and both had greater resources. Neither of them possessed territory overseas which could in any way compare with Britain's Empire, but in conditions of free trade an empire did not possess any outstanding advantage. Britain's chief advantage lay in the fact that she had had a long start and possessed by now an industrial tradition and well established markets. The challenge was formidable, but Britain as we have seen was already suffering from a misguided belief that she owed her supremacy to the fact that she was Britain. The USA and Germany proved this to be a fallacy by 1914, and in many ways long before that.

In the period 1870 to 1914 the world's manufacturing activity increased roughly more than four times. In 1870 Britain was responsible with France, Germany and USA for the manufacture of 79 per cent of the world's supply of manufactured goods. This concentration of production in a select few countries had only slightly decreased by 1914 when the figure had dropped to 72 per cent. More significant was the relative amount of manufacture in the countries concerned. In 1870 the USA had produced 23 per cent of this against 32 per cent by Britain; by 1914 the share of each country had changed to 14 per cent for Britain and 36 per cent for the USA.[4]

It is arguable that this changing pattern was inevitable. No one country could expect to dominate world markets indefinitely. Britain's command of world markets had happened only because she had industrialized first. As other countries industrialized so Britain's share of the markets was bound to decline. This is true, but it is questionable whether Britain needed to lose markets to the extent she did. How much of the drop in the share of world markets was due to reasonable encroachment by the USA and Germany and how much was due to the conservatism associated with Victorian prosperity?

These are questions that cannot be assessed easily. Some sort of answer can be found by looking at the evidence of productivity in the countries concerned, and at any emphasis on new industries, but even then the statistics can be very misleading. Comparison between the economic growth of one country and another is never very informative unless there is a reasonable common base on which to work. The stage of development at which the countries are when the period covered by the statistics starts is all important; unless the countries are at a comparable stage there is little validity in the comparisons.

The USA and Germany in 1870 were both a long way behind Britain. Both were able to take full advantage of Britain's long experience in industrialization and incorporate the latest technological advances in their new industries. Statistics show that both countries achieved a very rapid rate of growth in the forty years before 1914, but there is no value in saying that their rate of growth, expressed as a percentage with 1870 as a base year, was faster than that of Britain. It is better to look at industry in Britain to see whether it took up the challenge.

Iron and steel

In 1856 Sir Henry Bessemer read his famous paper on the manufacture of steel to the British Association at Cheltenham. This showed the way to production of cheap steel in quantity, particularly when Gilchrist and Thomas subsequently demonstrated in 1879 that, by lining the converter and adding lime, basic steel could be produced from iron ore of high phosphoric content. In 1857 William Siemens, a German who had settled in Britain, developed the open-hearth method, which introduced a method of manufacturing steel cheaply in quantity and with even greater control than the Bessemer process. Gilchrist and Thomas demonstrated that basic steel could be produced by the open-hearth method as well.

These developments came just at the right time for the USA and Germany. They were developing their metal industries so that no massive scrapping of plant was involved and they possessed both the capital and the supplies of iron ore. It was thus a British invention that made American and German steel expansion possible.

Britain on the other hand was not particularly anxious to pursue the new techniques. The capital invested in the iron industry at the time of the railway expansion was enormous, and British firms were not anxious to scrap it. Britain was producing wrought iron in quantity, and a change over to steel was highly inconvenient. The Bessemer process at first demanded non-phosphoric ores which were not common in England. This in itself was not much incentive to invest in steelmaking plant. Yet capital was invested, not in England but in Spain and Sweden, by British firms anxious to make use of the vast supplies of non-phosphoric ores available in those countries. Thus when the basic process was developed British capital was tied up elsewhere. It is therefore not surprising to find that in the early 1890s both Germany and the USA overtook Britain in steel production. By the turn of the century only 17 per cent of British steel was produced by the basic method. This suggests a conservatism on the part of the British, which is a telling example of the disadvantages of early industrial leadership.

Electricity

Just as cheap steel can be regarded as indispensable to twentieth-century industry, so electricity has become an indispensable source of power, heat and light. Britain was not quick to grasp the enormous potential that electricity offered, even though some of the most important advances in the development of electricity took place in Britain itself. Michael Faraday invented the electrical generator in the 1830s, and in the 1880s Sir Charles Parsons constructed a turbine which took Faraday's invention to the point where electricity could be generated in sufficient quantities to challenge the existing sources of power, heat and light. This development of electricity may have gone hand in hand with the increased demand on all sides for coal, because coal was needed to provide the power to turn the turbines; but it challenged the interests of the new gas industry. Gas had been a successful new industry in the earlier part of the nineteenth century. The construction of gasworks and the laying of gas mains had involved investment on a very large scale. Much of the capital equipment was comparatively new; some of it by now was owned by municipal authorities. Those who had put money into gas were alarmed at the prospect of the growth of an electricity industry. The invention of the gas mantle in 1886 (two years after the the invention of the turbine) gave hope that gas lighting would triumph after all; but it did not give encouragement to electricity.

The electricity industry was thus hampered from the start by vested interests. Furthermore the experience that the Victorians had acquired in the development of municipal gas and water undertakings prompted the attitude that electricity supplies should be on a municipal basis too, but many local councils considered the provision of electricity to be a very risky business and declined to promote any supply. Private companies took over but obtained permission to do so only on the understanding that the area supplied conformed to a local government area that could be the subject of subsequent municipal control. This ensured that the unit of supply was small, when the electricity industry is one that benefits more than most from the economies of scale. There was no attempt at standardization. Voltage supplies varied from one area to another so that appliances, plugs, sockets and so on were at variance with one another. By 1913 the whole of the British output of electrical equipment including electrical cables, was only just over a third of that of Germany. An industry that did not have a well organized expanding market at home could not expect to triumph in the export field.

Internal combustion engine

The internal combustion engine ranks with steel and electricity as a major contributor to twentieth-century economic development. We have seen how Britain was slow to react to the introduction of steel and electricity. Her reaction to the internal combustion engine was in many ways similar, although it must be admitted that the original indifference was eventually overcome. Legislation passed in 1865 restricting the speed of vehicles on the road (the famous 'Man with the Flag' Act) was not repealed until 1896. During that time the major inventions concerning the development of the internal combustion engine were made on the Continent. It is significant that Diesel, Otto and Daimler were all German.

The inference to be drawn from looking at the British approach to the newer industries at the beginning of the twentieth century is that Britain was not prepared to make much effort to change. She was already well set in her ways. What of the staple industries themselves?

Coal

Down to 1914 coal was enjoying buoyant markets. Production increased in volume and value, the labour force increased in numbers and as a percentage of the total working population. Maximum output was achieved in 1913 when 287·4 million tons were produced, of which 94 million tons went for export. In 1851, 216,000 men were employed in the industry; by 1913 there were 1,127,000 men, representing a tenth of the total male labour force in British industry. To all outward appearances the coal industry was thriving, yet all was not well. Productivity was declining and the productivity figure was more important than absolute volume. In 1871, 373 tons were produced per man per annum, but by 1913 this had been reduced to 260 tons.

Cotton textiles

The same might be said of cotton textiles. Although cotton goods achieved a dwindling share of the total of Britain's exports, overall production increased. Productivity did not show a corresponding increase. Much of the machinery in the industry had already done long service but while sales figures at home and abroad were good there was little incentive to modernize. Whereas in Britain one operative could control four looms, in the USA one operative had machinery sufficiently modern for him to control twenty. The failure to modernize was made more serious for the industry by the export from Britain of modern textile machinery to those developing industries that were likely to offer the most challenging rivalry in the future.

Agriculture

The prosperity of the mid-century was comparatively shortlived. The British farmer in the last quarter of the nineteenth century found severe competition from the USA, Canada and Argentina at a time when free trade was the unchallenged doctrine in Britain. The Americans were able to take advantage of growing grain in bulk in a climate and soil well suited to such an operation. They then transported it in bulk on the new railways to the eastern seaboard, whence it was taken in the new steamships to the ports of Europe, particularly to the ports of England where there was no tariff barrier. Grain prices fell. The farmer, if he could no longer compete in growing wheat, could turn to the production of meat. Unfortunately for him the New World was also bringing into use the grazing lands for which it has ever since been famous. This, in conjunction with the new invention of the refrigerated ships introduced keen competition in beef farming too. The effect was for British farming to be rationalized and thereby rendered more efficient, although not without the ruin of some farmers, the creation of agricultural unemployment and the depression of wages. Greater attention was paid to techniques in farming, in order to provide a greater yield; greater care was taken in breeding for meat, butter and milk, while wheat-growing tended to be confined to those areas where the British climate would permit a crop that was comparable with American grain. Just before the war of 1914, Britain was supplying all her own milk, nearly 60 per cent of her meat but imported nearly 80 per cent of her wheat. The figures in Table 2.2 show how the pattern of British farming was changing by the turn of the century.

Table 2.2

Acreage under cultivation in UK (million acres)

	1870	1895
Arable	24	23½
Pasture	20	27½

Source: 1900, Birnie, *An Economic History of the British Isles*, Methuen, p. 258.

Agriculture was thus one industry where the acuteness of the competition from abroad did not permit conservatism for long. There was no opportunity for a long, drawn out period while the farmer gradually accepted that the traditional market

3

had permanently declined. The adjustment was painful but fairly rapid. The outcome was a more efficient, more specialized industry and a redeployment of labour in the greater interest of the nation's economy. The same challenge was offered to the staple industries but not in such an acute form, and their reaction was therefore slower. The period of transition from the old outlook of anticipating easy markets and a few rivals to the new concept of fierce competition stretched well into the twentieth century.

Shipbuilding and shipping

The shipbuilding industry ran counter to the pattern of the other major industries during this period as it had done during the period of Victorian prosperity. Supplies of timber close to the coast had almost run out by the mid-nineteenth century, whereas in the USA there were ample supplies of timber ready for the construction of an American industry that would quickly eclipse the British. The British industry had been saved by the advent of first the iron and then the steel ship. Although the wooden sailing ship lasted into the twentieth century, the shipbuilders of the late nineteenth century concentrated on the metal steamship. A succession of inventions improved propulsion steadily until the superiority of this type of vessel was permanently established. This was an industry where Britain with its engineering tradition led the world. In America the industry was not so well placed geographically, with iron and steel plant and coal supplies not so conveniently close to the coast as in Britain. The Americans concentrated their efforts and their supplies of iron and steel on their expansion to the West, leaving the way clear for Britain to capture the lion's share of the world market. By 1914 the tonnage of ships produced in British yards was greater than that of all other countries in the world together. A similar preponderance existed in the carrying trade. British ships not only carried her own goods but also acted as carrier for much of the world's trade, as they had done ever since the days of mercantilism ended.

New outlook on Empire

One way in which markets overseas had been kept buoyant had been a deliberate change in the direction of trade. Britain could not control world markets, but it was possible for her to secure some control over the markets of her own Empire. The Empire took on a new significance at the time of the 'Great Depression' because of the possibility of new and more easily controlled trade. It is difficult not to be cynical about Britain's attachment to the idea of Empire in the last quarter of the nineteenth century. During the period of mid-century supremacy, when Britain had a commanding position in world markets, the colonies were regarded as a 'millstone round our necks' (Disraeli). When European and North American markets became more difficult as supremacy was lost, Britain 'discovered' her Empire, joining in the ignominious scramble for those parts of the world, particularly in Africa, that were still not divided among the great powers.

The office of Colonial Secretary became one of the most important in the Government, as was evinced by its Cabinet status. Joseph Chamberlain, one of the most influential politicians of the day, was colonial secretary during the vital period 1895–1903, bringing great authority to the idea of Empire. The Diamond Jubilee celebrations of Queen Victoria were not so much the occasion for the coming together of the heads of state of all Europe, as the opportunity for the leading figures of Empire to pay homage to the great white queen and to collaborate on economic matters.

In spite of a free trade policy Britain still had a tariff barrier, even though it was not nearly as high as earlier in the century. Now she could lower it still further for the Empire countries in return for special terms being granted to her own exports in those countries. This was imperial preference. There were opportunities of fresh markets for cotton textiles in the Empire and new areas for investment of British capital to give a prolonged lease of life to the pattern of industrial production and capital export of the earlier part of the century.

Table 2.3
Distributive value of UK exports, 1870–89

	To foreign countries	To British possessions
	£ million	
1870–74	175	60
1875–79	135	67
1880–84	153	81
1885–89	147	79

Source:*Fiscal Blue Book 1909*, quoted in Knowles:*Industrial & Commercial Revolutions*—Routledge.

The change in the attitude to Empire gave Britain in some degree a false sense of security. It helped to conceal the real facts about the shortcomings of her economy. When those shortcomings were made painfully obvious in the 1930s one of the reactions was to reinforce strongly the principle of imperial preference in an effort to restore the equilibrium. Imperial preference still remains, though the whole issue has been reopened in the light of Britain's desire to enter Europe.

The analysis of change

Britain's response to the challenge of the developing economic strength of Germany and the USA was thus a mixed one, but already there were signs that there would be very serious problems as the twentieth century developed. It is, perhaps, easy at this distance of time and with the consequent advantage of hindsight to point out the shortcomings of the pre-1914 economy. In this outline of economic development the factors that proved to be relevant to change have been singled out from the multitude of facts that had no bearing on change. This sifting of facts becomes more and more possible the farther away in time the period is. The cause is always much easier to analyse once the effect has been observed. In the nineteenth century and the early twentieth the economic factors of change could not have been nearly so obvious to those engaged in economic activity. The broad economic facts must have seemed very encouraging. The volume of trade, as we have seen, was steadily increasing; actual production figures showed a regular growth in all the major industries. London was still the undisputed centre of the financial world, the bulk of the world's insurance was transacted by British companies. Prices were reasonably stable, the unemployment level gave no cause for alarm and real incomes had been rising over a long period. There were those who in commenting on the economic state of affairs gave warning of the consequences of relying too heavily on industries that were either unsophisticated or extractive, but while there were markets for the goods made in Britain, and while profits were still to be made, the warnings tended to go unheeded.

By 1914 the foundations of Britain's economic problems had already been laid. The Pax Britannica was over, with Britain now no longer leader of the world economy but just one among equals. The ensuing war was to accelerate the changes; it did not initiate them.

3
The view from behind

The First World War was more prolonged than most people had anticipated and was on a scale that very few could have envisaged. Britain had never maintained an army in the field of anything like the size of the one that was mustered as the war progressed, nor had the cost of equipping an army ever been so enormous. The more sophisticated weapons, in conjunction with the tactics that trench warfare demanded, made the four years of fighting the costliest war that Britain had ever experienced. In 1914 Britain may have been wealthier than she had ever been before but a war of that magnitude was bound to have a lasting effect on her economy.

The diversion of economic effort from satisfying the country's needs in time of peace to providing the means to win a war involved such a drastic change of course that private industry was not capable of succeeding on its own. Here was an emergency where the application of state control was not seriously questioned. If maximum production of the vital products of war was to be achieved it was accepted that the government must adopt the necessary measures to secure efficiency. As the war progressed and the needs grew more pressing the state took control of the means of production to a far reaching degree. Winston Churchill, who became Minister of Munitions in 1917, wrote in *The Aftermath*: 'Nearly all the mines and workshops of Britain were in our hands. We controlled and were actually managing all the greatest industries. We regulated the supply of all their raw materials. We organized the whole distribution of their finished products.'[5]

In the interests of common victory the liberty of the individual was largely submerged. It is worth noting in passing just how efficient the British economy became in conditions where there was a common cause supported by the trade unions and the ownership of industry, both groups working in concert with the government. There were strikes it is true, but not many, and there was a minimum insistence upon rights and privileges; industry accepted gracefully measures of centralization unthinkable in peace time. Consequently productivity rose sharply as the war progressed and as more and more control was applied. The early transitional muddles were cleared up, and by 1918 the British economy had become very efficiently organized for the purpose of waging large-scale war.

This forced conversion to an efficient wartime economy was not necessarily of assistance to Britain when the return to peacetime conditions occurred in 1918. The loss of liberties that state control had involved was an irksome sacrifice that the people did not wish to continue once hostilities had ceased. The swing away from control was thus a feature of post-1918 Britain.

Government control of labour had served to expand some industries beyond their peacetime potential. Capital which could have been better applied elsewhere had been diverted to produce the weapons of war. Fixed capital equipment in many industries had been overworked and had not been replaced. Much of it was already out of date, but its replacement had not been possible in time of war.

The economic effects of the First World War were long-lasting, and most of them were damaging. Many of them were incalculable. No one can assess the damage to the country of the loss of three-quarters of a million young men in their prime. They represented 9 per cent of all men between twenty and forty-five. It is arguable that these would have been the men with initiative and enterprise who, in the 1920s and 1930s could have helped Britain to overcome the economic depression which was to be her lot. No one can calculate the effect on morale, and hence on economic efficiency, that the suffering of the survivors and the grief of the bereaved relatives involved. Only one thing is certain: an immense economic effort was involved not, as is customary, in order to improve the standards of living, but to waste all four factors of production on an enormous scale by holding living standards down; all the war equipment produced was designed ultimately either to go up in smoke or to find its way to the scrap heap. The same of course applies to the war effort of all the belligerent powers.

There were other more tangible economic effects. For four years Britain had not been able to export to world markets anything like the quantity of goods that she did in ordinary times, and her customers overseas could not be expected to wait an indefinite period for the resumption of deliveries. They were obliged to supply themselves or else to seek a new source of supply. The commonsense geography of supply and demand was brought into operation earlier than it might have done otherwise. The USA, which did not enter the war until April 1917, was well situated for supplying markets in Latin America; Japan, a belligerent with little to contribute to the fighting, was well placed for developing markets in the Far East. Continental countries with indigenous coal supplies saw the economic absurdity of importing coal from Britain. Other countries, deprived of the product of British industries, started establishing their own. Britain thus found herself in 1918 with a reduction in markets for her staple industries that was likely to be permanent.

The treaty of Versailles tended to aggravate the economic difficulties rather than alleviate them. Several new nation states were created with the economic barriers that are the concomitant of political frontiers. The free movement of goods through what had been the one economic unit of Austria-Hungary was now restricted by new political frontiers. Nation states strive for economic self-sufficiency and engender a spirit of economic nationalism which restricts the volume of international trade. One of the features of international trade in the interwar period was the formal abandonment of free trade by Britain and the retreat by most countries behind national tariff barriers.

The other disturbing economic aspect of the Versailles settlement was more deliberate. The creation of new economic barriers had been incidental to the over-riding intention to resolve political problems. The clauses that dealt with reparation were deliberately imposed, not just to make Germany pay for her sins but, on France's part at any rate, to ensure that Germany was weakened economically for a very long time. It was felt that an impoverished Germany would be in no position to threaten France for a third time. France was ready to accede to Britain's demand that Germany should be made to pay for the war, though the prospects of a European economic recovery without a prosperous Germany must have seemed remote even at the time. Nor was Germany the only country saddled with war debts.

Britain, while lending to her continental allies, had borrowed extensively from the USA. During the war she had covered part of her overseas debts by the sale of privately owned investments. It has been estimated that 10 per cent of the total of Britain's long term assets were sold and a further 4 per cent to 5 per cent of British foreign investment was lost by confiscation in enemy countries and in Russia.[6] Investment started again after the war, but Britain never regained the creditor position which she had held. The USA was now the chief creditor nation. None of the European belligerents was free from debt and the problems that arose from repayment (which was ultimately abandoned in 1932) served only to confuse still further an economic situation that was already unstable.

Perhaps the most unfortunate feature of the attempts to find a European settlement after the war was the failure of the USA to ratify the Versailles Treaty. Had the USA formally accepted some responsibility for the economic and political reconstruction of Europe after 1918 many of the problems would have been eased. The Americans, however, apart from a belated effort through the Dawes Plan to assist Germany, turned their backs on Europe, not realizing that a strong Europe would have been a great help to their own economy.

World economic development between the wars followed a pattern that might have been anticipated. There was a postwar boom which lasted for eighteen months until the summer of 1920, while the immediate shortages caused by the war were overcome. This boom was followed by a recession which lasted until the end of 1922. From then until 1925 an effort was made to restore international financial stability so that from 1925 until 1929 some growth in output and trade was possible. The recessions that began in late 1929 developed into the great slump and financial crisis of 1931, lasting until 1933, which we recognize now as the result of an attempt to return to pre-1914 conditions.

Prices collapsed, industrial output fell, international trade contracted, and there was mass unemployment in the capitalist world to such a degree that the countries involved were compelled to accept that new economic policies were necessary, and that no return to prewar days was possible. From 1933 onwards there was a slow recovery associated with the efforts of individual countries to pursue new policies to restore individual equilibrium. Unemployment fell, prices rose slightly and production rose, though international trade was slow to respond because the new policies concentrated on economic nationalism as a solution rather than on international economic cooperation.

Britain's economic development during this period followed the world pattern except that she did not enjoy to the same extent the partial recovery between 1925 and 1929 experienced in other parts of the world. Britain had individual problems which added to the difficulties created by the world situation. These problems and the policies adopted to deal with them must now be examined.

Decline of the old staples

We have seen how before 1914 there had not been the same impetus to change in Britain as had occurred among her new economic rivals. Modernization of the staple industries and investment in the newer industries had both been neglected. The effects of this dual neglect were now combined with the loss of markets caused by the war.

COTTON TEXTILES

The number of cotton spindles in Japan, China, India and Brazil has been estimated at about 10 million in 1913. By 1924 the number had risen to nearly 18 million; the number of power looms in India and Japan increased from 120,000 to 200,000 between 1913 and 1922.[7] It is not surprising that British exports of cotton textiles to the Far East dwindled and output remained well below the prewar level. The output of piece-goods (in yardage) in 1924 was 33 per cent less than in 1912, and in 1929 nearly a fifth less than in 1924. In 1937, the best year of the thirties, the total exported was only 52 per cent of the total export of piece goods of 1929 and a mere 29 per cent of the immediate prewar period.[8] Piece goods suffered the greatest decline, but yarn output and exports ran into similar difficulties.

The cotton industry was by the late 1930s no longer the major exporting industry it had been. The numbers employed in the industry had gone down from nearly half a million in the early 1920s to just over 200,000 in 1938, and the number of looms and spindles had been reduced by approximately one-third. This was a major contraction of great significance, because although the world cotton industry had also been affected by the economic depression of the war years, there was an overall expansion in world production of cotton textiles between 1918 and 1939.

The reasons for this decline have already been partly explained. It was predominantly in the export field (supply for the home market increased slightly during the period) where Britain could not compete successfully against countries which had the combined advantages of geography and cheap labour to give them low manufacturing and transport costs. Much of the machinery that Britain's competitors used had been manufactured in Britain and her skills had been faithfully copied, but the industrialization of cheap textiles was bound to take place in developing countries (it was Britain's first industrialized industry after all), and there was no moral or economic reason why it should be either regretted or opposed. The only choice left to the British industry was to turn to the high quality cotton goods which could still be sold to the richer countries and leave the cheap piece-goods to the new competitors in the Far East. This meant a very difficult transition, involving the closing down of many mills and the introduction of a variety of schemes to eliminate excess capacity. The mill owners and the workers in the industry had to face a constant threat of loss of earnings or even livelihood; the nation had to accept that an industry that had traditionally contributed substantially to the balance of payments surplus was now no longer able to do so.

COAL

The problems of the coal industry, which, like the textile industry, employed well over 1 million workers, were equally acute. In 1913, the year of peak production, Britain had produced about half the entire coal output of Europe and was responsible for 55 per cent of world exports of coal, even exporting coal to Germany. This meant a share of world markets which she could hardly hope to sustain and which was inevitably disrupted by the war. Poland, Holland and Germany offered an increasing challenge in European markets in the 1920s and 30s, securing an increasing proportion of a market that was not greatly expanding because of increased economies in the use of coal and the competition from other sources of power.

OTHER SOURCES OF POWER

Another complicating factor which was to affect the demand for coal was the competition from other sources of power. Oil in particular was starting to challenge coal at a particularly inconvenient time. The Royal Navy had converted to oil in the First World War. The mercantile marine of the world made the gradual conversion too as the advantages of and availability of oil became apparent. In 1914 94·6 per cent of the world's mercantile tonnage was coal-fired; by 1939 that percentage was reduced to 54 per cent.

Hydroelectricity became a feature of power supplies during this period. Although it never contributed a challenge to coal in the home market it did affect our exports of coal to Europe. Had there not been the expansion of the conventional electricity supply in the United Kingdom the coal industry would have been even worse off.

In electricity generation coal found a new customer whose demands were substantially increasing. Coal-fired power helped to offset some of the industry's market losses elsewhere, but even here, as in many branches of industry of all kinds, coal utilization was greatly improved so that less coal was required to do the same amount of work. Britain thus had a surplus capacity which demanded a high level of efficient production if depression in the industry was to be avoided.

Unfortunately the coal industry at this juncture was far from efficient. This was one of the problems that was particular to Britain in the interwar period, and which aggravated an economic situation already unhealthy due to world conditions. The great expansion of the coal industry up to 1914 had taken place while coal was comparatively easy to extract, and while markets were easy and accessible. In these circumstances volume of production had taken precedence over productivity. After 1918 the competition in export markets introduced an emphasis on productivity. The British industry was not geared for this. Some idea of the level of efficiency in the industry in the 1920s can be obtained from the fact that in 1927 the output per manshift was 20·62 cwt (compare 36·4 cwt in 1966). Whereas the European competitors were equally inefficient immediately after 1918 they were in a position to make some improvement. By 1928 there was one worker for every 5 tons of saleable coal in the United Kingdom whereas in Holland there was one worker for every 20 to 25 tons, and in the USA one worker for every 50 tons. These figures do much to explain why British exports of coal fell.

The chief reason for low productivity was the smallness of the operating unit relative to the area being worked. This had been a hampering feature of the British mining industry from early times. By the 1920s there were 1,400 privately owned collieries and 2,500 mines. The capital available for the industry was split into small quantities which made large scale economic development impossible. Mechanization on the scale that was taking place in the USA and elsewhere would have been possible only if there had been wholesale amalgamation by the coal owners, or if there had been nationalization.

The Sankey Commission in 1919 recommended that the industry should be nationalized, but this was not politically expedient. The major coal strikes of the 1920s were caused by the inability of the owners to find any solution to the problem of rising costs other than a reduction of miners' wages. Rationalization was a popular word of the twenties, just as nationalization was a popular word in the forties and modernization in the sixties, but there was more discussion and declaration of good intent than good practice with coal in the interwar period. Some amalgamation and a degree of mechanization did take place, but mainly in the newer fields; it was not taken far enough to make coal an economically viable industry. Many pits were losing money at the pit-head prices, the collieries remaining in business only because profit was still being made by the subsidiary companies that transported coal to the consumer. The Royal Commission of 1926 reported that

114 pits were operating at three shillings a ton loss. Of these 110 had a yearly output of less than 400,000 tons.

SHIPBUILDING

Bad as the situation was for the major staples of cotton textiles and coal it was even worse for the traditional British industry of shipbuilding. Unemployment in ship-building rose to 62 per cent in 1932 when the national average was 22 per cent although the numbers employed were fewer than in cotton and coal (320,000 in 1926). The Tyne and Wear shipyards suffered particularly though Clydeside, Belfast and the Mersey all shared in the misery of the worst depression the industry had ever ex-perienced. As with the other industries suffering from depression, this was caused partly by the circumstances of world wide dislocation of trade and partly by cir-cumstances peculiar to Britain.

In the period 1910–14 Britain had built 61 per cent of the gross world tonnage of merchant vessels launched, and the building of warships was proceeding apace. About one-fifth of the merchant tonnage built by Britain was exported. Britain's share of the market was, perhaps, unnaturally large, and some contraction should have been expected. Many of Britain's customers were deprived of bunkering coal during the war and changed over to diesel propelled ships. This gave them experience both in diesel propulsion and in ship construction, which they developed at Britain's expense after the war. Other countries realized too that it was dangerous to rely so much for shipping on a foreign country that could not supply in the emergency of war and therefore fostered their native industries, once more at Britain's expense. The subsidizing of foreign shipyards became a feature of the shipbuilding industry in the inter-war period and must be regarded as a factor in explaining Britain's difficulties. The government intervened in the 1930s and resorted to subsidizing British shipowners. It supported the closing of redundant shipyards which had been undertaken by a company formed by the shipowners (National Shipbuilders' Society) and directly subsidized tramp shipping. Owners who were prepared to scrap old vessels were helped to replace them with new ones, and a special grant was given for the *Queen Mary*, construction of which had been suspended by a hard pressed Cunard Line.

The improvement that resulted from this government action was not particularly impressive, perhaps because there was not enough of it. The government was having to spend so much to help overcome the worst effects of the depression that it could give only limited assistance to any one industry. The world depression in international trade affected all shipbuilding countries, and was a calamity that was beyond control, but there is evidence to show that Britain's troubles were worse than they might have been.

Costs in British yards were higher than elsewhere. The shipyard owners blamed the high cost of steel and quoted the cheapness of labour in overseas yards, but the

Scandinavian countries, with equally high labour costs and little or no subsidies, put up a better performance, while Dutch yards, using British material, built ships at lower cost. This pointed to the inefficiency of British yards. In times such as this when jobs were insecure there is a natural tendency for the individual unions to fight hard for the rights of their members to continue in outdated techniques if the introduction of new ones threatens to create unemployment. The number of unions involved was large, thus giving rise to restrictive practices and demarcation disputes which were bad for the industry as a whole.

The British yards in any case were hampered by the slowness of shipowners in making the conversion to diesel propulsion. With the superabundance of steam coal in Britain it was not unnatural that the owners were reluctant to go over to oil. British engineers were responsible for many of the technical innovations that were a feature of ship design during the interwar period, but foreign shipyards derived the major benefit. Thus Britain fared badly in comparison with her foreign competitors. By 1937 she was building only 61 per cent of the gross tonnage that she had produced on average every year between 1909 and 1913 (inclusive), whereas the other shipbuilding countries of the world by 1938 were building 100 per cent more than they had been building prewar. Japan and Germany made the running, even successfully tempting many British shipowners to place orders abroad rather than in British yards.

This latter fact is perhaps the most damaging of all in assessing the part played by the British shipbuilding industry between the wars. Britain, a maritime nation that owed its wealth to overseas trade, had been outpaced in an industry where she should have had all the advantages. The raw materials were readily available, there was a great pool of highly skilled labour and a fund of technological skill. With the long tradition of dependence on the sea there was not much excuse for failing to remain competitive. The organization and operation of the industry on the part of both owners and unions must be held responsible for allowing the industry to lapse so far. The coal and cotton textile industries could justifiably claim that external circumstances were primarily responsible for their difficulties; the shipbuilding industry was in difficulty because of internal inefficiency.

IRON AND STEEL

The other basic industry, iron and steel, suffered also from the effects of the war and the world economic depression. Capacity had been expanded, plant had been over-used, as had happened in other industries during the war, and after the immediate postwar boom, markets for British iron and steel proved to be difficult. There was something of a world revival between 1924 and 1929, but Britain's industry did not participate in this; in the early thirties the markets were so bad that the industry in Britain was on the point of total collapse. During the later thirties there was a world-wide recovery in which Britain had some share, but it cannot be said that the iron and steel industry fared well during the interwar years. It experienced the same unhappy combination of a high level of unemployment and a low profit level that was common to the old staple industries in Britain.

We have noted earlier that the production of basic steel, made possible by the Gilchrist-Thomas invention, was not taken up particularly in Britain. British steel production was concentrated upon acid steel which required iron ore of low phosphoric content which had to be imported. Germany and the USA, not having the same geographical advantage, developed plant for the production of basic steel using ores which they had in abundant supply. At first basic steel was regarded as inferior to acid steel but improvements in the techniques of open-hearth basic steel production had made basic steel an acceptable alternative to acid steel by the 1920s. Customers who had specified acid steel previously now turned to basic steel because the cost was lower. Two major customers in the home market for acid steel, the shipbuilders and the railway companies were suffering themselves from economic depression and, accordingly reduced orders for iron and steel. The industry thus had to face the fact that it was geared for the production of a kind of steel that was not so much in demand. In the past also there had been a huge market for wrought iron. Before 1914 Britain had produced 1,207,000 tons a year of puddled bar iron. Basic steel had, by the 1920s, proved to be a popular replacement for this to such an extent that in 1929 the British production figure was down to 158,000 tons. Britain's share of the world export market for steel fell from 21 per cent in 1929 to 17 per cent in 1938.

Apart from the difficulties indicated above the industry added to its own troubles. Costs of production were higher than elsewhere. This was due, no doubt, in part to the decision to take up the production of basic steel, but it was also caused by the failure to integrate production and amalgamate firms. The iron and steel industry is one that benefits from economies of scale but demands large sums for capital investment. Only the biggest firms can provide the capital necessary to build plant where the whole process of steel manufacture from the assembly of iron ore and coal to the completion of the steel product is possible on the same site. Some amalgamation did take place in Britain in between the wars. By 1930 twenty firms owned 60 per cent of the steel capacity of the British industry and 47 per cent of the pig iron capacity, but they were still not big enough compared with their German and American rivals. There was still too much old-fashioned and inefficient plant in operation which, because of the large capital sum needed for its replacement, was tending to perpetuate inefficiency. By 1939 the average British blast furnace was producing only 40 per cent of the product of its American counterpart.

It is not suggested that the capital invested in the industry between the wars was meagre—it was not: but the British industry had to undergo conversion, which it did reluctantly, while its rivals either expanded or reconstructed industries already geared for the product the market demanded.

Much of the British capital available to the industry was used piecemeal in the refurbishing of existing works. These works were sited for their convenience in producing acid not basic steel and were away from the major supply of Jurassic ore in Northamptonshire. Factors other than the major economic one intervened. For example the firm of Richard Thomas was unable, because of pressure from the trade unions and public opinion to site new works in Lincolnshire. Instead, in order to relieve the unemployment problem, the works was sited at Ebbw Vale.

The Government intervened to help the steel industry perhaps more than any other except agriculture. Its motives were to encourage the industry towards amalgamation and to protect it from foreign competition. When free trade was abandoned in 1932 a tariff of 33⅓ per cent was put on foreign steel and subsequently the Import Duties Advisory Committee agreed to raise this to 50 per cent provided the industry reorganized itself. The British Iron and Steel Federation had been formed in 1932, and this was able to negotiate an agreement with the European industry which had organized itself into a cartel. The agreement gave preferential terms to European steel in British markets, but limited severely the quantities of steel that could be exported from Europe to Britain. This helped towards the revival of the British industry in the late 1930s but did not encourage efficiency. In overseas markets, on terms of equal competition Britain's share dwindled.

AGRICULTURE

Agriculture too was hard hit by the interwar depression. During the First World War agriculture had been subject to a form of central control which had raised the level of production, regulated wages and guaranteed prices. The emphasis of the increased production had been on arable farming. When the war ended the industry prospered for a while but in common with others it suffered from the depression of 1921. Prices fell rapidly but government control had been withdrawn. Wheat, which had been at 86s 4d a quarter in 1920 was 40s 9d in 1922. The natural reaction of the farmers was to revert to pasture rather than arable farming because prices were better and pasture farming required less manpower. There was a steady exodus from the countryside which helped to swell the growing numbers of unemployed from the depressed industries. By 1939 agriculture was responsible for only 3½ per cent of the national income.

The principal reason for these difficulties was the overproduction of agricultural industries overseas. This was something that was beyond Britain's control. If home agriculture was to compete in the open market with foreign produce then it had to become more efficient. This could be done, however, only by increasing the size of the agricultural unit, which was small in comparison with some of its competitors. It is difficult to see how this could have been done without causing considerable social upheaval, unlike amalgamation in other industries which could have been achieved without much social disturbance.

The government paid particular attention to agriculture in the interwar period. In addition to the tariffs imposed in 1931 as a protection against foreign competition it subsidized the industry in several ways. Help was given to smallholders to encourage a movement back to the land, and agricultural land and buildings were given relief from the burden of rates. The growing of fruit for the canning and bottling industry was encouraged, and large-scale cultivation of sugar beet was introduced. In 1935 the British Sugar Corporation was formed, three of whose directors were government representatives. Wheat was subsidized, as also were oats and barley, cattle and fertilizers. Marketing boards, a significant departure from laissez-faire, were established for milk, potatoes, pig meat and hops. The boards were associations of producers who had compulsory powers to restrict output and maintain prices. But regulation, subsidy and control had little effect on the natural development of agriculture. 'There was no strategy, only a series of uncoordinated measures, mostly directed to propping up the status quo.'[9] Arable farming declined until 1939 when the effects of the corresponding decline in soil fertility were felt.

4

Progress – the newer industries

This account of why things went wrong in British industry presents a gloomy survey of economic progress. It is advisable perhaps at this stage to remind the reader of what was said earlier about the theme of this book, lest it be felt that so far there has been simply a catalogue of the mistakes and inefficiencies of our economic past. If economic circumstances had consistently played into Britain's hands, if the multitude of individuals responsible for achieving the country's economic growth had always been alert to the interests and needs of Britain, and if no wrong decisions had been taken, then economic progress would have been spectacular. No country, of course, enjoys such a bright future, but it is possible by looking back at economic development to see how progress was held back and to come to some conclusions why this was so. It is possible also to see why other countries were more successful. In doing this it must not be forgotten that, in spite of the difficulties and mistakes, at no time was there economic retrogression or stagnation. Britain, in common with other advanced economies was becoming steadily wealthier. The difficulties she encountered affected the rate of progress, and here we are outlining the factors that have been peculiar to Britain, but we must not lose sight of the overall advance.

The interwar period is a good example of this. In spite of the worldwide depression and the contraction and decline of her old staple industries, Britain achieved an increase in real national income over the period, as evinced by the rise in real income per head which made possible, for example, the growth of a prosperous home market for motor vehicles and the new consumer goods. While the old staples were in difficulties new industries and new fields of investment were emerging. New consumer goods industries appeared and absorbed some of the labour made redundant in the older industries, creating a demand for a whole variety of materials and components. Mechanical and electrical engineering were two branches of industry that experienced a healthy expansion; others were rayon, glass, paper, scent and soap, radio and gramophones, and the food trades.

Motor vehicles
The industry which affected economic development most of all was the motor vehicle industry. The increase in the numbers of vehicles produced between

1918 and 1939 almost speaks for itself (see Fig. 4.1). Rubber, glass, ferrous alloys, electrical components were just some of the items now much in demand. Oil refining offered opportunity for heavy investment, while road building provided employment rather as the railways had done the century before, even if not on the same scale.

Yet the motor vehicle industry was not a major exporting industry in the interwar

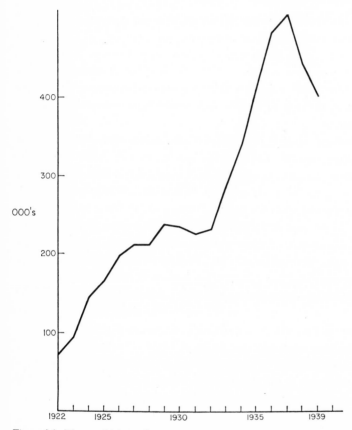

Figure 4.1. *Motor vehicle production in UK* 1922–39. Source: Key Statistics 1900–1966.

period, though there was a potential overseas market and British engineering tradition should have encouraged the overseas buyer to buy British. The fundamental reason for this was that Britain was slow off the mark.

By 1913 British motor vehicle production had reached 34,000 units per annum. This compared with 485,000 units in the USA. This huge discrepancy is undoubtedly partly accounted for by the much bigger market in the USA and the higher level of personal income, but not entirely. By the beginning of the century the Americans had already developed a components industry which involved a considerable degree

4

of standardization. Firms existed to supply several of the vehicle producing firms with carburettors, electrical components and so on, in standardized form. This meant cheaper production compared with the British method of each firm attempting to make its own parts. In Britain before 1914, the middle-class market, because of the high price of the motor vehicle, was hardly touched. Henry Ford in the USA had, of course, by this time introduced the flow production method which a huge market made possible.

The First World War hindered British vehicle production. Factories changed to the production of aero-engines and munitions, while the USA exported vehicles in large numbers to the Allies. Export markets were lost during the war, as with other industries, but at the same time the home market was substantially protected by the McKenna Duties (1915) which placed a $33\frac{1}{3}$ per cent ad valorem tax on car imports – a duty sufficiently high to remove any threat from foreign competition more or less permanently.

The components industry in Britain developed between the wars, with firms like Joseph Lucas expanding rapidly. At the same time many new firms entered the field, though many were to fail in an industry that demanded a high degree of engineering skill and good business organization. There were eighty-two assembly firms in 1922 but by 1929 these had dwindled to thirty-one. Of these Morris, Austin and Singer produced 75 per cent of the total output. The fewer the firms the better, from the standpoint of economic production. American flow production techniques could be operated if sales were sufficiently big. William Morris had attempted to initiate flow production in 1924, but not very successfully because of the size of the market. American methods were, however, gradually introduced during the 1920s as the market expanded. British producers offered to the public a wide variety of models which, because of the corresponding loss of the advantages of standardization, kept prices higher than they might have been. In the USA standardization was much greater, in spite of the much larger production. By 1939 in Britain there were twenty independent firms left in the industry. Six of these were responsible for 90 per cent of total output, but there was an important change from 1929. The prohibitive McKenna Duties had induced the Americans to invest inside Britain rather than attempt to bring in vehicles from abroad. Fords had developed their Dagenham factory, General Motors had bought up Vauxhalls and expanded production significantly. Of the six manufacturers mentioned above, Nuffield (Morris), Austin and Ford were the big three. Vauxhall, Rootes and Standard were all at much the same level of production but behind the first three. It is not surprising that, in view of the comparative efficiency of the USA car industry, it had secured such a footing in Britain by 1939.

The demand for cars in the overseas markets at this time, as demonstrated by the success of the Americans, was for vehicles of large horsepower and seating capacity. The major reason why British cars did not sell well abroad was because of their small size and engine capacity. The British industry concentrated on a product which was in demand at home but which was not much wanted overseas. The home demand for vehicles of this kind was stimulated by the taxation scheme then in operation which taxed according to engine capacity. The bigger the engine, the higher the tax. This also applied to insurance premiums. Petrol was not cheap, as in the USA, because it was not an indigenous natural resource, so that the emphasis was on the small car. British exports were largely to the Empire, where British vehicles were given preferential entry terms; 81·2 per cent of car exports from Britain in 1938 went to Empire markets, and this was not an exceptional year. The markets outside the Empire went largely untapped. British cars were made to run on the smooth modern road surfaces that were experienced in Britain in the interwar period; ground clearance did not have to be high and suspension did not have to be sturdy. On the rougher roads that were experienced abroad British cars did not fare so well, which was a further factor limiting their sales overseas.

When the slump came in the early 1930s, the British motor vehicle industry remained surprisingly buoyant compared with similar industries abroad. Production fell 15 per cent in Britain between 1929 and 1932 compared with 75 per cent in the USA. This indicates the leeway that the British industry had to make up in its own home market. After 1945 something was done about the leeway in overseas markets, although the great post-1945 expansion was difficult to foresee in the 1930s.

Electrical engineering

It has already been noted that by 1914 Britain had fallen behind the USA and Germany in electrical engineering, one of the most important twentieth-century industries. This failure to pursue vigorously the advantages of electrical power was continued during the earlier part of the 1920s. By 1924 electricity accounted for only 49·7 per cent of the total power consumed by British industry, where the comparable figure for the USA was 73 per cent. The traditional predominance of coal as a source of power was in part to blame. The history of steam power in the nineteenth century had wedded many manufacturers to old-fashioned machinery, thus holding back more efficient techniques of production, limiting the manufacture of electrical equipment and retarding the provision of a uniform system of electricity generation. Furthermore the multiplicity of small generating plants with different voltage supply hindered the expansion of the industry. Germany's exports of electrical equipment were twice as big as those of Britain by 1925 while the USA's exports were five times as large.[10].

The industry was boosted by the creation in 1926 of the National Grid. The geographical advantages of the size of Britain made a grid of this kind comparatively easy to organize and construct, providing a system which could be claimed as superior to any in Europe or the USA. A Central Electricity Board was set up as part of the rationalization scheme, small inefficient plant was shut down and large new generating stations were constructed to provide cheaper electricity. Total output rose from 6,600 million units in 1925 to 26,400 million units in 1939.[11]

Electricity was thus a success story in the interwar period. Electrical consumer goods were manufactured in appreciable numbers to supply a rising demand among the middle classes, whose incomes continued to rise. The manufacture of washing machines, electric irons, refrigerators and vacuum cleaners gave employment directly to many, and indirectly in those industries that supplied the materials of which these goods were made. The introduction of broadcasting in the 1920s, with its obvious connection with electricity, gave rise to the new industry of radio.

The demand for electrical engineering plant as more power stations were required encouraged the growth of electrical engineering firms with a corresponding growth in employment in the industry. By 1937 there were 367,000 insured workers in the industry.

Chemical industry

The greatly increased demand for chemicals during the First World War gave an impetus to the chemical industry in Britain which brought it more into line with the requirements of a modern economy. Britain, though pioneering some of the early discoveries (especially in dyeing) had not pursued their application but had left their development to others, particularly the Germans. The German supply was abruptly cut off in 1914 and obliged Britain to provide the necessary chemicals herself to win the war. Four firms in particular expanded in consequence and these were merged in 1926 to form Imperial Chemical Industries (ICI), a company big enough to match the size of European competitors, particularly those in Germany. The major interests of four firms give an idea of the chemical industry's production at the time. Nobel Industries were the most important firm in the manufacture of explosives; the British Dyestuffs Corporation Ltd was concerned with organic chemicals and dyestuffs; Brunner-Mond Ltd produced alkalis and industrial gases; and United Alkali produced much the same. Other products of the new firm ICI were fertilizers, phosphates, fine chemicals and drugs. The plastics industry was yet to be developed but it is worth noting that one plastic, bakelite, was in production in the interwar period and was used extensively for electrical fittings and small containers, thus initiating a new type of material which was to develop into an industry in its own right in the post-1945 period.

The chemical industry was also closely linked with the manufacture of rayon, which was the most important manmade fibre before 1939.

Building

The very large number of interwar houses that are recognizable today by their distinct (usually semidetached) style are evidence of another industry that flourished while other industries declined. Like the coal industry, the building industry employed materials and component parts which involved many other industries in its prosperity. Directly and indirectly the building industry gave employment to many thousands of people. Nearly 750,000 workers were directly engaged in all sectors of the industry, while another 300,000 to 400,000 were employed in dependent industries. Over 4 million houses were built in the interwar period. The boom in building, particularly in the 1930s, represented the fastest growth in the history of the building industry and must be considered as an important factor in mitigating the worst effects of the slump. 'Building employed only 6–7½ per cent of all insured workers in the 1930s, but it accounted for 20 per cent of the increase in employment in 1932–35, or 30 per cent if the increase in the indigenous building materials industry is included.'[12]

The cheap money policy which kept interest rates low during this period did not affect building societies particularly, and this contributed to the boom in housing. Their higher rate of interest attracted funds which made money available for mortgages. Rents remained high and many properties were built to be rented. Productivity was improved in the industry in the 1930s, which brought the price of houses down. Workers in the newer industries, experiencing deflation at a time when, for them, wages were not contracting, were in a position to demand new houses, especially as there had been little really significant replacement housing for nearly twenty years. The majority of houses built were small. The reduced size of the average family and the dramatic decline in the employment of domestic servants, coupled with the increasing rateable value of domestic property, created a demand for the small house placed on a small plot of land. Roughly 75 per cent of the houses built in England and Wales during the period were built by private enterprise. Some of these received a State subsidy. The other 25 per cent were built by local authorities –council houses mainly for rent.

Much of the new housing was built in the South-East and the Midlands, but particularly in the London area. This illustrates a most important feature of the interwar period (one that has had very marked repercussions ever since), the move of the population from north to south on a scale which compares with the movement in the opposite direction at the time of the economic expansion in the eighteenth and nineteenth centuries. 'In June 1923, the four Southern Divisions of the Ministry of Labour (London, South-East, South-West and the Midlands) contained 46·6 per cent of the insured population, and the rest of the United Kingdom (including Northern Ireland) the remaining 53·4 per cent; in June 1938 these figures had been almost exactly reversed, the south now having 53·9 per cent and the north 46·1 per cent of the insured population.'[13] The outer London area experienced a mushroom growth of housing estates. Wembley's population grew by 205 per cent between 1921 and 1931; Hornchurch increased by 166 per cent, Merton and Morden by 141 per cent and Hendon by 106 per cent.[14] New garden cities were established at Letchworth and Welwyn whilst elsewhere at Slough, for example, trading estates were built which offered factory accommodation to let, and which anticipated and

41

achieved considerable urban development. Birmingham attracted a similar industrial expansion to that of London, but not on the same scale.

The population drift southwards during this period was caused not so much by the change in location of industries as by the expansion of new ones in the south and the contraction and decline of old ones in the north. The reasons need to be found why the expansion took place in the south rather than in the north, where there was already a long established industrial tradition. The most important reason was the introduction of electricity. The original migration northwards had been made necessary because of the need to be near good supplies of flowing water and the need for coal as a source of power. Once industry was freed from the economic necessity of being near coal, it could site itself in areas where other economic factors could be used to advantage. The movement of population southwards started right at the beginning of the century. The population of Greater London grew by 1,600,000 between 1901 and 1938.[15] This coincided with the growth of the electrical supply system.

London attracted many light industries because of the size of the market it offered. Most of the new industries that grew in this period produced goods for home consumption. Anyone setting up a business or factory in the London area had the biggest market in the country on his doorstep, with commensurate savings in transport costs. Also, because of the large population already there, a labour force awaited the enterprising entrepreneur. Ultimately this labour force, which provided largely unskilled male and female labour, was in short supply.

For the few industries that required bulk raw materials London offered port facilities second to none. The paper industry was one of these. Most, however, were light industries which could take advantage of improved road communications to bring in component parts and distribute finished products.

London and the Midlands had every appearance of being prosperous areas and this in itself attracted the entrepreneur anxious to make a profit in the most likely market, so that prosperity snowballed. Meanwhile the other areas of Britain experienced a loss of population. Scotland, Wales and the north of England lost 950,000 between 1923 and 1931 and 260,000 between 1931 and 1936 (net emigration).[16]

An important feature of the new industries that has a bearing on the changing economic pattern of the interwar period, was the size of the firms involved. In all the expanding industries mentioned, except for the building industry, the big firm became the established economic unit. Names that are household words today, ICI, Nuffield, EMI (Electric and Musical Industries), came into prominence in the 1920s and 1930s; Courtaulds had already become prominent in 1904 when they secured the control of the rayon process. The capital base needed for these industries was large, but once formed there were important benefits from economies of scale. There was at first a fear of monopoly if firms grew too large. This fear was inherited from nineteenth-century economics, and from experience in the USA in the late nineteenth century when capitalism was unrestrained and the large firm had abused its monopoly situation. Monopoly had not occurred in British industry and until the 1920s there was a determination that it should not. The serious difficulties of the 1920s brought a change in attitude. The mood for rationalization coincided with the view that provided there were necessary safeguards a monopoly or quasi-monopoly was even desirable. The big firm was thus tolerated and in some instances, as we have seen, the Government actually encouraged amalgamations. This change in attitude was late compared with the USA and Europe, and explains in part why British industry found its competitors were more efficient. For example, in 1930 it took the twenty biggest firms in the industry to produce 70 per cent of the British output of iron and steel, whereas the same quantity of steel was produced by one firm in Germany, and in the USA one firm produced three times as much.

The British car industry, it has been noted, was dominated by six firms in 1939. In the USA there were only three really big firms by this time. One of them, General Motors, was alone responsible for producing nearly four times the number of vehicles produced by the entire British industry.[17] British industry thus had a long way to go to catch up its rivals. The growth of the big firm we shall note as a continuing tendency in the post-1945 era.

The significance of the interwar period

Now that more than a quarter of a century has elapsed since the end of the interwar period it is possible to see it as a very important time of transition. There is a striking contrast between the pre-1914 economy and the post-1945 economy; the period between the wars represents the awkward, embarrassing years when the need for change was slowly borne in on industry and those who controlled it, while the realization dawned that a return to the old ways and attitudes was not possible. The period 1918 to 1939 forms a bridge between the old and the new.

The failure of the old staple industries to contribute effectively to the export trade can now be seen as permanent. From 1918 to 1939 there was always the hope that once the worst of the slump was over, the upswing of the trade cycle would bring renewed prosperity. This was a hope sustained by the conservatism of industries where none of the people working in them could remember, nor could their parents, when the industries concerned had not been the mainstays of the British economy. The twenty-one years of the interwar period were needed to demonstrate that t' is was no longer true. They were years of reluctant change, with contraction and decline occurring parallel with expansion and enterprise. They were inevitably years of confusion and frustration, but not stagnation. Britain was in a sense a divided nation in that while so many people suffered from unemployment and low incomes, others achieved a higher standard of living than ever before.

The role of government

A further aspect of this transition period was the slowly changing attitude to the role of government in controlling the economy. As the effects of the changing economic pattern became increasingly and painfully obvious, so the Government's responsibility for doing something about it was increasingly acknowledged. The regulation of the home market, the support to be given to industry, the responsibility for relieving unemployment, the mitigation of the undesirable effects of the trade cycle, these were all accepted as matters to be resolved by state action. In the nineteenth century, when it had become apparent that laissez-faire of contract was leading to exploitation of the working classes, the state had been obliged to interfere to ensure reasonable working conditions and terms of employment. A succession of Factory Acts, Mines Acts and Workshop Acts had gradually established the right of Government to circumscribe employers so that minimum working conditions were assured. This was one way in which the state had already intervened in industry before 1914.

Between the wars the government embarked upon a further stage. When the old staples encountered protracted difficulties, the government intervened in one way or another in all of them in an effort to alleviate the worst effects of the falling markets. A Coal Mines Reorganization Commission was established to promote amalgamation within the coal industry, the iron and steel industry was assisted by tariffs and derating, the National Shipbuilders' Society was actively supported by government funds in its efforts to close down redundant yards, agriculture was given subsidies and help in other forms, as we have seen, and the cotton textile industry was assisted by schemes to buy up and scrap some of the excess capacity. The intervention was ad hoc and was not particularly effective but the acceptance of government responsibility here was important. It denoted a new attitude and one which was alien to the pre-1914 period.

This attitude was in line with the new approach to the familiar topic of free trade. The nineteenth century had been the century of free trade; Britain, clinging to the idea that her greatness stemmed from free trade, had let it carry on into the twentieth century. She was about the only country to do so, though the movement in support of protection was supported by one of the major political parties. Free trade became an election issue in 1923 but the Conservative party, asking for a mandate to do away with free trade, was defeated. Sheer economic circumstances forced a different attitude by the early 1930s. Intervention by the Government was then accepted as essential. When free trade was abandoned in 1931 it was the old nineteenth-century conception that was finally discarded. This was the conception of a worldwide trading area dominated by a Britain industrialized in advance of her competitors, and in a position to flood world markets with manufactured goods in return for the unhampered import of food and raw materials: the free trade of the age of mid-Victorian supremacy. In the interests of the promotion of world trade this loss was a fortunate development. Free trade can be successful only when the trading countries are competing from a reasonably comparable base of economic development.

In the 1930s free trade gave way to a form of economic nationalism which was practised just long enough for the shock of the slump to be absorbed. The way was then clear for a new movement to gain ground–the post-1945 movement to-wards free trade which we still have in our own times. This is a free trade movement more likely to succeed because it involves countries on a comparatively equal footing, no one country dominating as in Victorian times. It involves also, paradoxically, freedom of the individual firm or industry to trade within a much more tightly controlled economy.

Government influence over the national economy was exercised in three major ways in the interwar period. First, as has been noted, the Government assisted individual industries; secondly, by imposing tariffs it deliberately protected the home industries and this was perhaps where government intervention had the greatest effect. The third method was the attempt to control the economy by mone-tary and fiscal measures which were designed to counter economic depression and unemployment. We have become so used to the comparatively close control of the economy by the Government since 1945 that the duty of the Government to take what we now look upon as orthodox measures is questioned by few. There were few orthodox measures in the 1920s and 1930s so that government control was neither close nor very successful. The emphasis upon the type of control before and after the war is important in this context. Control of the national economy by fiscal and monetary methods has been the most important way in which the govern-ment has influenced economic affairs since 1945; before 1945 it was the least import-ant. There was a general assumption that the government should act, but because a situation of this kind had not occurred before, the government was not sure what to do. This is why government action at this time has been described as ad hoc because it was difficult to analyse change as change was taking place. It is easier now to see what was left undone and to understand what was wrongly done.

The orthodox approach to fiscal and monetary control of the economy, prior to 1939, is simply put. The focal problem was the maintenance of confidence in the currency, and the best method of keeping the £ sterling strong was to demonstrate to the world that Britain could balance its books. A budget deficit was, therefore, undesirable; although it might occur from time to time it should not be planned. This thinking can be explained by a fear of inflation which was heightened by the experiences of Germany and other countries where inflation ran wild, but it does not alter the fact that the aim for a balanced budget entailed a deflationary policy in a period of economic depression. In the light of the Keynesian policies that have been orthodox since 1945 this outlook now seems extraordinary. Keynes was, of course, advocating that the government should inflate, and should budget for a deficit, but although he was listened to and supported by the academics he was not supported by

45

the politicians. Other countries, notably the USA, Australia and Sweden, by a combination of good management and good luck applied comparatively correct inflationary policies. Successive governments in Britain increased taxation, reduced social benefits and cut back government expenditure. On the occasions when taxation was reduced, expenditure was correspondingly reduced to compensate for the loss in revenue. The most notable examples of reduced government expenditure were when the Committee on National Expenditure, led by Sir Eric Geddes, recommended in 1922 how £100 million could be 'saved' (the Geddes axe), and the Snowden budget of 1932 when, amongst other items, the salaries of civil servants and local government employees were cut.

It is not fair, however, to suggest that the pursuit of Keynesian policies in the interwar period would have resolved Britain's economic dilemma. Keynesian policies would certainly have helped but they could not have solved on their own the problem of economic depression combined with an adverse balance of payments that occurred in the slump of the 1930s. Since 1945 Keynesian policies have been applied in the context of inflation and occasional imbalance of payments, which presents a different problem from prewar circumstances. A deflationary policy promotes the double effect of reducing imports and curbing demand in the home market. If one of these is required and not the other a deflationary policy is bound to be working half the time against a successful solution. The prewar problem presented just such an embarrassment. Exports had fallen away, but until the imposition of tariffs in 1931 imports were virtually unrestricted. Imports did not rise particularly, but because exports were low the effect was the same as if imports had risen. The deflationary policies thus helped to control imports but worked counter to the pressing need to stimulate the home market.

The solution to the balance of payments problem became pressing in 1931. The crisis was induced partly by Churchill's budget of 1925 which brought Britain back on to the gold standard but at the same parity ($4·86) as when she had gone off it in 1914. The reasons for doing this were laudable enough, particularly the belief that Britain would accordingly provide stability to a shaky world currency exchange system, but the pound sterling was overvalued. It was too much to hope that the First World War had made no difference to the relationship of individual currencies to gold. Certain countries in following Britain back on to the gold standard readjusted their currencies so as to undervalue them – Japan and France were two of these – and they could now export more easily as their goods were attractively priced in foreign markets. Britain made exporting an unnecessarily difficult task because her goods were too highly priced in consequence of the overvaluation.

The serious imbalance of payments in 1931 compelled Britain to take steps to protect her economy. Free trade was abandoned as also was the gold standard. The £ immediately settled down at a more realistic exchange rate. The implications of this were farreaching. Now that the automatic mechanism of the gold standard had gone the currency had to be controlled, while at the same time the imposition of tariffs involved further control. In both instances the government had to assume the responsibility. This was a distinct move away from the orthodox conception of the role of government in controlling the economy. Since 1931 all British governments have been obliged to manage the currency and this has increasingly involved them in measures to protect the pound sterling from external pressures.

In 1932 an Exchange Equalization Account was established. Its purpose was to help stabilize the pound by purchasing or selling sterling according to the pressures of the market. This was the herald of the presentday system of exchange control through the nationalized Bank of England.

One other factor, an involuntary one, helped the trading position. Throughout the interwar period, particularly in the 1930s the terms of trade moved in Britain's favour. In this she was fortunate because the value of her imports was kept correspondingly low at a time when she could ill afford a high import bill. In fact, but for the favourable terms of trade, the trade balance problem would have been very alarming. If, in addition, Britain could have switched her surplus manpower from the old staples to the new industries the trade figures of the 1930s would have looked very rosy.

In assuming greater responsibility for the economy the government of the 1930s deliberately pursued a policy of cheap money. This is a policy which subsequently fell out of favour. Some facts about it are included here because they help to explain the modern technique of bank rate manipulation that has taken the bank rate to high levels over long periods. The bank rate was kept at 2 per cent from 1932 to 1939. The intention was partly to discourage the movement of 'hot money' which could confuse the currency situation at the wrong time and disturb confidence, and partly to reduce government expenditure by minimizing the outgoings on the National Debt. It was claimed also, that a low interest rate encouraged economic expansion, but economists are still in disagreement over the efficiency of such a policy. Certainly the post-1945 Labour administration accepted the opposite point of view and retained cheap money during a period of full employment and inflation. Since 1951 the bank rate has once again been used as a monetary weapon, the accompanying disadvantages being accepted as inevitable. The argument since 1945 has not been whether cheap money stimulates the economy in times of depression but whether or not a high bank rate in itself deters expansion in a period of inflation.

The impact of mass unemployment

The comparative inactivity of the government in the interwar years left the onus of coping with the human problems of change to the people themselves. The government provided only the framework for economic activity and left the owners, the managers, and the employers to work things out with the employees. The First

World War had left a legacy of class bitterness (the leadership in the war was casti-
gated by the rank and file), which was now carried on into the difficult circumstances
of the peace. Not only was political leadership questioned but the policies of owners
and management were denounced as unemployment grew. Figure 4.2 illustrates
the number of people out of work during the period.

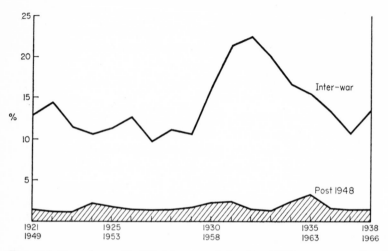

Figure 4.2. *Unemployment in UK, interwar period and post-*1948, *percentage of working population.*
Source: Key Statistics 1900–1966.

The mass unemployment between the wars was, it is true, especially bad in certain
industries, but overall it affected the unskilled worker and the working classes in
general rather than the middle classes and the white collar worker. As has been
noted above, there was a rise in personal income for many people, and a rise in
national income, but for the unemployed the level of income was wretchedly low and
their social status was degrading. It has been estimated that at the worst period of the
slump in 1932 nearly 3,750,000 workers (insured and non-insured) were unemployed
and their reaction to living in a society where for others life was increasingly prosperous may be imagined.

Industrial unrest was, not surprisingly, a feature of the period. Figure 4.3 illustrates
its extent. The hostility towards 'the bosses' became with many workers deeply
ingrained. Cuts in wages were hotly contested in an atmosphere of insecurity,
mistrust and suspicion. The relationship between worker and employer was at a
low ebb. The power of the trade unions was limited in a time of mass unemployment
and the collapse of the General Strike in 1926 made many of the workers resigned to
the inevitability of a system beyond their influence, but the bitterness remained.

The trade unions have been criticized since 1945 for their militance and selfish
pursuit, at times, of claims that are not in the national interest. Some allowance must

be made for a reaction to the experiences of the interwar period. There are still many people who can remember the circumstances of those times and the contrast between the prosperous and the unemployed. The experience of a long period out of work,

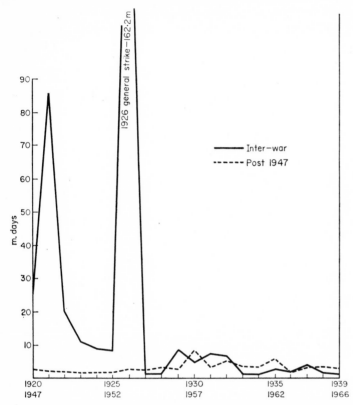

Figure 4.3. *No. of working days lost through industrial disputes–interwar and post-*1946. Source: Key Statistics 1900–1966.

especially if the worker has a wife and family to support, is not forgotten in a life-time, and some of the bitterness is handed on to the next generation. The events of the 1930s are not so distant that it can be safely said that they have no effect upon present-day attitudes of workers, management and government. Full employment since 1945 has produced a reactionary situation where the unskilled worker and the skilled artisan have achieved a startling increase in prosperity while the middle classes who did so well before the war have had to be content with a comparatively modest increase in their standards of living. Certainly for a long time after 1945 it was not accepted that full employment was a permanent feature of the postwar period. The unions, therefore, tended to press for high incomes, almost irrespective of the future consequences, in the belief that they should secure maximum rewards

49

for their members while the going was still good. The period that has elapsed since the end of the Second World War is now sufficiently long for that attitude to have partly spent itself, and a new attitude is evolving. This is discussed in Chapter 13. The point to be emphasized here is that the industrial unrest caused by the changing economic pattern of the interwar period had repercussions after 1945 that lasted a very long time; they are, perhaps, still with us.[18]

5

Postwar affluence

The effect of the war

In 1945 a responsible commentator on economic events could have been forgiven if he had forecast a gloomy future for Britain. The 1930s had been difficult enough. Six years of war had stretched the economy to a point where it was only natural to presume that recovery would be a very long struggle. The difficulties and disruption that had occurred after 1918 were expected by many people to recur, but in greater measure. There was, admittedly, the idealism customary during any prolonged major catastrophe, set on putting to rights after the emergency all the ills of society, but the memory of dashed hopes and disillusionment after 1918 had a sobering effect. In any case, the hard facts of Britain's economic plight were there for all to see.

Much of the capital equipment of British industry had been due for modernization or replacement by 1939. During the war this capital had been run down and could not be expected to continue much beyond 1945. The railways, for instance, had been overstretched as well as suffering considerable destruction from air attack, and without capital reconstruction on a massive scale were not in a position to provide the services so vital to economic recovery. The same could be said for most of the basic industries.

Much of industry had converted to production for war purposes when cost was secondary to the business of winning the war. Now reconversion had to be undertaken when cost was a prime consideration. Where was the money to come from? Half of Britain's overseas investments had gone to help pay for the war which had been costing in its later stages £12 million per day. The comfortable feeling that the trade gap was covered by profits from overseas investments had gone. It did not look as if expenditure would be covered by income. A debt had been built up in the war years, in spite of generous Canadian aid and the Lease-Lend system with the USA. By mid 1945 it was £3,355 million, the greater part of which was a debt to the Sterling Area. At the beginning of the century Britain had been a creditor of the USA; now she found herself in debt to India, Egypt and the Sudan.

As had happened after the First World War, the rest of the world, except the USA, was disorganized or completely disrupted. The chances that Britain could obtain the necessary raw materials or find the markets to help to restore the trade balance appeared slim. In any case, Britain's overseas trade was restricted by the fact that she had lost a quarter of her shipping, and the terms of trade were now set against her.

In spite of this inauspicious setting for the postwar era, in spite of the gloomy forecasts that the country would run into economic catastrophe (these were particularly prevalent in the USA), Britain passed into an age of comparative affluence at a pace of economic growth unprecedented when compared with the first half of the century.

Full employment has become the accepted condition of society. Only twice since 1945 has unemployment risen above the 3 per cent level and on each occasion only for a short period when a severe winter caused abnormal laying off of outside workers. The average rate of unemployment has been between 1 per cent and 2 per cent. The length of the working week has been gradually reduced, while increased holidays with pay have become a feature of modern industry. Primary poverty, so much a feature of earlier economic development, has been almost eliminated; incomes have been consistently at a high level and have risen at a pace that could not have been anticipated in 1945. This has meant a standard of living for the majority of people in Britain that until the 1950s had seemed to be possible only for the minority.

How much of this is of a temporary nature? History has shown that economic fluctuations can be violent and prolonged. Has the nature of capitalism changed so as to produce rapid unruffled economic growth in place of the increasing disruption of the trade cycle? Has the affluence of postwar Britain been brought about by a conspiracy of uncontrolled circumstances or by careful design or both? These are questions that we need to answer if we are to have confidence in the future of the British economy. If this affluence has come about by sheer chance, then the future holds no certainty that steady economic growth can be maintained; if this affluence has been brought about by a control over the economy (i.e. a manipulation of economic policies by successive governments or by a change in Britain's industrial structure), then there is a real hope that economic prosperity can be assured. In fact the answer lies somewhere in between. Britain's economy is a mixture of state control and capitalist enterprise. Capitalism has adapted itself to postwar conditions, accepting a fair measure of control by the state. The state on the other hand has accepted a much more definite and positive role in the economy but still relies very much on the willingness of the capitalist sector of the economy to accept voluntary self-control rather than centrally controlled state planning. The whole question of the control of the economy is in a state of flux and we shall need to examine it later on; meanwhile we must look at the factors that have been responsible for Britain's postwar affluence.

Reorientation of industry

At the centre of the economic troubles of the interwar period was the failure of the staple industries to provide the income from exports that they had traditionally achieved from the early days of the Industrial Revolution. Cotton textiles and coal in particular, which had been major export industries prior to 1914, were now, for reasons outlined in chapter 3, in no position to provide the major contribution expected from major export industries to the balance of payments. In 1913 textiles accounted for one-third of total British exports and nearly 44 per cent of manufactured exports, but by 1937 these figures had dropped to one-quarter and 33 per cent. The cotton industry itself was supplying only 13 per cent of total exports by 1937, but even so, apart from machinery it was the most important single item on the export list. After the war exports by 1948 had not exceeded two-fifths of the 1937 figures. Coal exports had dwindled from the record 94 million tons of 1913 to a mere trickle in the immediate postwar period.

As Table 5.1 shows, by 1945 there was an alarming deficit on visible trade. Because so many overseas investments had gone to pay for the war there was a greater need than ever for the visible trade gap to be brought under control by means of greatly

Table 5.1

Value and volume of external trade of the United Kingdom

	Value £ million		
	1938	*1944*	*1945*
Imports	919·5	1309·3	1103·7
Exports	471·4	266·4	399·4
Re-exports	60·9	15·6	50·8
	Volume Index no. 1938 = 100		
	1938	*1944*	*1945*
Retained imports	100	80	61·9
Exports	100	31	45·8
Re-exports	100	15	42·2

Source: Board of Trade.

increased exports. If the staple industries were no longer able to provide these exports, new industries had to take their place in the export field, and quickly.

The pattern of exporting industry has thus radically changed since the war. New export industries, particularly motor-vehicles, chemicals and the new branches of engineering have emerged as the staple industries. They have filled the gap left by the failure of cotton textiles and coal to cope with the mounting pressure for exports.

5

Before the war there had always been the hope that the fall in demand for exports was a temporary phase. Exports would ultimately revive, or so it was hoped, and coal and cotton textiles would be restored to their position of supremacy. There was thus a refusal to face squarely the fact that new industries were needed and that the decline of coal and cotton textiles was permanent. The war obliged industry to accept that change was necessary and that clinging to a forlorn hope was disastrous.

The new industries emerged, not as a result of specific planning, but by the forces of the market. The government encouraged an export drive imposed upon them by the blunt facts of the country's trading position. Controls, financial incentives and persuasion were used to direct as much as possible to the export trade, but the ultimate decision as to what was produced, how much was produced and how much could be sold abroad was left to the manufacturers themselves.

The public became accustomed to exhortations from the government to accept import restrictions in the national interest and to understand why so many of the consumer goods desperately needed on the home market were being exported. Press photographs of goods lined up on the docks awaiting shipment were meant not to make the consumer in Britain discontented but to demonstrate the vital importance of the export drive. 'Export or die' was a slogan of the time, somewhat dramatic, but an indication of the serious nature of the situation. The shops were poorly stocked. This was the age of austerity.

The British economy was thus forcibly made to alter its course. Instead of experiencing the normal gradual economic evolution, the slow pace of change as evidenced in the interwar period, Britain had to make a leap forward to avoid disaster. In this way it can be said that the war had a beneficial effect on the economy. Had it not been for the calamitous cost of the war Britain would have tended to rely on income from overseas investments rather than turn to new export industries. This would simply have put back economic recovery.

The war helped also in another way. The scientific and technological advances developed towards winning the war were now available for peacetime purposes. The industries that were likely to succeed in the export drive were those where sophisticated methods of production could be used. The damaging rivals to British exporters had proved to be the developing countries which had applied cheap labour to the basic but comparatively unsophisticated industries that we now associate with countries undergoing an industrial revolution. The developing countries could not hope to compete in the manufacture of sophisticated goods. Here lay Britain's strength and it is on this strength that she still relies. Britain's natural resources are few. Her prime resource is the skilled, educated, trained manpower which can keep its industries one step ahead of the developing countries with their advantage of cheap manpower in the less sophisticated export markets. Since 1945 Britain's particularly successful industries have been those requiring a high degree of skill in the techniques of production, or ones where the finished product is itself sophisticated. The success of these industries has contributed substantially to the eradication of mass unemployment. The sustained demand for labour in engineering, in the chemical and plastics industries, in the motor-vehicle industries, and also in the many industries which supply their needs, has made the application of government policies on full employment much easier than they otherwise would have been.

We have seen that the emerging postwar export industries required a scientific and technological base. Also, they required a very broad capital base. The new techniques of production called for costly capital equipment which could be used for production of goods on a scale commensurate with the wide markets envisaged at home and abroad. Once again this was a feature of the British economy which the developing countries could not emulate. Cotton textiles could be produced by a comparatively small firm with machinery that was relatively inexpensive; chemicals and motor-vehicles required a capital expenditure that could be financed only by a very large firm or a nationalized industry. A feature of British industry since 1945 has been the investment of capital on a huge scale. The big firm has emerged along with the new industries. The amalgamations, the mergers, the takeovers that have been taking place since the war have achieved a concentration of capital which has reached a stage where ICI for example finances most of its capital programmes from its own reserves. The big firm, backed by vast capital resources, producing sophisticated goods by highly advanced techniques, is the backbone of the export drive. The four most important industries in Britain, measured in terms of value of exports are all industries of this kind, as Table 5.2 shows.

Table 5.2

Value of Exports of the major industries of the United Kingdom, 1966

Commodity	*£ million*
Machinery other than electric	1040·7
Transport equipment	791·8
Chemicals	468·9
Electrical machinery apparatus and appliances	346·0
Textile yarn fabrics and articles	260·7
Iron and steel	214·8
Non-ferrous metal	191·4
Manufactures of metal	155·3
Petroleum and petroleum products	114·0
Coal, coke and briquettes	20·0

Source: *Annual Abstract.*

All these industries had their origins long before the postwar era. What has happened since 1945 has been that they have been greatly expanded from the solid foundations of a big home market by injections of private capital. Their postwar success can be attributed in part to the fact that these foundations had been laid earlier. Immediately after 1945, though they were short of capital, they found that the competition from other advanced countries (except the USA) was almost non-existent because of the disruption caused by the war. Even competition from the industries of the USA was not a serious challenge because of the acute dollar shortage. European countries might have preferred American goods to British but they did not have the dollars to purchase them. The dollar shortage may have caused very serious difficulties in other ways, but it did help Britain in these vital years of post-war reconstruction. The motor-vehicle industry, in particular, and the engineering firms found that markets were wide open. The privations and shortages of six years of war had led to a clamour for goods all over the world, and Britain was the one country in condition to supply at least some of this demand. British industry had been sorely stretched by the war and was in need of modernization and re-organization, but it was at least much better off than the industry of Europe and Japan which had suffered severe damage and in some instances total destruction.

Thus the new export industries were given every opportunity to expand and establish markets on which they have built ever since. Subsequently European and Japanese industries have recovered, so that from 1950 onwards there has been intense competition, but by 1950 British industry had had the opportunity to become firmly based and in a position to hold its own. Since 1945 there have been fluctuations in production, investment and demand, and these must not be forgotten when considering the progress of industry, but the point here is that when looked at in the perspective of two decades or so since the war the new industries have expanded rapidly, building on the base established from 1945 to 1950 to achieve a vital part in the prosperity of Britain.

There is, however, an urgency for Britain to keep modernized, with an emphasis on sophistication. The need for keeping one step ahead is still there. Professor Barna's evidence, quoted in chapter 14, shows that it is possible for even the most advanced industries to concentrate on the older more traditional commodities within the individual industries themselves, demonstrating the familiar resistance to change. It is not surprising to find that the need for modernization has been stressed over and over again by politicians of all parties, leaders of industry and economists. Without the constant effort to keep ahead through research, and willingness to invest capital in new techniques, Britain might well revert to her prewar dilemma. The national preoccupation with the balance of payments does perhaps demonstrate that the conservatism of the past is not as strong in present times.

The service economy

A fluctuating trade cycle has been a feature of capitalist economies ever since the expansion of trade in the nineteenth century. As world trade increased so the fluctuations of the trade cycle became bigger, with each depression causing more trouble than the previous one as the economies became more complex. The interwar depression was the biggest the world had known, with its attendant stagnation and mass unemployment. Yet since 1945 these fluctuations have not continued in the same pattern. The trade cycle is still there, but though it occurs with greater frequency the fluctuations are of nothing like the same magnitude. Previously the duration of the cycle had been of about nine years, but since the war it has been about four and a half years from peak to peak. Instead of involving alternating rises and falls of output it has consisted merely of alternating periods of faster and slower growth. This has been one of the prime causes of postwar affluence. Without economic depression there is not mass unemployment. Demand is steadily maintained because of steady income and with steady demand full employment is more assured. Demand is thus the key to full employment. It must be said straight away that the taming of the trade cycle since 1945 has been brought about primarily by economic policies pursued by successive governments. These policies, inspired by Keynesian economics, will be considered a little further on, but before that there is an interesting aspect of Britain's economy to observe that has a direct bearing on the trade cycle.

The working population of any economy is traditionally divided into three main groups: primary (agriculture and fisheries), secondary (mining and manu-facturing), and tertiary (the service and distributive trades). In the early stages of industrial development there is a growing preponderance of labour in the industrial industries, while agriculture is still very important. Labour is cheap, machinery is comparatively scarce and the country is poor. In a poor society there is insufficient wealth to provide capital for social services, scientific and industrial research and the many appurtenances of an advanced economy. A wealthy society, by contrast, can spend a smaller proportion of its income on the consumption of goods and more on services. Transport and communications, public administration, pro-fessional and financial services, catering, entertainment and the distributive trades feature more and more in the allocation of labour to occupations. The hallmark of a really advanced economy is for the majority of the working population to be in the service industries: a service economy.

Britain has a service economy but has had it only since 1945. It is possible to obtain only a broad assessment of how the structure of the working population has changed in Britain because the basis upon which the statistics have been collated has been changed several times since the earlier part of the century. The statistics in Table 5.3 should be treated with caution for that reason but they are sufficiently accurate to give a general impression of the growing importance of the service industries. The size of the working population has increased by 44 per cent in the last

5 Postwar affluence

Table 5.3

Distribution of manpower in UK – selected industries, selected years, 1911–66

000's

Manufacturing industries	*1911*	*%*	*1931*	*%*	*1948*	*%*	*1956*	*%*	*1960*	*%*	*1966*	*%*
Chemicals	155	0·85	229	1·1	444	1·9	530	2·7	531	2·1	528	2·0
Metal manufacture, machines, metal goods, implements, ships, conveyances	1,784	9·7	2,406	11·42	3,284	14·3	3,659	14·8	4,411	17·6	4,627	17·6
Manufacture of textiles	1,360	7·4	1,320	6·4	936	4·1	1,002	4·1	902	3·6	810	3·1
Manufacture of textile goods and clothing	1,168	6·3	897	4·3	662	2·9	716	2·9	591	2·3	552	2·1
Manufacture of food, drink and tobacco	563	3·1	709	3·4	723	3·2	939	3·8	815	3·2	841	3·2
TOTAL of all manufacturing industries	6,147	33·5	7,126	33·8	8,099	35·4	9,482	38·8	8,851	35·2	9,055	34·4
Mining, Agriculture and Fishing	2,800	15·3	2,612	12·4	2,110	9·2	1,982	8·0	1,404	5·6	1,058	4·1
TOTAL – manufacturing, mining, agriculture and fishing	8,947	48·8	9,738	46·2	10,209	44·6	11,464	46·8	10,255	40·8	10,113	38·5

Service industries

Gas, water and electricity supply	117	0·64	246	1·2	312	1·4	383	1·6	378	1·5	431	1·6
Transport and communication	1,260	6·9	1,443	6·9	1,808	7·9	1,758	7·1	1,707	6·8	1,629	6·2
National government services	452	2·55	610	2·9	696	3·0	583	2·4	526	2·1	579	2·2
Local government services	555	3·0	1,019	4·9	735	3·2	751	3·0	751	3·0	804	3·1
Building	950	5·2	1,149	5·5	1,463	6·4	1,578	6·4	1,459	5·8	1,725	6·6
Distributive trades	N/a	–	N/a	–	2,523	11·0	2,932	11·9	2,833	11·3	3,035	11·6
Insurance, banking and finance, professional, miscellaneous services	N/a	–	N/a	–	3,938	17·4	4,248	17·2	4,487	17·9	5,468	20·8
TOTAL of all service industries	5,912	32·2	7,096	33·3	11,475	49·9	12,233	50·1	12,141	48·0	13,671	52·1
Total working population[1]	18,351		21,074		22,904		24,681		25,100[2]		26,236[2]	

[1] For all years H.M. Forces and unemployed persons are included only in the figures for the total working population.
[2] For the years 1960 and 1966 employers and self-employed persons are included only in the figures for the total working population.
N/a = not available.

Source: *Annual Abstract of Statistics.*

fifty years. In the postwar period there has been a significant increase in female labour, full and part-time, which accounts for some of this 44 per cent. The manufacturing industries have increased the number of their employees by roughly 50 per cent, but the service industries have increased their numbers by well over 100 per cent. Mining, agriculture and fisheries have been the areas of decline. In the postwar period the most significant increase has been in the distributive trades and in those services under the heading Financial, Professional, Scientific, Catering and Miscellaneous. In the latter category there has been an increase in only ten years of 30 per cent. The figures for 1966 show that less than four out of every ten people in the working population are engaged in manufacture in conditions of full employment. In the USA this weighting in favour of service and distribution has gone even further and reached a stage where only 25 per cent of the working population are in the manufacturing industries.

The change is brought about by methods of production which greatly increase productivity: technological change, improved management techniques, automation, made possible by an education system that provides the necessary highly advanced skills.

The numbers employed in individual manufacturing industries change with the decline of some and the emergence of others. In Table 5.3 the sophisticated industries show an increase in the numbers employed over the period while coal and textiles show a decline. This is to be expected as part of the natural evolution of industry; it is a redeployment of manufacturing labour. The newer industries offer the most favourable prospects and readily attract both capital and labour. The important fact is that of the total labour force the proportion employed in the service industries is increasing.

The significance of this distribution of labour is that it has an effect on the severity of trade cycle fluctuations. The first section of the community to be affected by the downswing of the trade cycle is that which is directly engaged in manufacture. If there is to be unemployment it will appear here first. However, if the majority of people are not engaged in manufacture this reduces the number of people immediately affected. The majority of people will still be receiving the same income and will be spending as they always have done, and thus sustaining demand. If the downswing of the trade cycle were prolonged, the service and distributive industries would be hit by the depression too, and demand for goods would not be sustained; but with economic policies applied by the government to minimize the trade cycle fluctuations, the effect of the service economy is to cushion the impact of the downswing and help keep things going until these policies arrest the depression. The more advanced an economy becomes the more it protects itself against the trade cycle. It is worth noting in this context that because many of the service industries have a lower productivity their labour costs are comparatively high, especially since the introduction of the selective employment tax (SET). The effect of this is for the less efficient ones to disappear (e.g. domestic service, which used to employ one-tenth of the whole working population), or to be mechanized (e.g. the telephone), while the efficient and essential ones remain. Thus many of the services are by now essential to the working of the economy, and labour in them would not be dismissed in a trade recession.

The SET was introduced in 1966 as a matter of policy to slow down the growth of the service economy. The tax was assumed to be the concept of Professor Kaldor, Economic Adviser to the Treasury, who in a subsequent inaugural lecture (Causes of the Slow Rate of Economic Growth of the UK, November 1966) asserted that the rate of growth of manufacturing production was likely to exert a dominating influence on the overall rate of economic growth. He argued that as there was a shortage of manpower in the manufacturing industries in Britain a selective employment tax would attract labour from the service industries into the manufacturing industries which were the industries chiefly involved in exports. The tax has been controversial ever since but because it raises £200 million per annum is unlikely to disappear. It is too soon to assess its efficacy but it is evident that it will only slow down the rate of growth of the service economy not reverse the trend discussed above.

It may be argued that the USA with its advanced service economy has none the less a high rate of unemployment compared with Britain; but this unemployment is not due to economic depression. The USA has experienced in the last few years for the first time in any country, an unemployment problem during the upswing of the trade cycle. This is a phenomenon caused by automation and highly mechanized techniques, not by falling demand.

Economic policy since 1945

One of the most important factors in achieving postwar affluence has been the pursuit of economic policies devised by Lord Keynes. The Keynesian revolution in economic thinking has been accepted by successive governments, irrespective of political colour, as a basis for overcoming chronic mass unemployment. Keynes worked out his theories in the interwar period when the predominating problem was the high unemployment rate coupled with the stagnation of the economy. Because these policies have been so successful since 1945 there is a temptation to wonder how governments and others influencing economic development during the interwar period could have been so inept. Their activities seem now to be naive if not foolish.

But it is unfair to judge policies of a bygone period by the standard of present knowledge and thinking. The climate of opinion at that time must be taken into account. 'The shortcomings of economics are not original error but uncorrected obsolescence.'[19]

Every period will look inadequate or even primitive when set against the new knowledge and ideas of succeeding generations. Undoubtedly generations of the future will look back to our own times and wonder at our inability to detect the right methods for overcoming difficult problems.

Economic policies are influenced very much by past events. Because the past is easier to understand than the present it is natural to apply to contemporary situations policies designed to avoid recurrence of past troubles. Meanwhile the contemporary situation is producing changes which demand new policies to meet them. This time lag is taken up with arguments both public and private, academic and political over possible new policies. New ideas take time to be assimilated and accepted. Thus economic policies always tend to be one stage behind events. It is necessary to understand this if we are to understand the policies that have been applied since 1945.

Keynesian principles have given a technique to the management of the economy which is far superior to prewar policies. Governments since 1945 have accepted a much greater degree of responsibility for the state of the economy. The climate of opinion has changed so that full employment has become the accepted basis on which the economy of the country is to be built. Any government is now deemed to have an obligation to achieve full employment from a moral point of view as well as from the economic desirability of the most efficient use of all the factors of production. The effort to achieve full employment has involved a much closer control than ever before in the effort to balance demand and supply in a steadily expanding economy.

The contrast with the years before the Second World War is marked. Then, interference in economic affairs by the state was increasing, but in desultory fashion. The intervention was ad hoc, in an effort to put right what had already gone wrong, rather than to control the equilibrium by any system of integrated economic policy. The 1930s were the times when the rights and wrongs of more effective use of monetary and fiscal policies, which meant greater government control, were being debated. The post-1945 period has seen their universal acceptance.

Management of the economy through Keynesian policies has involved control of demand and hence an ability to minimize the effects of the trade cycle. This is not the place to outline the complexities of Keynesian theory, but briefly Keynes advocated using government control over public expenditure for stimulating investment during the times of economic depression and obtaining, through the multiplier, an expansion of demand until a condition of full employment had been reached. Once full employment had been reached the technique was to balance the economy in the context of steady growth, by the same careful control of investment in the public and private sectors.

The practical application of Keynesian policies has become familiar to all, particularly to the taxpayer at Budget time and to those who control industry. The management of the economy calls for a flexible monetary and fiscal policy and hence a flexible taxation system. The Budget is no longer simply a statement of proposed government expenditure and anticipated revenue, but an instrument for

controlling the volume of money in circulation, encouraging or discouraging investment, affecting savings and influencing exports.

The government has become the biggest spender in the economy and is therefore
in a position to control more than ever the volume of money in circulation, and
thereby the level of aggregate demand. Government spending on goods and services,
including transfer payments (subsidies, benefits, pensions etc.) had risen to nearly
38 per cent of the gross national product by 1967. Taxation policy has become of
very great importance. The type of tax and the use of revenue have to be blended to
provide a net effect which will either stimulate or dampen down the economy according to the need.

The government of the day is expected to interfere in these spheres of the economy
in order to control the balance of payments and to achieve steady economic growth.
Statistics, carefully compiled and analysed, are now used to assess growth and to
determine what measures are needed to ensure steady economic growth. In 1941
for the first time an official estimate was made of the national income, in order to
find how much of the country's economic effort would be directed to winning the
war. Since then the measurement of the national income and hence the national
product has become central to the control of the economy. Postwar governments
have had a much clearer up-to-date picture of the country's economic health than
was ever available to prewar governments. In 1958 quarterly figures were introduced.

The ability to measure economic growth has in turn led to the automatic assumption that each year will bring increased growth: if the growth is not appreciable,
particularly when compared with countries of similar standing, the common view
(sometimes held quite unjustifiably) is that the economic policies of the government
of the day are in part responsible.

The government must also manage the currency; failure to maintain the exchange
level of the pound is regarded by many (once again somewhat unfairly) as the failure of
the government and its policies. The devaluations of 1949 and 1967 were particularly
damaging to the Labour governments responsible for them. This charge upon the
government to maintain a steady increase in the standards of living and sustain the
pound is a measure of the increased responsibility of state for economic control.

The devaluation of the pound sterling from $2.80 to $2·40 in 1967 came only
after the European central banks had made strenuous efforts to support the pound
and when the International Monetary Fund had indicated its willingness to make a
further loan. The difficulty for the Labour government was that in all probability
it would have been obliged to guarantee stringent measures to curb spending at
home in return for this financial backing. No government likes to feel that the control
of its economic policy at home is in any way dictated by external agencies; the
alternative was devaluation.

The reason for the devaluation in 1967 was the prolonged balance of payments
deficit. Confidence in the pound was lost as the country seemed unable to produce

63

evidence that it could quickly emerge from the poor state of its trading figures, which had been gloomy since 1964. Devaluation carries with it psychological over-tones that distort the real facts; national prestige is affected and popularly the country is supposed to be 'down and out'. In fact devaluation is an economic adjustment that may have short-term repercussions on standards of living (slowing down the rate of increase only) but which may have salutary long-term effects. The reasons

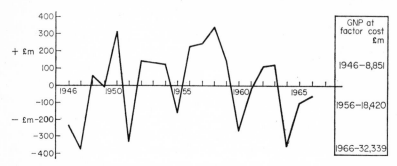

Figure 5.1. *UK Balance of Payments* 1946–1966 (*current balance*). *Source:* Key Statistics 1900–1966.

for the prolonged balance of payments deficit are manifold; many of them are touched upon in the last chapter of this book in that they are involved in the problems of inflation and the rate of economic growth, but devaluation must not obscure the fact that the UK balance of payments figures since 1945 (current balance) have been up almost as much as they have been down and have been accompanied by reasonably steady economic growth (see Fig. 5.1).

It is possible to overemphasize the importance of postwar economic policies in the context of postwar affluence. 'The purely intellectual change, which is popularly labelled the Keynesian Revolution is not the decisive factor. Something more is evidently required than a knowledge of techniques.'[20] Keynesian policies have dealt successfully with the interwar problem of unemployment but fresh problems have emerged, notably the problems of inflation and productivity, which have be-come the urgent problems of our time. But these are the problems of economic growth which are easier to bear than the problems of economic stagnation. The period of sustained economic growth which has gone on since 1945, aided by the Keynesian revolution, has minimized business risks and thereby helped to perpetuate itself by encouraging incentive to invest.

The need to control the problems of inflation and productivity has led to even closer involvement of the government in economic control and planning. In 1962 the National Economic Development Council (Neddy) was established to consider the growth plans of the different sectors of the economy and to work out the implica-tions of an annual growth rate in gross national product. The brief that it was given

Table 5.4

The relationship between stocks and balance
of payments

Year	Stocks £ million	Balance of payments £ million
1960	591	−275
1961	319	− 5
1962	95	+101
1963	157	+107
1964	524	−393

Source: *Key Statistics*, 1900–1966.

meant that NEDC would have to investigate most sectors of the economy. The
Council consists of twenty industrialists, trade unionists and independent members,
with the Chancellor of the Exchequer as chairman. Subsequent Economic Development Committees were set up (little Neddies) to study ways of improving the
efficiency of firms in particular branches of industry. One problem with which the
little Neddies have become especially concerned is that a high level of stock usually
accompanies a balance of payments deficit. This is the stop part of stop/go (see
Table 5.4).

Every time there is a rise in economic activity stocks build up and an adverse
balance of payments appears. This is a problem that has to be tackled at the level
of the individual firm as well as at a national level, and hence it interests the EDCs.
This collaboration between government and industry to consider future economic
implications is far removed from the lack of coordinated effort before the war.

High incomes

Demand in the postwar economy had been maintained, as we have seen, by full
employment and the service economy. It has been greatly stimulated too by the
high level of incomes compared with the prewar era. High incomes are brought about
by a number of factors, one of the most important of which is the simple one that
with the natural process of economic evolution the country is becoming wealthier.
It seems to be a feature of modern advanced economies that the pace of economic
growth breaks into a gallop. Rostow has described this as a period of high mass
consumption. This stage of economic evolution is reached when incomes are high
enough for the mass production of consumer durables to be worth while. Refrigerators, washing machines, cars etc. become common household possessions. The
Americans reached this stage in the interwar period; Britain achieved it in the late
1940s: the Soviet economy is now poised for a similar expansion.

Capital is important here. There is enough capital to permit rapid economic expansion while sufficient income is still available to permit a high level of consumption. There is undoubtedly a connection between economic growth and capital accumulation (see p. 217). A poor country with very little wealth to set aside for future production will accordingly make slow economic progress. Economic history shows us that the more capital there is available the greater the pace of economic change. Britain has by now amassed a vast quantity of capital and is creating more and more each year. If Britain devotes 15 per cent of her income to capital goods this represents, in value, very much more than say a 25 per cent saving out of income by a poor economy. Thus she has reached a stage where she can afford to consume goods in quantities sufficient to give a high standard of living while there is still enough saving to finance economic expansion. There is disagreement over how much investment should take place in relation to consumption in Britain, but whatever the ratio the volume of both is very high. There is also some argument over the common assumption that it is the quantity of capital that determines the pace of economic growth, but there is agreement over the close association between the two. In the stage of high mass consumption the wealth of the country is so great that incomes are high while capital accumulation is also at a high level. Standards of living are raised. This means that there is more money for people to spend on an increasing diversity of goods, which in turn means more incentive to invest and the availability of more capital for that investment.

A rise in income applied at the bottom of the income scale has a more positive effect than at the top. A poor man will respond to an increase in income by spending most of his increase. As with society in general so with the individual, experience shows that savings increase only as income increases. In the early stages of rising income the individual spends his increase on goods of which he has long been deprived. Only as he acquires a higher standard of living does he save an increasing proportion of his income. To take the extreme, a millionaire would not be tempted to spend an increase in his income of £5 a week, but for someone earning £10 a week an increase to £15 would encourage a spending spree. In the interwar period an increase in incomes as advocated by Keynes would have stimulated the economy. In the postwar period rising incomes have provided the necessary stimulus to sustain demand.

But high incomes are not just the result of economic growth. There has been a redistribution of wealth in British society whereby a greater proportion of the national income has been shared amongst the lower income groups. There is nothing like the disparity between rich and poor that existed at the beginning of the century. The disparity then was probably greater than at any time in the economic evolution of this country and this has now been recognized as both social injustice and poor economic organization. It has been estimated that in 1911–13, 1 per cent of the population of the country owned 65 per cent of all personal property.[21] L. Chiozza

Money in his book *Riches and Poverty* in 1905 pointed out that about half the national income went to only one-ninth of the population. This was the result of the concentration of wealth during great economic expansion of the Victorian era into the hands of comparatively few. The rich had a high income to use in a society where domestic service was cheap and where industry manufactured the necessities of life for home consumption and export. The market for consumer goods had not yet developed. The mass of the people earned sufficient only to provide themselves with a meagre standard of living which provided little in the way of spare pocket money. The work of Seebohm Rowntree in the investigation of poverty in those times is well known. In his investigations in York in 1898 he estimated that 27·4 per cent of the population of that city were living below the poverty level that he had set as a minimum necessary for the health of the individual. The principal reason for that poverty, he discovered, was the low wage of the bread winner. In the village of Ridgmont on the Woburn estates of the Duke of Bedford at that time, four-fifths of the population were living below the poverty line while the Duke was receiving an annual income of £20,000 from his Covent Garden estate alone. Wealth was badly distributed, and maldistribution was slowing the pace of economic growth and depressing the standard of living of the majority. Capital needed to be concentrated so that a proper level of investment could be achieved, but the incentive to invest was not as great as it should have been because the market was not there.[22]

The Liberal government of 1906 adopted an attitude to redistribution of wealth on social grounds which has been accepted and implemented by all succeeding governments irrespective of party. The social justice of this is not our problem here. We are concerned with the economic consequences. The redistribution has been achieved by the double method of progressive taxation in conjunction with the setting up of welfare facilities that form the foundation of the income of people at the lower end of the income brackets. Fiscal measures have been used for this purpose. The Chancellor of the Exchequer has become a latterday Robin Hood, taking money from the wealthy and redistributing it among the less well-off in the guise of welfare facilities. The progressive taxation system has now been in operation for over sixty years, making a steady contribution to the rising living standards of those with comparatively low incomes, enabling them to spend more and thereby sustain demand. The economic effects are cumulative. The longer the redistribution goes on, the greater the effect on incomes and the economy in general. The measures taken have increased steadily in quantity as well, the state gradually controlling a greater proportion of the national income. The Budget of 1898 involved approximately £102 million; the Budget of 1967 involved £10,278·9 million. In 1900 only 5 per cent of the national income was taken in taxation; by 1938 nearly 24 per cent was going to the state and by the 1960s this has increased to 34 per cent, if the social security contribution is taken into account.[23]

The welfare facilities have grown from the introduction of old age pensions in 1908 and the beginnings of national insurance in 1911 to the welfare state which took shape after 1945. The level of taxation has increased accordingly. Income tax in 1906 was ninepence in the pound; by 1938 it had risen to 5s 6d and since 1945 it has never been below 7s 6d. Surtax was 6d in 1913 but since 1945 has been at 10s at the top level, although the base at which surtax becomes payable has been raised. Death duties, introduced in the late nineteenth century as a device for accumulating revenue, have been used as an integral part of the progressive taxation system. Just as income has been taxed on the principle of redistribution so has personal property. Between 1930 and 1938 the state took one-fifth of a fortune of £100,000 and one-half from the heir to £1 million. After 1945 this was raised to one-half of £100,000 and to four-fifths of £1 million. Board of Inland Revenue figures show that approximately 41 per cent of all direct taxation is paid by 3 per cent (approx.) of the taxable population (1964).

The postwar period has thus seen a marked increase in levels of taxation following the gradual introduction of progressive taxation from the beginning of the century. Assessment of the effectiveness of this is difficult. There has been some controversy over the Inland Revenue statistics on the grounds that tax evasion, both legal and illegal makes the statistics misleading.[24]

E. Cooper-Willis,[25] estimated that by 1926–28 the personal property owned by 1 per cent of the population had been reduced to 57 per cent of the whole and that by 1946–47 this figure was down to 50 per cent. As for national income, according to *The Economist* the share of the national income going to wages after direct taxation increased by 25 per cent between 1939 and 1949. During the same period the share going to salaries had fallen by 2 per cent and the share for profits, interest and rents had fallen by 23 per cent. The Financial Secretary to the Treasury, in a written reply in Parliament in 1961 said that between 1938 and 1960 the value of dividends had increased by 190 per cent but over the same period the increase in earnings had been 384 per cent.

Rowntree made two surveys subsequent to his enquiry into poverty in 1899. The preponderant cause of poverty in his first survey had been low wages. In his second survey one-third of the cases of poverty were, so he found, due to low wages and another third due to unemployment. In 1950, in his third survey, where the percentage of the population living in poverty according to his definition was down to 2·77 per cent, low wages as a cause had disappeared and two-thirds of the poverty was due to old age.

Our own experience of society demonstrates the extent to which primary poverty has been abolished. National Assistance, family allowances, National Insurances, the National Health Service and its free medicines have largely done away with situations where individuals or families were faced with a financial emergency with which they could not cope. The necessity to keep a minimum level of savings for fear of the proverbial rainy day has gone for many people. People still save of course, and those savings are needed to finance expanding investment, but the purpose of saving (Keynes's precautionary motive) is now to increase the security that the state provides. The security is important because a climate of security encourages economic activity. If the individual is assured of a basic income minimum he will dispose of the rest of his income with greater confidence than he would do otherwise, and in the process gives some stability to the pattern of demand. In a sense the state engages in compulsory saving for the individual and provides him with necessary amenities which, were he to pay for them himself, would represent a substantial part of his weekly, monthly or annual earnings. The smaller the income, the greater the percentage of his income these amenities represent. Redistribution of wealth has thus contributed to high incomes and the creation of demand.

In seeking the reasons for high incomes since the Second World War we must also take into account the part the trade unions have played. They must take some of the credit for the creation of the Welfare State in Britain, though the social conscience and Parliament must take prior claim. The unions, however, have played a central role in the rise in wages since 1945; they have been able to do this because of the position of authority a trade union must have in a modern society in conditions of full employment. Wages are the price of labour. As with any other price in our economy, where prices are left to the forces of the market, the price of labour is determined by supply and demand. Because demand for labour since 1945 has been great and the supply of labour, particularly skilled labour, has been short, the unions have found themselves with great bargaining power. One of the major problems since 1945 has been to keep wages, as part of the national income, within the bounds of increases in national productivity, but because the share of national income that wages enjoy is increasing this is not an easy problem to solve. What is relevant is that that share has been increasing, in part through the work of the trade unions, and higher real income has been the result. There is thus a situation where full employment has given the unions strong bargaining power which has raised the share of labour in increasing prosperity, and thus in turn has stimulated demand and helped to maintain full employment.

The shortage of labour brought about by the policies of full employment has induced many married women to take up full or part-time work. Unlike the interwar period, when there was some social stigma attached to the married woman at work because it was seen to be a public admission that the family could not otherwise make ends meet, the postwar period has produced conditions where such work is socially acceptable. A wife at work is now taken to be a sign either that an adequate income is being supplemented in order to provide extra comforts, or else the wife needs the daily social stimulus that she cannot find in ordinary household duties. Whatever the reason for married women going out to work the result is that the household income increases–a further explanation of the high incomes since 1945.

Increased productivity

In an economy where full employment has been achieved the dominating factor in the pace of economic growth is the introduction of new and cheaper ways of doing things. Technical innovation is of paramount importance. In Britain since 1945, while full employment policies have been implemented, while incomes have been raised, new techniques of production have been introduced which have greatly increased productivity. The pace of technical innovation has increased at a rate greater than ever before. The Second World War was responsible for a great jump forward in the use of new materials, the development of electronics, the techniques of engineering and the expansion of the chemical industries. 'Scientific research, at first regarded as a supplementary aid to productivity improvements is being increasingly recognized as the spearhead of industrial progress and improved living standards.'[26]

There has thus been a greater emphasis in the postwar period on the education of scientists, technologists and engineers. The expansion of higher education has placed stress on technology and scientific research so that several of the new universities brought into being in the 1960s have evolved from colleges of technology, and it is in technology that their main strength lies. Further, the growth of the big firm, a feature of postwar development, has created a situation where industrial research can be financed. The small firm cannot afford to run research programmes. British efforts at research may look small in comparison with those of the USA, but this is an indication of the degree of research that is possible as the wealth of a country increases.

The result of this growing emphasis on technical innovation has been a stream of new materials and a variety of new techniques. 'Over the present century technological progress has been so rapid that more than one quarter of the goods produced in Europe today, and an even higher proportion in the United States, either did not exist fifty years ago, or were only in their experimental stage of development.'[27] These new materials and techniques are making possible not only improvements in style and performance of products but also reductions in the cost of production. Manmade fibres are an important example, and the use of plastics is in particular an illustration of the virtue of search for economic substitutes.

The most important advance in techniques of production has been the introduction of automation. Whereas the mechanization of industry in the eighteenth century replaced human physical labour, automation in the twentieth century is also extending human mental capacity. Of the four factors of production three (land, labour and capital) have always proved, in one way or another, capable of expansion or more intensive use. The fourth, organization, was the one which appeared to have definite limits. Automation, through the use of computers, extends the scope of the human mind so that hitherto impossible organizational problems can be solved or difficult laborious ones can be enormously speeded up.

The use of computers is the most advanced form of automation, but there are other forms as well. Transfer processing is one, where several processes of manufacture are performed by machine without any human handling. This is to be found in manufacturing industry, particularly where machined component parts are necessary in quantity. Automatic assembly is another form of automation where component parts are assembled by machine, as for example in the radio and television manufacturing industry, where the component parts of receivers can be added by machine to printed circuit bases. Another form of automation is to be found in those industries which are involved in continuous processing: oil distillation, steel strip rolling, chemical processing are good examples. In this case the automation takes the form of controlling within prescribed limits by electronic sensing devices the various inputs of materials throughout the production process. The common denominator of these different forms of automation is that they are a considerable advance on the mechanization introduced in the Industrial Revolution, whereby the simplest operation associated with the division of labour was taken over by machines. Automation in any form takes over several of these operations.

In the areas of manufacturing industries where it can be applied automation can greatly increase both the speed and volume of production while at the same time achieving a degree of accuracy which human labour cannot match. In an economy where full employment has been achieved automation can solve a labour shortage. Indeed some of the impetus towards automation since the war has come from the fact that labour has been in short supply.

The part that automation is playing in increased productivity must not be overestimated. It is not a panacea for all productivity problems. It has been estimated that the industries in which automated processes can be used employ about 40 per cent only of the manufacturing labour force of the country or 15 per cent of the total labour force.[28] But where automation can be employed productivity is invariably greatly stepped up and thus further economic growth is achieved.

International cooperation

However successful the economic policies pursued at home to maintain full employment and to encourage rising incomes, the fact cannot be escaped that Britain depends for her existence on export trade and the import of raw materials. That is, she is dependent for her livelihood upon other economies which are outside her sovereign control. Throughout the long history of economic evolution the predominant attitude has always been that each nation must look to itself in economic affairs and that the economic misfortunes of one country are the economic gains of the others. While Britain was developing as a trading nation before the Industrial Revolution the spirit of economic nationalism was intense. Competition was cutthroat with no regard to the economic consequences of the failure of one or more of the trading nations. 'The trade of the world is too little for us two, therefore one must down', wrote Samuel Pepys in reporting a discussion with Captain Cook on rivalry with Holland. The nineteenth century was the century of free trade, which suited a dominant Britain but did not satisfy the developing countries who wished to establish new industries of their own. Until 1945 there was little evidence that attitudes to international trade had changed much. The economic disruption of the interwar period was partly caused by the deliberate intention of those responsible for the Versailles Settlement for political reasons to reduce Germany, the major central European power, to a weakened economic condition. With the onset of the slump in the early 1930s the major reaction was to withdraw behind the barriers of economic nationalism once again and let each country fend for itself. The USA had shown during this time a reluctance to become involved in the economic condition of Europe, except through private investment, and it was the withdrawal of this that hastened the catastrophe of the early 1930s.

There is some evidence that by the latter part of the 1930s international cooperation was being considered more seriously, but the postwar period has seen recognition at last of the need for as much common agreement and control in international trade as is compatible with the idea of international trading competition. Just as individual economies based on private enterprise have come to accept the need for a degree of state control, so the trading nations of the capitalist world have accepted that some degree of international control is necessary, though nothing like the degree that the internal economies experience. In this way the fluctuations of international trade which vitally affect Britain's economy have been tackled more successfully.

The USA led the way after the war, albeit a little reluctantly at first, by lending large sums of money, and subsequently giving generous economic aid, to Britain and Europe in order to expedite recovery from the disruptions of the war. There may have been political motives, but the economic consequence was that by the early 1950s Europe was able to stand on its feet again, to the benefit of the whole trading world. This made an impressive contrast with the economic dislocation of the 1920s. From the American aid, the Marshall Aid Plan, sprang the Organization for European Economic Cooperation (OEEC) which was necessary for the sensible allocation of aid in the interests of the European economy. This compelled Europe to get together to consider economic problems. The OEEC was reconstituted in 1961 to form the Organization for Economic Cooperation and Development (OECD) which has much the same function of encouraging European economic cooperation.

The movement towards economic unity in Europe is familiar enough although Britain has been tardy in showing willingness to join. Parallel to this movement have been international agreements and international trading organizations all of which are designed to improve international collaboration and to avoid a return to economic nationalism. The International Monetary Fund (IMF) was set up as the war came to an end in an effort to avoid the worst repercussions of a currency crisis in any trading nation that contributed to the Fund. Britain has had recourse to the IMF on several occasions since the war in order to obtain backing for sterling and hence avoid a run on the pound. Not every member country has abided by IMF rules and its role of 'umpire' has sometimes been ignored, but in the main it has functioned as intended when it was set up at the Bretton Woods conference in July 1944.

The European Monetary Agreement, the successor to the European Payments Union, is a European organization intended to ease the currency problems of Europe. Its work is supplementary to the IMF.

The General Agreement on Tariffs and Trade (GATT) was established to lay down various principles of trade policy and to encourage methodical reduction of tariffs throughout member countries. In this it has achieved a measure of success.

These are the main organizations, but pervading the whole field of international trade and international monetary problems there has been since 1945 a common realization that stability and growth are best achieved by cooperation. One country's difficulties are now looked upon as the concern of all the trading nations. It is understood that one country, particularly a major trading country in difficulty, can be a calamity for the rest. The tremendous financial backing lent to Britain in the sterling crisis of 1964–65 is an illustration of this. An example in the opposite direction is the revaluation of the West German mark in 1961 because West Germany had at that time an embarrassing surplus in her balance of payments. This has created a climate of confidence in international trade which helps to promote expansion.

The activities of General de Gaulle in the 1960s have marred the otherwise encouraging picture of international economic cooperation since the war. French policy seems to have been politically motivated in a spirit that is more reminiscent of the bad old days of nationalist rivalry than the modern concept of fruitful co-operation. De Gaulle's policies are apparently aimed at changing the international price of gold, which has been at $35 an ounce since 1935, and at overthrowing the reserve currency system; this would mean a return to the gold standard. Since 1967 France has refused to contribute to the support of the world price of gold through the London Gold Pool. Hitherto she had joined with the central banks of Britain, the USA, Italy, Belgium and Switzerland in an international effort to stabilize the world's gold market. There were repercussions of this when sterling was devalued; a run on gold took place which forced the Americans to sell large quantities of gold in defence of the dollar reducing their reserves to the lowest level for thirty years. De Gaulle has also steadfastly opposed Britain's entry to the Common Market thereby delaying the biggest experiment in international cooperation of all.

The overall picture of international cooperation is nonetheless an encouraging one. There has been wide recognition since 1945 that economic nationalism is a danger to the economic stability of all. The close cooperation that has been practised since the war has helped to smooth the path of economic growth.

There is thus no one simple factor to explain the postwar affluence of Britain. A combination of factors is involved which together have brought prosperity and rapid economic growth in spite of short-term setbacks and long-term difficulties.

Now that the factors that have contributed to the moulding of Britain's economy have been outlined we can consider both the extent to which the individual present-day industries are affected by economic evolution and the nature of their main problems. Although as we have seen Britain is a service economy the wealth of the country accrues primarily from manufacturing. Unless the major industries are increasing their productivity or new industries are appearing, the standards of living of the country will not be rising; if an industry declines and there is no expanding industry to replace it the nation can expect to be poorer. There is no natural law that provides Britain with eternally profitable industries; indeed, as we have seen, the pattern of industry is constantly changing. An awareness of change and an ability to take an advantage of it has never been an outstanding British characteristic. The following chapters indicate but not measure the reaction of British industry to change in modern times. The size of industry is now such that the achievements, the setbacks and the problems of Britain's industry are the vital concern not just of those who own, manage and work in industry but of the whole nation. A strike in the motor vehicle industry, declining orders in the shipyards, a new steel-making process, the amalgamation of big firms in the chemical industry, the advance of micro-electronics and so on, are all now a concern of the nation's wellbeing from which the individual citizen cannot escape.

6

Fuel and power

Fuel and standard of living

As a nation becomes industrialized and its standard of living starts to rise, so the demand for fuel is rapidly increased; that demand goes on increasing even more rapidly as a nation moves into the stage of a highly advanced economy and achieves a very high standard of living. The purpose of economic activity is to make life more comfortable and to reduce the proportion of man's effort which has to be devoted to manual labour. The whole conception of raising the standard of living is basically one of reducing physical labour in conjunction with a higher income in order to provide relaxation in the increasing hours of leisure. This means higher productivity, which in turn means increasingly complex machinery, for it is the machine that takes over the hard physical labour even if, until automation, it replaced it with the boredom of repetitive work.

Fuel provides the energy originally provided by manpower, and that energy provides heat, light and power, which are fundamental to raising living standards. The *per capita* consumption of fuel is a sure guide to the level of productivity of a nation. The American worker, for example, has 200 times as much power working for him as a worker in Nigeria, with the corresponding startling difference in standards of living.

Access to an adequate supply of fuel has always been a prime requirement of any developing nation, and in the past this has usually meant coal. Britain, relatively to territorial size, has been endowed with a more plentiful and accessible supply of coal than any other nation in Europe, a major factor in the Industrial Revolution, as we have seen. There is still sufficient coal in Britain to provide 200 million tons per annum for 400 to 500 years. The predominance of coal as a source of power and its place as a major industry in Britain lasted right through the nineteenth century through to the second half of the twentieth, so that any consideration of fuel must start with coal. This is not to lose sight of the other sources of power which have now nudged coal from its traditional position of supremacy; these will be considered later.

Coal

The coalfields that were worked in quantity in the early stages of the coal industry were those where the coal was shallow and where the quality of the coal was suited to the purposes for which it was to be used. The Northumberland and Durham

Figure 6.1. Coalfields of Great Britain.

coalfield, because of the accessibility of the coal and the comparative ease with which it could be transported by sea from Newcastle to London, was the most important coalfield until well into the nineteenth century. For a long time this was the field responsible for the major proportion of British exports of coal. By 1850, the North-East was still responsible for 63·6 per cent of total British coal exports. It was only by 1880 that exports from South Wales equalled those from Northumberland and Durham.

The South Wales coalfield was one of those where, because iron ore was either close to or bedded with good coking coal, there was rapid development from the eighteenth century onwards with the demand for iron as well as coal. The Shropshire and Staffordshire coalfields were of this kind also. With the invention of the hot blast furnace by Nielson in 1829 the poorer quality coals could be used for ironmaking, which made possible the rapid development of the Scottish fields, particularly in the West. Coal was exported too from the coastal fields of Scotland. The Lancashire coalfield developed with the cotton textile industry and, except for a small export through Liverpool, supplied the home market.

SHIFT IN GEOGRAPHICAL EMPHASIS

Export of coal grew impressively in the latter half of the nineteenth century in conjunction with the rapid increase in production in the home market (Table 6.1). It has already been noted how, with the expansion of output, productivity ultimately declined. This needs to be linked now with the shift in geographical emphasis in the working of coal. The coal measures that were worked first of all, those where the coal was accessible or readily exportable, were at a marked disadvantage as the twentieth century progressed. The collapse of the export markets for coal combined with the inefficient application of capital rendered many of the collieries no longer economically viable.

Figure 6.1 shows the major coalfields of the British Isles. The coal measures worked from early times are illustrated in conjunction with the coal measures that have now become important with the changing position of a coal industry that has to be highly productive. Most of the English coalfields today consist of two parts: the older shallower part which is now uneconomic because of exhaustion or working by small inefficient units, and the newer deeper part recently developed because of the more modern techniques required to reach coal overlain by rocks. The Scottish field has

Table 6.1

Coal output pre-1914

	Million tons	*Proportion of output exported* %
1850	49·4	6·8
1870	110·4	13·4
1900	225·2	25·9
1913	287·0	32·4

been worked extensively, first in the West and then in the East, but the remaining measures are in millstone grit and limestone and have proved uneconomic. The South Wales field produces special quality coal, especially anthracite and steam coal, but the extensive working over a long period has rendered much of that field uneconomic too. The South Wales field suffered particularly in the interwar period, as did Northumberland and Durham, from having relied so much on exporting coal.

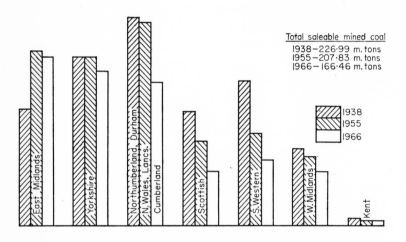

Total saleable mined coal
1938 – 226·99 m. tons
1955 – 207·83 m. tons
1966 – 166·46 m. tons

Figure 6.2. *Production of coal in Britain* 1938, 1955 *and* 1966 *by coalfield.*
Source: *Annual Abstract.*

Thus the presentday coalmining industry reflects the contraction of export markets and the need to work measures which have not suffered from prolonged exploitation. The most important coalfield today is that of York, Derby and Nottinghamshire. This field and the West Midlands field are the only two that produce coal at below the national average cost. Yorshire and the Midlands are now responsible for over half the coal produced in Britain (see Fig. 6.2).

TWENTIETH-CENTURY DEVELOPMENT

The coal industry in the twentieth century thus inherited from the previous century the twin problems of the contraction of export markets and the shift in the industry's geographical centre. The industry was geared, as a result of nineteenth-century expansion, for an export demand which declined rapidly after 1914, and was equipped to extract coal in the least economic coalfields. Inevitably there was profound upheaval while the industry came to grips with the change. For the most of the interwar period unemployment in the coal industry was over 20 per cent.

Those in employment were faced with a steady deterioration of their wages and a pressure to work longer hours. Relations between miners and owners had never been cordial from the days of laissez-faire in the early nineteenth century. Now the relations became very bitter. 1921 saw a prolonged strike and 1926 brought the General Strike, when the other unions came out in support of the miners who were resisting another cut in pay. The General Strike lasted only nine days but the miners stayed out eight months until in despair they were driven back to work on the owners' terms.

It is in times such as this that attitudes harden and bitterness finds a place in industrial relations. Undoubtedly the attitude of the presentday miner to wage claims, mobility of labour and pit closures is coloured by what has happened in the past. What the miner wanted to see, long before it came, was the end of the private ownership of coal. Although there were many factors involved, to the miner the only answer was nationalization.

SECOND WORLD WAR

Some account has been given in Chapter 3 of the failure to cope successfully during the interwar period with the problems inherited from the nineteenth century. The effect of the Second World War was to extend the coal industry to a point near to breakdown. Government control was essential for the production of coal in sufficient quantities for the war effort; 200,000 Bevin Boys were conscripted into the pits to overcome a labour shortage induced by allowing too many miners to join the armed forces early in the war. A Ministry of Fuel and Power was established in 1942 to coordinate in particular the work of the mines, but mechanization of the pits was difficult in time of war and not only did overall production decline but so also did productivity. When the war finished it was imperative that something drastic be done to the industry if it was to survive at all.

SINCE 1945

The Labour government, as one of its first major economic operations on taking office, passed the Coal Industry Nationalization Bill, which established the National Coal Board. Coal production in 1945 was down to 175 million tons, which meant that Britain was now producing insufficient coal for her own needs let alone those of her overseas customers. An attempt was made to keep open the markets abroad which Britain would need as her industry was modernized and became more productive, but it became apparent fairly soon that the struggle would be to satisfy customers at home. Expansion of production could come only as a result of long-term capital investment. Short-term there could be only acute shortage and frustration. The winter of 1946–47 was a particularly cold one. The sea round the coasts froze. The demand for coal outstripped supply and industry in many areas had to close down pending arrival of fuel ordered months before. Power cuts were the order of the day. This was a far cry from the pre-1914 days when cheap coal had been available in abundance. Exports of coal were now negligible, just at the time when the drive for exports was so important to overcoming a difficult economic situation in Britain. It even became necessary to import coal.

This was a crucial period for the coal industry. There was some irony in the situation. All through the interwar period there had been capacity to produce but a shortage of markets; in the immediate postwar period there was a fierce demand for coal but an incapacity to produce. Mining labour was scarce and the miners, remembering the unemployment of earlier days resisted efforts to import foreign labour. Miners' wages rose rapidly with the price of coal until, in comparison with other manual workers, the miner was highly paid. Even this did not attract the required number of workers into the mines.

Capital investment in fuel and power

As coal seemed unable to produce the fuel and power required, other sources assumed a greater importance. Oil, gas, conventional electricity and, in the long run, nuclear power were now looked to as alternatives to supplement supplies from an inadequate industry. The attractions of other fuels became more obvious once coal was in short supply.

These were the circumstances prevailing when farreaching decisions had to be made about the supplies of fuel and power. Long-term planning was essential and this meant investing very large capital sums. The government made these decisions about coal through the National Coal Board (NCB), about gas through the Gas Council, about electricity through the Central Electricity Generating Board (CEGB) and in research on nuclear energy through the Atomic Energy Authority (AEA). Only in oil were the decisions made by private enterprise. There was no overall planning. Private and public enterprise could both foresee an expanding demand for its particular fuel or source of power, and each went ahead with its own schemes.

Table 6.2 shows the size of the investment in the individual industries in a ten year period after the war. Of all the expenditure in the U.K. on machinery and plant from 1945 to 1964, 25 per cent was by the fuel and power industries. Most of this investment programme meant government control of capital investment in a way that was unthinkable even in the interwar period. The state had made significant progress in the control of the nation's economy. This degree of state control was accepted without any serious challenge. No government has ever sought to divest itself of control of the fuel and power industries, and the right of the government to that control is quietly accepted.

Investment on this scale means planning years ahead, estimating demand, trying to anticipate changes in the pattern of consumption. Government policy was to allow

Table 6.2

Gross fixed capital formation in the United Kingdom

Industry	1952	1953	1962	1953/62 (incl.)
			£ million	
Coal mining	40	55	82	824
Mineral oil refining	40	33	17	245
Gas	46	47	55	496
Electricity	159	180	409	2,906

Source: *Bulletin for Industry*, April 1963.

the industries maximum commercial freedom and flexibility of operation compatible with their social and non-economic responsibilities. There was to be free competition even among the nationalized concerns of coal, electricity and gas.

Back in the late 1940s it was difficult to foretell whether demand for fuel would be demand for coal, oil, gas or electricity. The only safe assumption was that demand for fuel would expand rapidly.

Modernization of the coal industry

The National Coal Board published its long-term plans in 1950. Broadly its intentions were to close down the uneconomic pits gradually. The capital made available to the industry was to be concentrated in those areas, shown in Fig. 6.1, where modern intensive mining methods would pay best. This meant in practice a great concentration of effort in the York–Derby–Notts coalfield, and a steady contraction of the older traditional mining areas. The plan which aimed at completion by 1965 involved expenditure of about £1,000 million and envisaged a production of 240 million tons per annum.

PIT CLOSURES

The run down of the uneconomic pits was to be carefully phased so as to reduce unemployment to a minimum and give miners the chance to be absorbed into the industry in another region. The nationalized mining industry could have been made economic long before the first year of profit in the 1960s if all uneconomic mines had been closed rapidly, but the human problem involved precluded any such thing. Apart from anything else the miners' unions would not have stood for it. Even in 1966 protest marches of miners were still being made through the streets of Westminster and petitions were still being handed in to M.P.s about the too rapid closure of uneconomic pits. In any case a whole area would not simply suffer the shutting down of its principal source of income. New industries had to be introduced which would absorb the labour force, before an area could free itself from dependence on coal. In South Wales and in Scotland, both heavily dependent areas, other industries have been steadily introduced, but these things take time. It did mean, however, that as late as 1964 about 150 collieries, accounting for some 20 per cent of output, were still failing even to cover their running costs.

The man who was ultimately put in charge of implementing the modernization plan for coal was Lord Robens. He had been a miner in his early days, and a successful minister in the postwar Labour administration; apart from being well qualified for a difficult job he was acceptable to the miners' unions. It is greatly to his credit that during the modernization there was nowhere near the industrial unrest that had characterized the industry for most of the century.

Throughout the 1950s production of coal rose and productivity made rapid progress. Britain moved away from her position as one of the least productive coal-producing nations to reach the position in the 1960s of the most highly productive country in Europe. Output per man-shift in 1945 was 20 cwt; by 1967 it had reached 36·4 cwt per man-shift. In 1965 the world's first automated coalmine was completed at Bevercotes in Nottinghamshire, a symbol of the modern appearance of Britain's coal industry.

At last it seemed as if the right things had been done. The industry based on the one natural resource this country has in abundant quantity had been streamlined and revitalized, and had thrown off the insecurity and turbulence that seemed to have dogged it through the first half of the twentieth century. The irony of the situation was that the right things had been done, but perhaps too late. The problems inherited from the nineteenth century had been overcome, but new twentieth-century problems had arisen.

Effects of competition

While this transformation had been taking place in the coal industry the effects of the investment in other sources of fuel and power had become evident. It had become slowly apparent that the share of the market that coal had enjoyed was dwindling. The market was expanding rapidly but demand was increasing for the competitors of coal much faster than for coal itself.

Oil

The biggest challenge to coal, developed largely since 1945, came from the oil industry. The figures in Table 6.3 show that the market for oil in terms of coal equivalent had reached well over half that of coal by 1966. These figures include the use of oil for motor transport, but this represented only 25 per cent of the total consumption. Oil was being increasingly used in industry for a variety of purposes.

Furnaces were oil-fired, gas was made by a new process using oil, electricity was generated in new oil-fired power stations, space heating in industry and in private houses was provided by oil, petrochemicals were made from oil, and the diesel locomotives on the railways replaced gradually the old steam ones. Oil was challenging coal in all its uses.

The attraction of oil, ease of handling and cleanliness, outweighed the disadvantages of its use. The chief disadvantage seemed to be a political one. After the war the political situation in the Middle East, the source of most of Britain's oil

Table 6.3

United Kingdom consumption of primary fuels

	million tons coal equivalent	
	1952	1966
Coal	204·1 (88·43)	174·7 (58·6)
Oil	25·7 (11·13)	111·7 (37·6)
Nuclear and Hydro electricity	1·0 (0·44)	10·2 (3·4)
Natural gas	—	1·1 (0·4)
Total primary fuel use	230·8	297·7

Figures in brackets show % of total consumption.
Source: Ministry of Power.

threatened to disrupt oil supplies. Added to that, there was a strong argument against importing large quantities of fuel when the emphasis of Britain's economy should have been on exports. The crisis at Abadan in 1951 when the British refinery was nationalized confirmed the danger of investing large capital sums in countries which might not remain always on friendly terms.

The problem was resolved in two ways. The oil companies decided to build new refineries in the United Kingdom. This meant that at least the capital equipment involved in refining was permanently under their control. Secondly, the discovery of large oil reserves on a worldwide scale meant that oil companies had to compete to sell oil. If oil companies were nationalized, selling the oil on the world market would have constituted a major problem for the countries responsible for nationalization. The pattern thus developed of importing crude oil in large quantities to be refined at huge new refineries built on the coast. Overland oil pipelines were built to supply inland depots. Large advertising programmes began to persuade the consumer of the convenience of oil.

The price of oil because of the discovery of large reserves, fell in relation to coal and has been favourable to oil ever since. This had a great impact on the fuel market.

The discovery of oil under the North Sea would increase this favourable relationship. Some oil has already been discovered and there is a chance that it will be discovered ultimately in quantity under the North Sea.

The formidable challenge of oil to the coal industry compelled the government to evolve ways to prevent the too rapid encroachment of oil upon coal markets. Conversion to oil was checked in government departments and conversion of power stations to oil firing was deliberately held back. This helped a little. The tax on oil was stepped up. Currently there is a 2d per gallon duty on fuel oil, as well as 3s 11d per gallon on petrol, and this must be regarded as a form of inverted subsidy to the coal industry.

Use of taxation of this kind has spread government control over all the fuel and power industries. If in conjunction with this it is remembered that the government obtained a controlling interest in BP it will be seen how by the 1960s the government had a command over the supplies of fuel and power which enabled it to issue a White Paper on fuel policy in 1965 (Cmnd 2798) in which for the first time plans were set out for the industry as a whole.

Nuclear power

By the 1950s, nuclear electricity had come into the picture to challenge coal as a prime source for electricity generation. The principle of nuclear fission was discovered in 1938. The war greatly accelerated the development of what was to be a new technology and an entirely new source of power. The many basic and difficult problems of design and technology were overcome in a period of time surprisingly short, when the general pace of commercial application of scientific discovery is considered.

In 1955 a White Paper was issued on a *Programme of Nuclear Power*. The nine power stations envisaged in this plan were to supply 5,000 MW. Their fuel was natural uranium. In the early stages of development a great deal was said about the cheapness of nuclear energy, and perhaps too much was expected of it. Until nuclear power stations had actually been built and put into operation it was not possible to estimate the cost of the electricity they would produce. The running costs could perhaps be calculated reasonably accurately, but not the capital costs. There were inevitable delays while snags were overcome, snags that were bound to happen in the development of a technology so new.

The capital cost proved to be very heavy, which made the overall cost of generation of electricity by nuclear power greater than generation by the traditional method. Much depended upon the life of the reactors. The original calculations were based on an assumption that the life of a reactor would be twenty to twenty-five years; this made the capital cost high. Conventional power stations were designed to last longer than this and hence were cheaper. Results from Calder Hall, the first reactor to be put in operation on a commercial scale (though essentially it was a prototype) suggest that a reactor will in fact have a much longer life. If this is the case, nuclear power generation even of the earlier stations measured over a longer period, will be economic. Capital costs have come down as lessons have been learnt by experience.

Berkley, one of the earlier nuclear stations, cost £185/KW. Wylfa, the last station of the original programme has cost £103/KW. At the same time thermal efficiencies have gone up from 24 per cent to 33 per cent.

Conventional coal-fired power stations became much more efficient during this period also, by improving their techniques of coal utilization. This enabled them to face up to the challenge from nuclear power, but at the same time it meant that they demanded less coal than they would otherwise have done. The coal industry suffered all the way along the line.

Of great significance is the fact that in 1965 a contract was placed by the CEGB for a new type of nuclear station. This was the Dungeness B station with the advanced gas cooled reactor (AGR) developed by the AEA. The order was placed after normal competitive tendering by established firms, the choice was made on straightforward commercial merits. This means that AGR is much more economic, and, in fact, will produce electricity more cheaply than the coal-fired stations. The White Paper on fuel policy referred to earlier estimated that, in consequence of the AGR, the second nuclear programme, to be put into operation 1970–75 would be extended from 5,000–8,000 MW. Capital cost for Dungeness B will be £78/KW and the efficiency will be 41 per cent. Another feature of AGR is that its safety characteristics are so good that nuclear stations can in future be built nearer to the centres of population, thus reducing the costs still further.

Another important prospect for nuclear energy is the Dragon High Temperature Reactor developed by the AEA at Winfrith Heath. Originally a Euratom British development, this has been taken over by AEA and promises to be the next step in the development of gas-cooled reactors. This is designed, it is hoped, to produce very hot gas from the Dragon reactor which can be used to drive a gas turbine generator directly without having recourse to heat exchangers. This would considerably reduce the generating costs.

The AEA is also well advanced in its research in fast reactors. This is a stage of nuclear energy development which promises even greater success than AGR. The fast reactor system involves the use of plutonium as a fuel, but each fast reactor breeds more plutonium than it consumes so that the system can become self-supporting in fuel. Fast reactors of this kind will permit much more electricity to be generated from a given quantity of uranium (the original source of plutonium) and will enormously increase the scope of nuclear power based on foreseen uranium resources. There is great hope that the fast reactor will generate power at substantially lower fuel costs than any other system, including AGR.

The first reactor of this type, an experimental one of 60 MW, has been in operation since 1963 at Dounreay. A second experimental reactor of 250 MW is to be built, also at Dounreay, and will, it is hoped provide the experience for designing the power stations of the later 1970s.

Gas

Oil and nuclear power have developed as a real challenge to coal in a comparatively short space of time. It is significant that so much of this chapter should have been devoted to fuel and power other than coal, even though coal has been used for hundreds of years while oil and nuclear power have made their mark only since 1945. Natural gas has made its mark even more recently and yet must be considered seriously when the fuel and power of this country are under consideration. The pace of technological change seems to have broken into a gallop.

Until the late 1950s the image of the gas industry was of one based on coal and an inheritance from the Victorian era. 'Gaslight' was a fine example of Victorian melodrama. Then came what was virtually a technological revolution, coupled with an intensive advertising campaign which transformed the image of the industry into one of efficiency, speed and convenience which could compete favourably with oil.

All this was achieved through reorganization, new sources of supply, and new techniques of production. In 1953 there were 900 gasworks in commission. By 1962 this number had been reduced to 350. The remaining plants were the bigger ones with reduced costs of production through economies of scale. The proportion of gas supplied from the traditional coke ovens had gone down. By 1964 one-third of all gas originated from sources outside the gas industry. Gas from the refining of oil was taken over by the gas industry and converted and purified for domestic consumption. Another source of supply was the vast quantity of natural gas in the Sahara which, because of technological advance, could not be exploited on a commercial scale. The gas (methane) is liquefied and transported at a temperature of $-161°C$ ($-258°F$). The Gas Council brought into operation two tankers which by 1966 were supplying about one-tenth of all British gas supplies. The methane, regasified at Canvey Island, was distributed through a pipeline network covering the whole country. The cost of gas imported in this way was cheaper than producing gas from coal in this country.

In 1964 the Gas Council announced a new technique, the Catalytic Rich Gas (CRG) process, which revolutionizes oil purification. This process produces non-toxic and highly pure gas direct from light petroleum distillate. Costs of the process are very low; in fact it is the cheapest known method of producing gas as opposed to tapping natural gas and is even cheaper than importing methane.

NORTH SEA GAS

In 1965, one year later, came the discovery of substantial quantities of natural gas under the North Sea. This has set the seal on the success of the gas industry and has necessitated a reappraisal of fuel policy and threatened even more the future of the coal industry.

The North Sea gas find was prompted by the discovery in 1959 of the second largest natural gasfield in the world at Gröningen in Holland. While plans were being drawn up for piping gas from this field to Britain there was hope that the field in Holland was part of a much bigger field that stretched out under the North Sea, but exploration could take place only if there were international agreement on ownership of rights to explore. A Convention which was ratified by twenty-two countries and came into force in June 1964, established the ownership of the sea on the Continental Shelf.

A median line was drawn halfway between Britain and her neighbours, allocating to Britain 100,000 square miles of sea, which was divided up on a grid system into blocks of about 100 square miles each. The British government granted licences of two kinds; one was for exploration, to cover search and drilling only, the other to cover full production, which permitted the holder to take and sell whatever oil or gas he might find. Rights to the chosen area were to last for six years and after that the licensee was to have an option of a further forty years. The exploration licences cost £1,000 a year, those for production £6,250 per year for a 100 square mile block. The government was to get a royalty of $12\frac{1}{2}$ per cent of the value of oil or gas found. The Gas Council and the National Coal Board have both taken out licences, the former having already been associated with a successful strike. This has so far proved a satisfactory arrangement to all concerned and has produced a fuel industry, brand new, where from the start the government has a moderate degree of control, thus conforming to the pattern of state influence over the fuel and power industries. It has, as we shall see, given the government via the Gas Council very considerable power in the vital decision of the price of North Sea gas.

The first North Sea rig began drilling at the end of 1964. The first strike, by BP came in October 1965, and by mid-1966 with four bores successful out of twelve it was evident that the hopes of a large North Sea field were justified. In May 1966 there was a successful strike on land at Lockton in Yorkshire which, because of the cheapness of land drilling and pipe laying, will produce gas at the cheapest rate of all.

The full extent of the North Sea find has still to be determined. Most experts believe that taking the area as a whole there will be as much gas as in the Gröningen field. This has a coal equivalent of 1,100 million tons.

IMPACT OF NORTH SEA FINDS

The question that North Sea gas raises is the effect that it will have on forward plans for the fuel and power industry. As has been already observed planning involves the investment of enormous sums of money, many years in advance of the provision of the fuel and power that it will provide. By 1965 the government and private enterprise were planning in terms of well into the 1970s and beyond, commissioning the supply of capital equipment involving many hundreds of millions of pounds. Scrapping such expensive equipment would be foolhardy unless North Sea gas were superabundant and ridiculously cheap, but even modifying plans would prove expensive.

The impact North Sea gas was to make would depend upon the quantity of gas discovered, the size of the increasing demand for fuel and power in Britain, and the price of the gas itself.

COMPARATIVE SIZE OF THE NORTH SEA FIELD

The quantity of gas found under the North Sea is not so vast that it will constitute anything like the major source of fuel and power in Britain. When natural gas was discovered Britain was using 1,000 million cubic feet per day of gas from all sources, which represented about 5 per cent of Britain's total fuel consumption. It is anticipated that from 1970 onwards, three to five times this amount will be available for a period of twenty-five years. The supply of natural gas is therefore a supplement to existing supplies of fuel and obviously the normal expansion of demand for gas will absorb some of the surplus. If the normal market is demanding 2,500 million cubic feet per day by the 1970s, then up to the same amount again will be available to compete with other sources of fuel. In terms of coal equivalent this represents about 34 million tons which in turn is roughly one-fifth of total coal production in the mid-1960s. North Sea gas is, therefore, a useful find but not revolutionary. It suggests that there will be a small surplus of fuel and power in Britain, so that one or other of the sources will have to be cut back.

Competition amongst the four sources

The decision as to which source has to be cut back is largely one of price. If gas is brought in at a cheap price to the consumer it will challenge existing markets for coal, oil and electricity. Certainly natural gas will be cheaper than gas acquired from any other source. Before the arrival of natural gas the average making cost of gas was $10\frac{1}{2}d$ a therm and the selling price was $1s$ $10d$ a therm. Natural gas is, of course, ready made but the costs of exploration, conversion of appliances and pipelaying are heavy and greatly influence the price. Taking these costs into account (and they could be £2,000 million), sales to big industrial users could be as low as $4\frac{1}{2}d$ per therm, but this in turn depends very much upon the price that the Gas Council agrees to pay for the gas from the producer groups. BP, who made the first strike, were paid $5d$ per therm, but the general price is expected to be half of this.

How does $4\frac{1}{2}d$ a therm compare with other fuels? It is marginally the same as fuel oil, but it must be borne in mind that fuel oil is taxed; if that tax were maintained it could be regarded as a subsidy for natural gas as well as coal. The cheapest price for coal to industrial users is $4d$ per therm, but this is only where the Coal Board is supplying to a power station situated right next to a coalfield so that coal is very vulnerable in the competition against the surplus supply of natural gas. Electricity would be affected where it provided a similar service to natural gas, particularly in domestic heating and cooking. The cheapest electricity to the domestic consumer is over 2s per therm, whereas natural gas might ultimately be 1s 2d per therm or even 8d per therm on central heating.[29] Any challenge to demand for electricity is, as we have seen, a challenge to coal; from this it must be concluded that the coal industry has had its troubles aggravated by the discovery of North Sea gas.

The future of the coal industry

In the light of these rapid developments in alternative sources of fuel and power, the position of the coal industry has been substantially changed. For the two hundred years of tremendous economic growth since the beginning of the Industrial Revolution, coal has been the unchallenged provider of fuel and power. The industry has seen many changes in fortune, but now, when it is at a peak of efficiency, its position of domination has been strongly challenged. It is an economic fact that not all the coal that can be produced is now required.

Not surprisingly there have been conflicting opinions on the role the coal industry should now play. There are those who have argued that the industry should be contracted to match short-term estimated demand with supply; there are those who have said that long-term plans should include provision for a buoyant or even expanding coal industry because the demand for coal will be sustained over a long period of time. There is unquestionably a need for coal for a long period ahead. The CEGB will soon be consuming 50 per cent of all coal produced from British mines, and coal-fired power stations which have a life of 30 years or so exist in numbers sufficient to guarantee a market for the NCB until, perhaps, the nuclear power stations ultimately succeed them; but it is difficult to see where else the Coal Board would find a market beyond this.

In the White Paper on fuel policy the government in 1965 plumped for reduction of output of coal from the 200 million tons per annum that could be produced to 175 million tons. In a reappraisal of the fuel and power situation in Britain in 1967 when the size of the North Sea discoveries was becoming clearer, the government announced a modification of these plans. This involved a reduction of coal production by 1970 to 155 million tons per annum and a reduction of 135,000 in manpower in the coal industry. The CEGB and the gas industry were asked to use an extra 6 million tons of coal per annum up to 1971 in order to avoid too quick a rundown of the coal industry. It was assumed that by then the capital cost of modernization would have borne fruit; coal could be extracted efficiently and comparatively cheaply for use primarily in generating stations and coke-ovens, though a market of 30 million tons for domestic use was still anticipated. Future electricity generating stations were, however, likely to be nuclear powered because the technology of nuclear power indicated that these stations would be markedly more economic than coal-fired stations.

So fast was the pace of change (particularly in nuclear technology and in the development of North Sea gas supplies) that a further White Paper on fuel policy was published late in 1967 (Cmnd 3438). This substantiated the earlier governmental review of the move 'from a two fuel (coal and oil) to a four fuel economy'. The government's objective of cheap energy was clearly stated. 'We should take full advantage of nuclear power, North Sea gas and oil.' A planned contraction of the coal industry

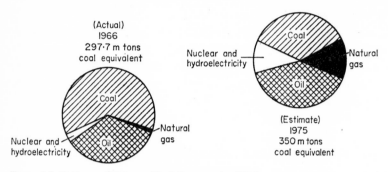

Figure 6.3. *Patterns of Primary Fuel Consumption* (*UK*).
Source: White Paper – *Fuel Policy*, Cmnd. 3438.

was envisaged, anticipated coal production being down to 120 million tons by 1975 and the labour force being reduced by 35,000 per year up to 1970–71. Oil would increase its share of primary fuel consumption to 42 per cent by 1975, and the government would encourage companies to build refineries in this country.

Natural gas was to be brought in rapidly although this would mean a shorter life for the gas fields. 'Most of the natural gas available will go to the premium markets where it will largely be displacing oil, but there will be some supplies to bulk industrial users, to assist the early build up in supplies, and to balance the load thereafter. In these markets there will be some displacement of coal as well as oil.' Consumption of natural gas was estimated at 50 million tons coal equivalent by 1975, but this estimate assumed that more gas would be discovered for that figure to be reached.

The plan for electricity was that 'for future power stations the government have now decided that the generating boards should base their choice of fuel on an economic assessment of the method of generation which will enable them to supply electricity at the lowest cost consistent with security of supply and load balancing. . . . Nuclear stations will predominate in new capacity planned for the coming years, but there will continue to be scope for some new conventional stations at specially favourable sites.'

The coal industry is, therefore, faced with a challenge that has not only already toppled it from its position of dominance but will also reduce coal to second position as a primary fuel in Britain by the 1970s. Coal will still be important for a long time, but it can never hope to recover from the developments of the second half of the twentieth century.

In the 1970s the coal industry will be competing, without the bolstering of disguised government subsidy and capital grants, on its own merits. Whether this means further contraction or whether the fully modernized industry will then hold its own remains to be seen. At least the industry will have the dubious satisfaction that its difficulties are caused by inescapable twentieth-century technological progress and not, as in the middle of the century by inefficiency, complacency and inertia.

7

Iron and steel

The iron and steel industry is the one old staple industry which has retained its relative importance in the economy in spite of the setbacks of the interwar period and the intense competition of an increasing number of producer nations. This reflects the value of the material properties of these metals in the working and fixed capital of the nation's economy. It is sometimes said that most of everything that works in the economy – except people – is made of steel, and as a broad generalization this is true. No other material that possesses the durability of steel or its capacity to withstand the hard wear that the friction and pressures of machinery demand can be produced so cheaply in quantity. There are other metals which may possess qualities that are superior in some ways, and the modern plastics industry has shown how steel can be replaced in what are, so far, comparatively minor uses, but steel is still easily the most important industrial material of the twentieth century.

A highly productive iron and steel industry is thus of great importance to a modern industrialized country, if only to supply the needs of the home market. Even so, it is sometimes argued that because profits are low, compared with other industries, resources should be progressively withdrawn from steelmaking in Britain and diverted to newer more profitable industries, but this is an argument hard to sustain. There are not many advanced nations which do not produce their own iron and steel in quantity. Switzerland, Denmark and Norway import much more than they produce, but they do not have the other major industries, particularly engineering and motor-vehicles, of the size that Britain promotes. Britain's balance of payments problems would be seriously exacerbated were she to require large imports of iron and steel. 'With home consumption of steel in 1975 running at the rate forecast even a halving of home steel production would involve adding some £500 million a year, at the very least, to Britain's import bill.'[30]

The emphasis of this century has been on steel rather than iron. Iron is still made in quantity but mostly as an integral part of the steelmaking process. Henry Bessemer in 1856 demonstrated how acid steel could be made cheaply in bulk, and within twenty-five years of that date came the open-hearth process and the discovery of how to use either method to make basic steel, called Thomas steel on the Continent. These have remained, until very recent times, the main steelmaking techniques.

It might be useful at this stage if something were said about the traditional steel-making processes, as the raw materials required have such an important bearing upon the development of the industry.

The raw material of steel is, primarily, pig-iron made from iron ore. Iron ore is iron oxide combined with other materials such as phosphorus, manganese, sulphur, alumina and silica. If the ore is placed in a blast furnace the iron can be drawn off in liquid form, but it still retains the sulphur and phosphorus and has a high carbon content. Scrap iron or scrap steel is a secondary raw material that can be used with or in place of pig-iron. When the pig-iron and/or scrap are treated either in a converter or in an open-hearth furnace, the carbon content is reduced to a predetermined level and the other impurities are removed, thus producing steel. For special steels other materials can be added. The Sheffield area is the centre for the making of special or alloy steels in Britain. It has a worldwide reputation for high quality steel but, because the greater proportion of steel produced in Britain is common steel, this chapter is concerned with that kind and not special steel.

The terms 'acid' and 'basic' steel indicate the type of ore used in the making of pig-iron. Acid steel is produced from iron ore of low phosphoric content. Ores of this kind are not found in large quantities in Britain, so that acid steel production has always demanded the importation of foreign ore. Basic steel is produced from ores with high phosphoric content of which there is a plentiful supply in Britain, though their iron content is low. It can be made in either an open hearth or a Bessemer converter, both requiring to be lined with a basic material which can take up the phosphorus from the iron during the conversion. Lime is added as a flux.

The open-hearth method involves the use of a regenerative furnace, temperatures in which range from 900° to 1650° Centigrade at different periods of the process, which lasts eight hours or more. The advantage of this method of making steel is that there is ample opportunity for taking samples of the metal for testing so that open-hearth steel, acid or basic, can be made to well-defined qualities.

The Bessemer process is very much quicker than the open-hearth process, a converter being capable of producing over 25 tons of steel in ten minutes. The molten pig-iron in the converter is subjected to a blast of air (nowadays oxygen enriched air or steam oxygen) which oxidizes the silicon, manganese and carbon. Phosphorus can be removed after blowing. The speed with which this operation takes place makes the quality of steel not so well assured, but it has the advantage that the fuel consumption is not so high as with the open hearth.

The making of basic Bessemer steel proved for a period to be unreliable in that part of Britain (Middlesbrough) where the indigenous supplies of ore were being used. The high sulphur and alumina contents of the Cleveland ores led to such a wide variation in the quality of the pig-iron that the steel made from it could not be relied upon to be of consistent good quality. For ten years, from 1924 to 1934, no basic Bessemer steel was made in Britain at all. The method was started again in Corby and at Ebbw Vale in the late 1930s; it had then been made reliable by means of charging the furnaces with prepared ores and by treating the pig-iron with soda ash to deal with the sulphur problem. Even so, by 1945 only 6 per cent of the steel produced in Britain was in Bessemer converters. The Bessemer process has never featured very largely in the British industry.

The electric furnace was introduced after the First World War; this can be run entirely on scrap charges and produces high quality steel, but the high consumption of electric power and electrodes did not, for a long time, make it an economic proposition except where high quality steel was particularly needed.

The fact that steel is made partly from scrap has a direct bearing on the process selected for any steel plant. Scrap is created in the actual process of steelmaking; it is in fact essential to remove impurities in the ingots and is too valuable to waste, so that there is an economic virtue in a process that uses a significant quantity of scrap. The openhearth furnace and the electric furnace, in fact, demand large quantities of scrap, in order to remove impurities in the ingots, but the basic Bessemer process can take very little. This is another reason why the basic Bessemer process has never dominated steel production.

The steel from either open hearth or converter is poured into ladles and then teemed into moulds where it takes the form of large solid ingots. While still hot the ingots are rolled or pressed in a series of processes which give the metal the required shape and size, sometimes as an intermediate product, sometimes (in an integrated works) as the finished article.

The outstanding requirement for practically all the processes of steelmaking is heat in large quantities. In the early development of steelmaking coal was the sole source of heat, but now there are others. The blast furnace requires large quantities of good coking coal; oil is sometimes used. The open-hearth rolling and pressing processes also require heat in order to keep the steel condition sufficiently workable for shaping.

The new techniques of production and their significance are reviewed later in this chapter, but first the pattern of the industry that has developed in consequence of over 100 years of the traditional techniques must be traced.

The influence of history on the location of the industry

From what has been said about the techniques of manufacturing steel it will be apparent that the size and location of plant are of great economic importance. The sheer weight and bulk of the materials being handled and the very high temperatures involved in steel manufacture necessitate the employment of plant of substantial size. The larger the blast furnace, the lower the labour costs and the less the radiation losses. The same applies to rolling mills, particularly now that they are mechanized. Once an industry has incurred heavy capital expenditure in an area, provided that the market for the finished product remains or expands, the likelihood is that the industry will stay in that area, even if the supply of local raw materials, the original reason for the siting of the industry, is exhausted.

Internal economies become apparent as a steelworks grows; the improvement of techniques, the enlargement of existing units and plant and improvements in the balance of operation between various pieces of equipment can all be implemented at an existing site. External economies too can be achieved as the area adjusts itself to the special needs of the industry. Thus the iron and steel industry experiences more than most industries a geographical inertia.

The location of the iron and steel industry today reflects this inertia. New compulsions have occurred for the manufacture of these metals in different parts of Britain as time has gone by, but the original sites have remained, in most instances, as thriving centres of the manufacture of metals. Originally, after Darby's invention of smelting with coal, the industry expanded rapidly in those areas where there was a combination of good coking coal and iron ore. These two materials had to be available in the same location because poor transport facilities did not allow the cheap movement of any raw material in bulk form. England was endowed with two areas, South Wales and the West Midlands, in particular, where iron ore was bedded with coking coal; it was in those areas that the early demands for iron were met. By 1830 two-fifths of the total supply of pig-iron in Britain was being produced in South Wales and one-fifth in Staffordshire. Scotland too had bedded ores which were worked at the famous Carron works near Falkirk, but the quality of the ore was not as satisfactory as in England. However, the invention by Neilson of the hot blast in 1828, making the use of inferior ores possible, led to the rapid rise of the Scottish industry. By 1857 Scotland, South Wales, and the Midlands were together producing about half the total world supply of pig-iron.

Inevitably the supplies of bedded ores in the coal measures started to dwindle even before the great steelmaking inventions had been made. The ores that were most accessible had been mined, and though there were still many hundreds of millions of tons remaining they were in thin seams and at considerable depth. Their iron content was 30–38 per cent, another reason why extraction was becoming relatively uneconomic. The large capital investment in ironmaking plant was not, however, to be wasted. These areas started to import foreign ores.

In the 1850s the bedded ores of the Jurassic rocks which had been strangely neglected for centuries were brought into use. These ores were rediscovered when a railway cutting was made. They were all lean ores of 23–32 per cent iron content, but they occurred in thick beds and were near enough to the surface in most places to make open-cast mining possible. They stretched in a band, though not continuously, from the Cleveland Hills in Yorkshire to the Banbury area in North Oxfordshire.

The important difference between them and the ores previously used was that they were not present with coal. The nearest coalfield was Durham, which possessed high quality coking coal. The development of the North-East as a major iron and later steel-producing area dates from this time. By 1870 it was the most important iron producing region in the country.

When the acid steel processes of Bessemer and Siemens were made popular the Jurassic ores, because of their high phosphoric content, could not be used for steel-making. For a brief period the two regions of Britain which had deposits of haematite (ore of low phosphoric content) came into their own. The more important of these was Cumberland with ore within a few hundred feet of the surface but not close to coking coal, and the other was Llanharry in Glamorgan, also bedded in coal measures. British haematite had an iron content of 50–55 per cent.

By the 1880s basic steel could be made using the lean ore. We have already noted that Britain had nonetheless invested in iron ore production abroad (see p. 19). Thus parallel with the development of the North-East industry based on Jurassic ores, there was an increasing supply of foreign ores which were of comparatively high iron content and were an economic proposition. The supply of iron ore was thus threefold – the ores bedded with the coal measures, the Jurassic ores and the imported ores. Broadly speaking the industry has moved from one ore supply to another, but has continued to thrive in all those areas in which it has been established. The way in which the emphasis on ore supply has changed in the last fifty years or so is shown by the following figures:

Table 7.1

Home iron ore production and imported ores – selected years

| | Thousand tons | | | |
	1913	1937	1956	1965
Haematite	1,767	857	323	261
Jurassic	12,572	12,919	15,793	15,007
Coal measures	1,542	178	–	–
Others	116	260	129	147
Home	15,997	14,214	16,245	15,415
Imported	7,230	6,950	13,737	17,936

Source: L. D. Stamp and S. H. Beaver – *The British Isles, Annual Abstract.*

In the twentieth century a new feature has been the siting of steel works on the Jurassic field. The attraction of this has been caused partly by the fact that whereas originally the amount of coal consumed per ton of pig-iron was about ten tons it

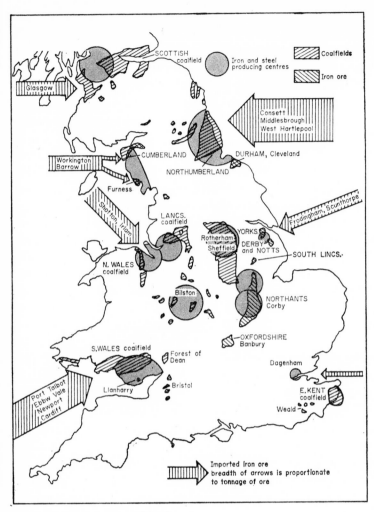

Figure 7.1. Britain's Iron and Steel.

has now fallen to just under one and a half tons in contrast with the amount of iron, which has remained almost stationary at an average of two to three tons. There is an obvious incentive here to site steelworks near the ore rather than near the coal. Since the Jurassic ores are lean it is in any case uneconomic to transport them far. British steel production today is thus centred in coalmining areas, on the Jurassic Field, and in coastal regions where deep ports exist for imported ores. Some steel-producing plant, sited originally because of coal and bedded ores, is surviving only because of proximity to the market and the availability of scrap. Bilston in Staffordshire is perhaps the best example of this. Other plant exists because of its coastal situation. North Lincs (Scunthorpe which also uses home ore), Teesmouth,

97

South Wales, North Wales and Cumberland now all rely heavily on imported ores. The major integrated steelworks (largest in Europe) at Corby is sited on the Jurassic Field so that in contrast to the others the original reason for its siting is still valid.

Since 1945 the importance of foreign ores has been growing so fast that another shift in emphasis of the location of the industry has emerged. The most important areas are those where there is a good supply of coking coal near to the coast and it looks as if these will be the areas in which the expansion of the next few decades will take place. The reasons for the increasing use of imported ores need to be examined.

In the first place, production of home ore supplies, in spite of vigorous efforts since the war, has not expanded sufficiently to meet the needs of the industry. Also, the foreign ores have the great attraction of being much higher in iron content than the British lean ores, so that the coastal works have been attracted to importing high quality ores rather than using lean ores where so much of what is being transported at high cost is wasted. Even the steelworks sited in home orefields are now at a disadvantage. The cost of processing the ore before and during the blast furnace stage has raised the capital cost of ironmaking to as much as 70 per cent higher than at a comparable new works based on imported ore; also, the coking coal requirement per ton of iron produced is about 6 cwt a ton higher. Finally there has been a remarkable increase in the availability of foreign ores.

World reserves of iron ore since 1945

Until 1957 there was a growing shortage of iron ore on a world scale. World steel production was increasing (between 1946 and 1962 it more than trebled, from 110 million tons to 361 million tons) and prices of iron ore were rising accordingly. Since the availability of scrap always tends to lag behind the demand for it, this rapid postwar expansion of the industry demanded more and more pig-iron, and, hence, iron ore. A worldwide fear was expressed that there was likely to be a long-term shortage of good quality iron ore. The Americans had consumed during the war no less than 340 million tons of high grade Lake Superior ores, and there were few supplies of ore of that quality left in the USA. We have seen how Britain had very little left in the way of rich iron ore and the European continent and Japan were in a similar position.

The world shortage promoted a search for new ore reserves with results that were quite dramatic. High quality ores were sought that were near to the coast and, preferably, near to deep water, as it was becoming obvious that transportation of iron ore in bulk, if it was to be economic, would have to be done in very large ore-carriers. New deposits satisfying these requirements were discovered in Labrador, on the West Coast of Africa, Venezuela, Brazil, Chile, Peru and Australia. At the same time the USSR, China and France intensified their own home production of ore making certain of their self-sufficiency.

The result was that the world reserves of good quality iron ores more than doubled from about 100,000 million tons in 1950 to about 250,000 million tons in 1962. Not all of these ores are readily accessible, but it is now estimated that the reserves will last, at the present rate of consumption, for over 250 years. The chief exporting countries, France, Sweden, Canada, USSR and Venezuela, are responsible for 60 per cent of world exports, while Britain, West Germany, USA, Belgium and Japan each import over 15 million tons annually. The consequence of this large increase in world reserves has been to change the market for ore from a sellers' to a buyers' market. In the space of five years, for example, the price of ores imported to W. Germany fell by 27 per cent[31] whereas during the same period the cost of home ore rose by 10 per cent. Similarly in Britain the imported ore price index fell from 100 in 1957 to 72 in 1965, while the home ore index rose from 100 to 126. Foreign ore has thus become more attractive on what looks like being a long-term basis.

Deep water berthing and large ore-carriers

The effect of this has been to raise the issue of facilities for the deep water berthing of very large ore-carriers. If Britain is to concentrate more and more on the use of high quality foreign ores the coastal sites which she now has must be able to contend with bulk supplies on the same scale as her Continental rivals if she is to remain competitive. Ore-carriers of 60,000 tons are being put into use which at present cannot be berthed at any steel port in Britain. Rotterdam is being developed by a consortium of Continental steel producers with a view to handling 15 million tons of ore per year from carriers of this size. An indication of future trends is the contract, signed in 1966 by the Steel Company of Wales, for the supply of 475,000 tons of 64 per cent iron-content ore from Australia, at the rate of 160,000 tons per annum.[32] This ore is so low in phosphorus content it can be fed straight into the furnace and will provide the company with $7\frac{1}{2}$ per cent of its requirements. However, because 60,000 ton ore-carriers are to be used the ore will have to be shipped to Rotterdam whence it will be transshipped into smaller boats (10,000 tons) to Port Talbot. Several of the British steel ports are now planning to enlarge their facilities in order to accommodate supplies direct. Port Talbot and Newport plan facilities to take ships of at least 65,000 tons and if necessary up to 100,000 tons. The Tees is being widened and deepened in its lower reaches for a similar purpose and plans exist for the Clyde and Immingham. It is likely too that deep water facilities will be provided on the Mersey. Thus the five areas likely to be the most important steelmaking centres in the future are South Wales, North Lincolnshire, Tees-side, North Wales and the Clyde.

The changing emphasis in the location of the industry helps to emphasize the main problems that the industry has to face. If it is to be competitive the industry must be organized into steelmaking works which provide minimum total costs per ton of output. The ebb and flow of raw material sources, the fluctuations of locational advantages and the rise and fall of the markets have all to be set against the fact that capital costs are enormous. Steel plant set up at very considerable cost may soon be inefficient compared with its competitors if techniques change. There is thus always a danger that for one of several reasons the capital invested in such large sums is at great risk. The only way in which this danger can be combatted is for continuous adjustments to be made in response to the continuously changing technological and market situations. In the past the changes have been gradual and the industry has been able to absorb their impact. Market changes produced difficulties, as we have seen, in the interwar period, but the pace of change has increased since 1945. Not only has there been the growing emphasis, already noted, on the supply of foreign ore, but technological advance has been impressive.

New techniques

New techniques have been applied in all areas of production. In ironmaking there has been a marked economy in the blast furnace process by preparation of the ore before it is charged to the furnace. Ores are now carefully crushed and sized and the fines are agglomerated by sintering. This leads to a concentration of the iron content as well as to improvement in physical properties. Furthermore the new technique of incorporating in the sinter mix the limestone required for furnace slag control, has reduced the weight of the material charged to the blast furnace, thus reducing the coke requirement per ton of product. This in turn has reduced the sulphur input to the furnace so it has been possible to increase the iron content of the charge. The whole process favours imported ores because of their much higher iron content,

Table 7.2

Blast furnaces

	Burden weight cwt/ton of iron	% Sinter in burden	Coke rate cwt/ton	Annual production furnace/1,000 tons
1957	49·7	26·6	17·9	146
1960	45·4	41·5	16·5	185
1964	40·7	59·6	13·9	257

Source: 'World of Steel', *Financial Times*, 28 March 1966.

especially since the introduction of pelletizing on the site of ore extraction. Pelletizing is a technique of treating the ore by removing impurities before transporting the ore to the steelworks.

The Bessemer process, as we have seen, did not prove very popular in Britain. Only 6 per cent of steel production in Britain was by the Bessemer process in 1945.

It had two serious limitations. The method of air blowing could be used only when the phosphorus content of the pig-iron was between 1·6 per cent and 2 per cent and the steel always contained a relatively high proportion of nitrogen which rendered soft steel liable to brittleness. Since the war it has been accepted that the remedy for both these limitations is to replace the air blast by an oxygen blast. The standard of oxygen-making processes has been developed to supply oxygen in gaseous form in bulk quantities (tonnage oxygen) at a much lower cost than the normal liquid oxygen delivered in cylinders.

Thus in recent times the open-hearth process has come to be looked upon as a slightly old-fashioned method of making steel even if oxygen is used, as it is, in the process. In 1945 approximately 88 per cent of British steel was produced in open-hearth furnaces and as recently as 1960 the figures stood at 85 per cent. By 1966 the figure was 63 per cent with every sign that this was a permanent downward trend. Its place is being taken by the LD converter (named after Linz and Donawitz, the Austrian towns where the technique was first developed), which uses tonnage oxygen. The technique involves blowing oxygen through a lance which is lowered into the converter so that oxygen is directed on to the surface of the molten metal at supersonic speed, penetrating the iron and converting it to steel. This can produce 100 tons of steel in an hour compared with 20–30 tons in the traditional open-hearth furnace. The steel it produces is high quality and the capital costs are low. At first it could produce only low carbon steel but improvements have now been applied which have made all types of steel, except stainless steel, possible with an LD converter. Its one drawback is that only 25 per cent of the raw material consumed is scrap.

Before the LD converter's ability to make all types of steel the Kaldo converter was put into use in some steelworks. This also uses oxygen, but the converter is inclined at an angle and revolves. It has the advantage that it consumes 40 per cent scrap, but it has a much higher rate of refractory wear. It is unlikely therefore that any more Kaldo converters will be installed in Britain.

Meanwhile electric arc furnaces are becoming more popular. At first they were used primarily for alloy steels because of the high cost of electricity but the size of these furnaces has now increased to make them economic in the production of carbon steels. It is possible to charge them with 100 per cent scrap; in this way they can be complementary to steelworks with LD converters which do not use so much scrap. The running costs of the two processes are comparable. Even the electric arc furnace is now being challenged by the FOS (fuel, oxygen, scrap) process which replaces the electrodes of the electric arc by a Shell oxygen/oil toroidal burner to heat the scrap. This process, developed by BISRA (British Iron and Steel Research Association) will be cheaper than the electric furnace and is another example of the competition between sources of fuel in postwar Britain.

One other new process which could revolutionize steelmaking has undergone trials at Millom in Cumberland and is now being produced by full-scale plant at Irlam. This is the continuous process of spray steelmaking, which eliminates conversion into ingots and rolling. Molten iron is passed through oxygen jets which burn out impurities and instantly atomize the metal into fine droplets which ultimately fall into a receiving ladle. The big advantage of this process is that the capital cost is less than one-third that of installing an oxygen process. The ultimate aim is to achieve a continuous flow of molten steel as opposed to the batch system which has prevailed until now. This would, of course, greatly accelerate the pace of steelmaking. In the manufacture of special steels there is the new vacuum treatment which excludes possible contamination from air and produces very high quality steel.

A feature of the modern steel mill is the use made of automation. The continuous processing, which is what steel rolling is, lends itself to automation. It is possible for the whole process of very many operations to be controlled automatically to within very narrow tolerances. Computers are used on-line to control plant and off-line for coordination and production planning.

The new processes described above have all been applied in the 1960s (the oxygen converter during the 1950s). After a period lasting 100 years or so when the Bessemer converter and the open hearth were the unchallenged processes of steelmaking, new

Table 7.3

The pattern of steelmaking processes 1960–65 and estimated 1970 percentage of total crude steel production.

Process	1960	1963	1965	1970
Open hearth	84	77	63	45
Oxygen converter	2	10	20	40
Electric FOS	7	9	13	15
Others	7	4	4	–
	100	100	100	100

Source: *Stage 1 Report*, BISF, p. 100.

techniques have suddenly arrived in number. This makes the problems of capital investment even more acute and underlines the necessity for coordinated decision-making on the enormous expenditure involved. Expenditure on development schemes from 1956 to 1965 was £1,070 million. In a modern steelworks up to £15,000-worth of equipment has to be provided for each employee. It takes a long time to plan, build and bring into operation an integrated steelworks, and the size of works is likely to increase. The Committee of the BISF recommend that existing integrated works should be expanded 'to sizes appreciably larger than the present works'. For wide strip mill works it envisages a minimum capacity of 5 million ingot tons by 1975 (there were none in 1966 over 4 million ingot tons).

Organization of the industry

Ever since the 1930s the need has been recognized for planning in the industry. As we have seen (p. 33) the difficulties encountered in the 1930s compelled the industry to rationalize production. The National government of 1931 increased the import tariff on steel only on the condition that satisfactory progress was made in the preparation of a scheme of reorganization and in putting the approved scheme into force. In consequence the Iron and Steel Confederation was formed to consider the reorganization schemes and to represent the industry in its talks with the Imports Duties Advisory Committee which was intended to look after the public interest.

Thus the steel industry has had, since the 1930s, a special relationship with successive British governments whereby the individual firms have surrendered some of their autonomy. Its development from that time has been undertaken in consultation with the government and its prices have been worked out centrally. The IDAC and the BISF came to accept the need for close cooperation and the concept of dual control at the centre took root. It was agreed that prices should be set according to ascertained costs, and in reviewing broadly the position of British steel the IDAC made recommendations that were the start of long-term planning. After the war, the Labour government announced its intention to nationalize the industry but did not have the opportunity to do so until 1951. In the interim the first Iron and Steel Board was established, but this did not have either statutory powers or effective control over some vital interests of the industry, so the BISF went very much its own way.

Nationalization was effective for a mere eight months and then the returning Conservative Government fulfilled its election pledge to denationalize steel, but they did not destroy the special relationship. A second Iron and Steel Board was set up in 1953 which was similar in its purpose to the prewar IDAC. The duality of central power was continued with the BISF acting as a trade association and the Board looking after the public interest. The special relationship was by now reasonably clearly defined. The task in initiating investment proposals was the responsibility of the individual firms who alone had the detailed knowledge of what was involved. The proposals were then looked at carefully by the BISF in terms both of their technical and economic merits, and were then subject to the scrutiny of the Board which paid close attention to any possible restrictive practices and ensured close attention to the national interest. The industry was under a moral obligation to cooperate with the Board's recommendations because the government was making special tariff concessions over steel. The five development programmes for steel since 1945 were made on these principles. The programmes were initiated in 1945,

103

1952, 1957, 1961 and 1964, each one stressing fast expansion: the first set a target of 16 million ingot tons and the fifth planned a production of 33 million ingot tons for 1970.

Meanwhile rationalization was carried through as production was expanded. In ironmaking, while output increased from 7·8 million tons in 1946 to 17·5 million tons in 1965, the average number of blast furnaces in blast was reduced from 98 to 66, and the number of works involved was reduced from 53 to 30. In steelmaking over the same period the output of steel rose from 12·7 million tons to 27·0 million tons, but the number of ingot-making works was reduced by five and the number of steel furnaces fell from 567 to 468.

The world market for steel

By the late 1960s the changing situation in the supply of raw materials and the capital demands of the fast changing techniques has created a situation where further rationalization is necessary. A surplus world steelmaking capacity has emerged, particularly as a result of the forceful expansion of the Japanese industry, making world steel prices highly competitive.

Table 7.4 below shows how world markets have developed in recent years. From 1956 to 1964 Japan raised its exports by 5 million finished tons. Britain did well to

Table 7.4

UK share of world steel market (in percentages)

Exporter	1956	1960	1964
UK	12·7	12·5	12·2
ECSC (excluding intertrading)	53·1	54·7	42·8
USA	20·8	11·6	10·6
Japan	6·1	8·7	21·6
Austria and Sweden	5·5	7·1	7·3
Canada, Australia, South Africa	1·8	5·4	5·5
Total above	100·0	100·0	100·0
Total above – million product tons	18·67	23·29	28·45

Source: *Stage One Report*, BISF, p. 114.

maintain a relatively stable share of the world's markets. British exports during the period rose from 2,105,300 tons to 3,481,000 tons but of greater importance to Britain was the fact that the percentage of exports to the Common Market countries rose from 14 per cent to 32 per cent whilst exports to the Commonwealth declined from 52·4 per cent to 38·4 per cent. This was an encouraging performance at a period when the greatest market potential lay in Europe.

The British industry can maintain this position only by keeping up with new techniques which involve costly changes and call for larger integrated works. The LD converter, for example, is a technique of steelmaking that raises the optimum size of steel plant; also, as we have seen, the increasing need to rely on imported ores demands large integrated steelworks in the areas of deep water ports. As Table 7.5 shows, there has been a great increase in the capital employed in steelmaking in Britain but the return on the capital employed has been declining because of world surplus capacity. The need to employ even greater sums of capital means that a greater return can come only from increased economies of scale. There were by 1967 all the signs of an impending world wide recession in steel. Demand in the home market has fallen because of the credit squeeze which had reached peak proportions in 1966. The capital-intensive nature of the industry makes steel very vulnerable in times of economic recession. It is a costly business to have expensive

Table 7.5

Total capital employed and profits of fourteen major steel companies

Year	Capital employed (£ million)	Profits after depreciation but before interest and tax (£ million)	Return on capital employed %
1956	625·7	94·0	15·0
1957	738·1	110·7	15·0
1958	803·5	108·8	13·5
1959	871·8	111·4	12·8
1960	991·5	141·0	14·2
1961	1,158·2	103·7	9·0
1962	1,282·0	64·1	5·0
1963	1,353·1	58·2	4·3
1964	1,386·1	85·1	6·1
1965	1,403·9	85·1	6·1

Source: *Stage One Report*, BISF, p. 134.

plant being used at only 70 per cent capacity, and discourages further capital investment.

Renationalization

It was at this juncture, 1967, that the Labour Government implemented their promise to renationalize steel. Some amalgamation had already been started. The three firms of Dorman Long, Stewarts and Lloyds and the South Durham Steel and

Iron Co. had already merged, though the process of reorganization could not have progressed very far before the Iron and Steel Bill was passed.

The decision was as much political as it was economic. The Iron and Steel Federation inevitably felt that the change of control would be to the detriment of an industry in which they had had a large measure of control in the past. Mr N. C. MacDiarmid in a celebrated statement at the Annual General Meeting of Stewarts and Lloyds in February 1967 said: 'A government appointed Corporation will be protected from the rigorous disciplines of competition, will be insulated from the need to justify its claim in the market place on investment grounds to a share of scarce resources and, however well managed, will be shackled in the exercise of its commercial judgment by the ball and chain of "the wider national interest" which is to be defined at the diktat of a Minister of the Crown for the time being in office.' Mr MacDiarmid had by then been appointed vice-chairman of the Organizing Committee which was to undertake advance planning for the proposed National Steel Corporation. The Labour Government on the other hand argued that the election which they won in 1966 was fought with steel nationalization as part of their programme. The principal argument in favour of nationalization is that only with central control of capital can rationalization of the industry properly be achieved. There are those who argue that nationalization of steel is a logical evolution from the period of the special relationship.

Government control of one of the major manufacturing industries constitutes a significant advance in a long evolutionary period of government controls. Apart from Austria, Britain is the only advanced nation with a steel industry that is predominantly state owned. For the first time outside the Communist world, a steel industry has been taken over on economic and political grounds where there are no special circumstances prevailing (as there were in Austria in 1946). On the other hand, both France and Germany have supervisory systems, that is a special relationship exists, and in Japan there is a tolerant attitude by the state to supervised cartels. In the USA there are economic guide lines, tax concessions on depreciation and periodical adjustments of steel prices by the Federal Government, so it can be said that state control of some kind or another exists in all the major steel producing countries. The choice in Britain has been between one nationalized concern, itself divided into groups, or a few very large firms formed from the major companies. Whatever the structure the unit has to be very large to conform to the new demands on capital.

Protracted argument and deep-seated controversy are a feature of economic change. The arguments about government control of industry have been going on for most of this century, and ground has been steadily yielded by those who have supported laissez-faire principles. Small wonder that the argument over steel nationalization should be so fierce, and that the industry should pass in and out of public ownership for a period before the issue is finally resolved.

In 1960, when the special relationship still existed in the British industry, the Conservative government authorized the loan of £120 million to Richard, Thomas and Baldwin (the one firm that had been left in public ownership in 1953) and Colvilles, the private enterprise Scottish firm. The loan was intended to make possible the building of two continuous strip mills in areas (South Wales and Scotland) where there were social as well as economic location factors involved. Conservative back-benchers contended that the money should have been raised on the open market and that this indicated that R.T.B. should have been sold back to private enterprise. The Labour opposition argued that if Colvilles could not raise the money on ordinary private enterprise terms the firm should have been taken over by the state. The loans, however, were made, and the mills were built, and in the event it seemed that the finely balanced argument over the source of the investment was largely academic.

It is arguable that the actual ownership of the industry is now of secondary importance to the main problem, which is how best to secure maximum efficiency in an industry that accepted its responsibilities to the nation a long time ago, but where the level of capital investment is so large that miscalculations can be disastrous.

When renationalization took place in 1967, the fourteen major steel companies once again passed into government control. The economic climate was unpropitious for expansion, devaluation taking place later on that year. It was to be expected, therefore, that steel production would fall. Capacity utilization was down to 76 per cent by the end of the year and production fell by 4 per cent compared with the previous year. The cuts in the capital expenditure of the nationalized industry that followed devaluation included one of £10 million in the steel programme. It was hoped that this would be offset by a production increase achieved by offering discounts to major customers (particularly the motor vehicle and shipbuilding industries) and by the increase in national output that would follow devaluation. It was evident that the cyclical nature of the industry was still the dominant factor in the production of steel. It is too soon to comment upon the efficacy or otherwise of renationalization.[33]

8

Engineering

The engineering industry came into being at the time of, and as a consequence of, the Industrial Revolution. At first it was concerned exclusively with the construction of capital equipment for the manufacturing industries of the day, particularly the textile industry, and as such its boundaries were easy to define. The economic growth of Britain hinged very much then upon the development of engineering and has done ever since, but the boundaries of the industry are now more difficult to determine. There is an engineering content in most of modern industry; even with the steady change of emphasis from manufacturing industries to service industries engineering has kept pace and is firmly implanted in both. The rationalization of office routine or retail distribution is now, through the computer, as much the province of the engineer as the manufacture of textiles or the development of a national transport system.

The industry has thus gone far beyond the limits of simply providing capital equipment. The uses of steam and electricity as sources of power have taken engineering into the transport industry, the provision of fuel and power, and the world of consumer goods. Although much of the market is due to derived demand there are now many engineering products, such as cars and television sets, which are supplied direct to the consumer. This dual role as manufacturer of capital and consumer goods makes it a key industry, whose productivity and wellbeing are of central importance to the economy. It has been observed elsewhere how important it has become that Britain should keep up with the rate of technological advance. The shortage of natural resources in Britain, and the need to export goods in increasing quantities in order to sustain a very high standard of living, places a heavy burden of responsibility on engineering. Unless the industry manages to keep to the forefront in technological change, not only will its own markets suffer, but so also will those of practically the whole of British industry. A modern steel mill, for instance, in order to sell its product against fierce competition from abroad, must have the most sophisticated equipment available; process plant of the latest kind is vital to the chemical industry and to power stations; automated equipment of all kinds is the product of engineering firms.

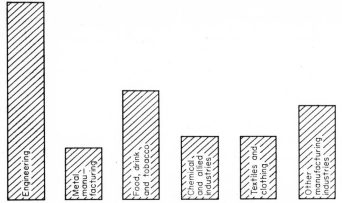

Figure 8.1. *Value of total output of British manufacturing industries* 1966.
Source: *Annual Abstract*.

The diversity of engineering is so great that a survey of the whole industry is not possible here. However, some reference can be made to the major sectors. Motor vehicles and shipbuilding are dealt with in chapters of their own while electrical engineering and machine tools are considered in the succeeding pages. An assessment of the significance of the industry to the economy can be made by reference to Figures 8.1 and 8.2, which illustrate the importance of engineering products in Britain's export programme in the total output of Britain's manufacturing industries.

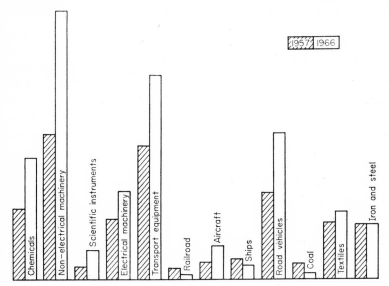

Figure 8.2. *Value of exports of British manufacturing industries* 1957 *and* 1966.
Source: *Annual Abstract*.

Electrical engineering

The demand for electricity has increased tremendously as the century has progressed; there is no need to emphasize how dependent the economy has become upon it as a highly convenient source of heat, light and power. Since 1945 the demand for electricity has increased by 8 per cent per annum until very recently, while the appropriate expansion in the market for generating equipment and electrical machinery and apparatus has been implicit in that demand. If exports of all electrical goods are considered (Figure 8.2 embraces only electrical machinery) total exports of the industry in 1966 reached £406 million, representing a little over one-sixth of the total output of £2,400 million for that year and roughly one-twelfth of the value of all UK exports. The importance of the industry becomes increasingly clear if it is realized that one-third of the new capital equipment for British industry was supplied by electrical engineering firms in 1966.

It is misleading, however, to treat the industry as a whole. The variety of electrical goods and equipment has become so farranging that there are subdivisions of the industry which are industries in their own right. Thus there is the electrical plant and machinery industry, which is concerned with plant for power generation, transmission and distribution; electronics and telecommunications which have made spectacular advance since the war, and the manufacture of domestic electrical appliances which has greatly expanded since 1945 as the high level of personal incomes has been achieved. The manufacture of electric wires and cables has also grown in importance. While there has been overall expansion in the industry the pattern within the industry has been changing, as Table 8.1 shows.

Table 8.1

Changing pattern of electrical engineering production

| | Percentage of total output | | |
	1948	1958	1966
Electrical machinery	54	49	35
Allied plant and equipment			
Electronics and telecommunications equipment	20	30	41
Electric wires and cables	19	11	13
Domestic electrical appliances	7	10	11

Source: *Census of Production*, BEAMA figures.

1. ELECTRICAL PLANT AND MACHINERY

Of the three branches of electrical engineering the plant and machinery sector is the oldest. Methods of electricity generation may have changed but the need for generating plant has remained unaltered. As might be expected the growth rate of the machinery sector is now the steadiest in the industry because it has settled down to the role of a traditional industry supplying a regular but increasing demand at home while competing hard to retain a reasonable share of world markets. Future demand for electricity is assured and can be calculated, within reason, comparatively easily, so that although the growth rate is still impressive it is not as dramatic as in electronics or as sporadic as in domestic appliances. The pertinent problem is now the control of investment in order to match the calculated increase in demand.

Size of firm

Electrical machinery is manufactured by a large number of firms. Much electrical plant is specific, calling for specialization, but the bigger the plant the fewer the firms that have sufficient resources to cope with orders of this kind. The size of the generating sets that are required for modern power stations is such that the number of firms capable of taking on contracts to supply has been reduced to three (GEC/ AEI, EEC* and Parsons). These three firms, however, do not specialize simply in heavy electrical equipment but produce electrical equipment of all kinds, including small electric motors, electronic equipment and domestic appliances. This has produced an industrial structure that is by modern standards rather clumsy. Although on the heavy equipment side there has been, of necessity, a streamlining of the number of supplying firms, there are too many firms engaged in the manufacture of all smaller electrical machines and plant. For instance; 'there are said to be sixteen firms in Britain making high-power electrical transformers, while in West Germany there are only six. There seem to be thirty firms making the smaller distribution transformers where six might do. And so on.'[34] There is, therefore, scope for further amalgamation and absorption of specialist suppliers if the British industry is to increase its efficiency. The German industry makes an interesting comparison. It is dominated by two major firms, but each complements the other in its specialization as opposed to the major British firms which tend to compete. The merger of AEI and GEC in 1967 was an important step towards rationalization but produced a giant (the third largest electrical firm in Europe and the second biggest manufacturing company in the United Kingdom) which 'makes everything electrical'. The result of this may be that further streamlining will take place and the heavy generating side of AEI will be sold to English Electric.

Productivity

The Economist estimate of productivity in 1966 (see p. 209) rated electrical machinery as the industry that compared the least favourably with foreign industry. It claimed that just over four men were needed in Britain for every one man working in the USA. The size of the unit of production must be regarded as one reason for this. Also, because the supply of much electrical machinery is set against a derived demand there are fluctuations in orders which are difficult to control. Firms find that at

* Since this was written the merger of GEC/AEI and English Electric has been announced.

111

times they require as many workers as they can get in order to manufacture equipment for a particular contract date. Subsequently, during the periods of comparative lull, they are loth to release their surplus labour in case they cannot re-employ them when the next batch of orders appears on their books.

The CEGB monopsony

The market for heavy electrical plant in Britain is unusual. There are three major suppliers, as has been noted, but there is only one buyer, the CEGB, whose programme of increasing the installed capacity of the electricity supply system provides the sole outlet in Britain for heavy plant sales. This presents obvious difficulties. When there is a single customer and several suppliers, the suppliers have to accept that the customer has a commanding control over not only the quality of goods supplied but their price and delivery date as well. It is possible for the CEGB to demand equipment which is specified in detail (the specification might even be the work of its own designers), thereby giving the supplier little scope for movement or initiative in design; even worse from the supplier's point of view, he may have to work to a different specification for the same product in the export market, losing in the process the standardization that could, perhaps, otherwise have been achieved.

The need for larger generating sets has meant that even before a power station has been completed, work has started on the design and construction of a bigger one. Fifty 500 megawatt single-shaft generating sets will be in service by 1970, but already full technical specifications have been issued for the first 660 megawatt units and 1,000 megawatt single shaft machines are envisaged for the 1970s. The nuclear power stations are correspondingly big. Indeed the bigness of the earlier nuclear stations combined with the newness of the technology involved the major companies in heavy losses, and even now the industry is saddled with a very costly programme of nuclear research. The sheer size and cost of the plant involved has had the effect of reducing the number of orders: the bigger the generating plant the longer the interval between the orders. The three big firms are thus faced with the fact that the loss of a contract is a much more serious affair than it used to be. There can be a gap of three years or more between one order and the next. No one firm has emerged as a price leader so that all are in a poor bargaining position from almost every point of view when they negotiate contracts. In Germany, on the other hand, the supply authorities are almost entirely in the hands of private enterprise and there is a very close link between them and the manufacturers, so that German firms make higher profit than those in Britain. The British system is a mixture of private enterprise and nationalization which has yet to be rationalized. Perhaps the way out would be for contract procedures to be worked out between the government and the major firms to ensure full and efficient use of productive capacity.

This brief reference to the problems of the electrical plant and machinery sector of the industry must not place the achievement of the postwar period in the wrong perspective. Very real technological advance has been made since 1945. The very large generating sets, for instance, were not designed and constructed without immense technical problems being overcome, while the British nuclear power programme was from the outset and still is the biggest in the world. Britain's transmission system operates at 400,000 V and uses overhead lines that can carry 1,800,000 KW and as such is the most powerful in the world.

2. ELECTRONICS

The electronics industry has expanded since the war at the annual rate of 9 per cent. In 1965 the value of its total output was £560 million, of which over one-quarter was exported. This level of production was well over 50 per cent above that of four years earlier. The industry has been right at the front of technological advance since 1945, providing computers, communications systems, industrial process control, navigational aids and so on, apart from consumer goods such as radios and television sets. It owes its origins largely to the British development of radar during the war, though much of the subsequent invention has been done outside Britain, particularly in the USA. The transistor, for instance, which has so boosted the components side of the industry, was invented in the Bell Telephone Laboratories in America in 1948. Technological advance in electronics is so rapid that obsolescence is one of the industry's problems.

The British success in electronics can be measured by the fact that Britain is second only to the USA in the value of goods produced and exported. In so many of the 'league tables' of productivity and economic growth Britain is so well down the list, that it is encouraging to find her well placed in an industry fundamental to future economic expansion. It must be admitted, however, that the British industry is only one-tenth the size of that of the USA. The Americans present a formidable challenge both at home and overseas. Three of the largest American firms 'each sold as much in a year as the total output of the British electronics industry'.[35] American exports have secured 60 per cent of the world export market and in Western Europe 'the proportion of American owned companies in the production of electronics capital goods is between 15 per cent and 20 per cent'. This daunting American share of the world market in electronics is the biggest difficulty for British manufacturers. The Americans have a much bigger home market while the US Defence Department greatly stimulates the growth of the industry by awarding attractively large contracts for the American defence and space programmes; the Americans are also able to afford expensive research programmes. There is a danger that the British industry will be ultimately engulfed by the sheer size and volume of the American effort.

There are at the moment three main sectors of the electronics industry. Consumer products (particularly radio and television sets) constitute one, while the other two, capital goods and components, may well merge in the future. This indicates the speed of technological advance. Electronics equipment has until recently consisted of discrete components brought together and wired into circuits. There have thus come into being two manufacturing groups, one for the components and one for the completed circuits. Micro-electronics, which is a very recent development, now offers a technique of manufacture which forms the whole circuit of wiring and components at the same time. This is done either by depositing thin films of suitable materials on glass or by forming the circuits on or within a tiny 'chip' of semiconductor. The structure of the electronics industry is thus likely to change although it is not clear whether the two groups, components and capital equipment, will merge or whether one will take over the other.

Consumer products

These account for approximately one-fifth of the total output of the electronics industry (1965: 22 per cent). The difficulties faced by this sector of the industry are similar to those of domestic appliances manufacture which are dealt with later in this chapter; they are therefore not discussed here. Technical innovation can give impetus to the market, but growth in this sector is much more sporadic than in the rest of the electronics industry. Between 1964 and 1965 the value of total sales of electronic consumer products dropped from over £81 million to about £71·5 million with the industry working well below capacity. Colour television, inaugurated in 1967, will perhaps give this sector the boost that it requires.

Capital goods

On the other hand capital goods have shown a dramatic rate of growth. Deliveries of electronic capital goods rose from £49·7 million in 1958 to £268·4 million in 1965. The biggest single item is radar and navigational aids which have secured 30 per cent of the world export markets. About 75 per cent of all ships with marine radar use British equipment, as do most of the world's civil airports outside the USA. Computers are of course counted as capital equipment. Britain's is the only independent computer industry outside the USA, but exports represent only 8 per cent of the world total. America's predominance in the field can be shown by the fact that Britain has imported 50 per cent of its computers.

American firms also predominate in radiocommunications equipment, but the development of the GPO telecommunications network has created a demand for capital equipment in this field. In 1965, for instance, the GPO placed orders for the first series of production electronic telephone exchanges which constitute part of a development programme that will last several years. Microwave techniques are being developed for trunk communications, with a network of towers being built for this purpose. The annual expenditure on equipment by the GPO is over £200 million per year. The development of satellite telecommunications also offers a market for British industry in that terminals will need to be built as the satellite system expands.

Industrial control systems which are the basis of automation have rapidly become important, particularly in process engineering; production for these shows a sevenfold increase between 1960 and 1965. It has been estimated that the three firms of Elliott-Automation, Ferranti and English Electric have accounted for about 13 per cent of world installations of electronic industrial control systems while AEI Automation and General Electric Automation (now merged) are manufacturers too. The development of direct digital computer control has made it possible for this type of control to be applied to almost all new process plant of significant size. Already the steel industry, the oil industry, the electricity supply industry, the chemical industry and the radio telescope at Jodrell Bank, have installed digital computer control; there still exists a very big market potential in Britain let alone the export markets for further application.

Meanwhile the introduction of microminiature techniques is rendering existing equipment obsolescent almost as soon as it is installed. The Ferranti Argus 400 was, for instance, the first UK microminiature control computer in production, replacing the transistorized Argus 100. In comparison it was 'thirteen times faster, being capable of over 80,000 additions per second, approximately ten times as reliable and sells at two-thirds of the price. Incidentally it is so small it can be carried about in an attache case, consumes the same power as a 100 watt bulb and works equally well at $-10°C$ and at $60°C$.' [36] Digital computers of this kind originally differed so much from conventional computers that they were not manufactured by the computer industry. They are now much more like the conventional computer but the five firms mentioned above particularly involved in industrial control systems have already gained a commanding lead in making them. These firms, the 'automation companies' have also specialized in making the 'software' (the system design and programming), thereby producing a control system to suit the requirements of individual processing operations and diminishing the probability that the conventional computer manufacturers will gain an increasing share of the market. There are those who believe that four firms are too many if the American challenge is to be met, so even this most advanced sector of the electrical engineering industry is subject to the criticism that the full advantages of economies of scale are not being obtained.

Components industry

The conventional components industry produces passive components (e.g. capacitors, resistances and transformers) and active components (valves and transistors). The 1965 output was valued at £250 million.[37] The same thing can be said of the structure of components industry as of the capital equipment sector. There are over two hundred firms, ranging from the very big to the very small. This fact, taken in conjunction with the advance in micro-electronics suggests that some rationalization is bound to occur. The cost of producing a microcircuit is high, but it can be offset by large-scale production. This means that a firm has to find the capital necessary for new plant and skilled staff. The small firms cannot cope with this. Technical advance is so fast, and the American advantage of size is so overwhelming, that the British tradition of allowing the industrial structure to evolve by competition, the less active firms falling by the wayside, is probably too slow. American firms have the constant stimulus of orders for the aerospace industry; many of these emanate from the Defence Department which, for example, in 1965 spent $2,300 million on electronics research and development; the British industry has a very limited stimulus of this kind because the British aerospace industry is so very much smaller. The investment in research and development has to be provided largely by the firms themselves but also by Government departments. The Ministry of Technology sponsors the industry but the role of government in precipitating the formation of a streamlined industry faster than would naturally occur is not yet clearly outlined. Purchase of shares by the government in any firm or a government subsidy raises a hot political issue. Meanwhile the American industry threatens to encroach upon existing and new market prospects. Some British firms have already yielded to the situation by producing advanced design circuitry under an American licence. Ferranti, for instance, have taken a licence from Fairchild. Well over half of British needs for microcircuits is being met by imports; seven American firms export to Britain and two have assembly plants here.

Reviewed as a whole, the electronics industry emerges as one of Britain's fastest developing industries with an enormous potential for assisting productivity and raising standards of living, provided it can cope with the American challenge. Its future seems to lie in the selection of particular fields of specialization which can be developed to supply world markets, particularly when the question of whether and how government aid should be applied has been resolved.

3. DOMESTIC ELECTRICAL APPLIANCES

The postwar redistribution of wealth and increase in incomes has paved the way for a remarkable expansion in ownership of consumer durables – the period of high mass consumption. Many of these durables are electrical appliances; the 1950s saw a mushroom growth in sales of vacuum cleaners, refrigerators, washing machines, etc. Table 8.2 demonstrates this.

The increase in manufacturing capacity thus demanded has changed the manufacture of domestic electrical appliances from being a subsidiary part of the electrical machinery industry to an industry in its own right. The demand has been met by a supply of goods made by the old established firms and by the many new firms that have entered the fray since 1945. This development bears several parallels with the motor vehicle industry but its development is condensed into a much shorter period. Both industries have made tremendous growth because of the arrival of high mass consumption, and both are concerned with the assembly of component parts; indeed, the two industries are in a sense competitors, because they are vying with each other for the increased savings of all income groups that is now available for spending on these products.

One aspect of the industry makes it different from most of the manufacturing industries: it is not a major exporter, nor does Britain import many appliances of this kind. Approximately 80 per cent of the industry's production is for the home market and 95 per cent of the domestic electrical appliances sold in Britain are also

Table 8.2

Percentages of households owning various appliances

	1938	*1948*	*1963*
	(a)	(a)	
Refrigerators	3b	2	33
Washing machines	3½	4	50
Vacuum cleaners	27	40	77
Cookers	18	19	35
Water heaters	n.a.	16	44
Fires	n.a.	64	72
Irons	n.a.	86	78
Steam irons	n.a.	n.a.	25

a Households wired for electricity only
b This figure includes gas apparatus
n.a. Not available

After T. A. B. Corley, *Domestic Electrical Appliances.*

made in Britain. This is a fact that has affected government economic decisions that concern the industry and one that causes particular problems. The inflation that has bedevilled the economy since 1945 has been partly a demand inflation, which has been countered by government control of personal spending. This has affected several industries, none more so than the domestic electrical appliances. Between 1951 and 1960 controls over hire purchase of appliances were altered eight times and purchase tax rates six times. If an industry relies so much upon the home market as this one does, then intervention of this kind is bound to disrupt sales and make a mockery of long-term planning; it will also inevitably affect the structure of the industry, as we shall see.

The manufacturer of consumer durables has to accept that he is making goods in advance of receiving orders for them. In order to make his product attractive in price to a potential customer he must be prepared to make it in sufficient numbers to achieve economies of production that can reduce the price to the correct level. This means gambling that there will be the demand for a supply that is provided well in advance. In conditions of rapidly expanding demand such as the postwar period has witnessed, the gamble has been attractive to many firms. Mr Kenneth Wood, for instance, anticipating the demand for electric food mixers, started production in 1947 with a capital of £800 and has established a very successful business. At the other end of the scale, Hoover, already a household word in vacuum cleaners before the war, opened two new factories in 1946, one to make washing machines. Lec Refrigeration Ltd, began making refrigerators in 1946. All these companies were making goods for stock, anticipating sales that would clear stock as fresh appliances were made. Stock can be carried within limits, at the factory, and also at distribution outlets.

The fluctuations of stop–go upset this process of growth and calculated risk. If there is recession in trade the first of the manufacturing industries to be affected are those making consumer durables, along with motor vehicles. Consumer durables are still regarded as luxuries and, because they are durable, they can be made to last longer if the consumer's money is tight. The bigger the firm, the greater the quantity of stock that has to be stored in lean times and the more difficult it is to amend production runs which depend upon a regular flow of component parts ordered well in advance. Similar problems exist, only in reverse, if there is an increase in the pace of economic growth.

Small firms either adjust swiftly to the changes in demand or go out of business; the big firms bear their losses and hope for a brighter future. The lack of export outlets for this industry gives little or no flexibility to sales difficulties at home. The stop–go economic policies of successive governments since 1945 have been formulated on the theory that falling home markets would inspire greater export performance. Put the other way, this means that when there are high levels of demand at home, the pressure on supply discourages exports. Certainly, the instability of the home market in domestic electrical applicances seems to have discouraged exports, though there is a school of thought that suggests that the cause of a poor export performance is the low relative growth rate.[38]

In 1963 there were twenty-five firms sharing 74 per cent of total sales of domestic electrical appliances all of them employing more than 400 workers: in addition there were about 140 smaller firms.[39] This is the range of the size of firms engaged in this manufacture. Among the big firms are those that make other forms of electrical equipment (e.g. GEC/AEI, and English Electric) and two (Hoover and Belling) that do not. No one firm dominates the market, nor do a select few. The variety of goods is huge. 'Of the forty appliances on the market in 1962, the 175 British manu-facturers, plus a number of importers, supplied between them 728 separate brands of appliances and 3,106 different models of these appliances, an average of 4·3 models per brand.'[40]

The situation is thus rather like the motor vehicle industry in the 1920s before the emergence of the big five in the subsequent decade. The small inefficient firms will probably be submerged by the effects of the fluctuation of the economy while the dwindling number of specialist firms will compete with the electrical giants whose efficiency is, perhaps, affected by the fact that if they lose profit temporarily because of the reduced pace of economic growth, their domestic electrical appliance division can be sustained for the time being by the strength of the other divisions of the company. Thus in common with much of British industry and the rest of the electrical industry there is a need for rationalization.

Machine tools

A machine tool is essentially a power driven machine used for cutting and forming metal. Fundamentally it is capable of six operations: drilling and boring, milling, turning, planing and shaping, grinding, and shearing and pressing.[41] Its importance to the manufacturing industries is inestimable since it provides the wherewithal for making components and 'machines to make machines' accurately with the minimum reliance upon human labour. The machine tools industry was established in the nineteenth century, but it was not until after the First World War that special-purpose tools were developed, designed for a narrower range of operations. These were followed by 'specific' machine tools which were more specialized still, but economic only in manufacturing industry where the large firm predominated. Today machine tools are in many cases automated highly complex pieces of machinery that are linked with the electrical engineering industry in their manufacture. This highly specific aspect of machine tools has militated against the big firm in the past because it was difficult to achieve economies of scale when in so many instances the individual customer had to be catered for. Now, however, machine tools are being made in sufficient quantities for bigger firms to emerge. 'Nearly three-fifths of total production is handled by half-a-dozen sizeable organizations; and perhaps a half of the industry's labour force comes under their control.'[42] Even so there are many small firms with a secure place in the industry. The industry is thus made up of many firms, none of which dominates the market.

If the British economy is to increase its rate of productivity the machine tools industry obviously has a most important role. In a sense, the more machine tools that can be sold to the home market the better; in theory each machine tool sold to industry releases labour and increases output. In 1965 just over 75 per cent of production in Britain went to the home market; this may seem encouraging but the picture is not necessarily as rosy as this suggests. Machine tools depend very much upon the wellbeing of other industries. Expansion in any of the manufacturing industries will promote sales of machine tools, but recession inevitably causes a decline in sales. Thus the industry's peaks and troughs generally follow those of the major industries, but with greater fluctuations. Overall growth in production since the war in the industry has hovered around 2 per cent but yearly changes have rarely been less than 5 per cent and have even mounted to 15 per cent. This is an economic fact that is very difficult for the industry to counter, except perhaps by long-term planning with the users.

In fact the key to the success of the machine tool industry in Britain lies with the user as much as with the manufacturer. We have noted the propensity of the British manufacturer to cling to the past, and this is illustrated by the way in which outdated machinery is kept in operation when more sophisticated machines would make production a more economic proposition. A 1960 report discovered that three out of every five of the 1,234,000 machines in use in Britain were out of date.[43] A Management Consultants' Association in 1965 found a similar situation, reporting that firms were unaware of the benefits which the greater use of modern machine tools would achieve.

NUMERICAL CONTROL

With the rapid growth in automated machine tools it has become more important than ever that firms should be aware of what these modern tools can do. A numerically controlled machine tool is controlled by a computer which can be programmed with the drawing board details of the article to be manufactured. Then by means of servomechanisms the machine can reproduce all the operations necessary for the performance of the job. Sensing equipment automatically corrects for slight deviations. Different programmes can be fed into the same control unit and a wide variety of different components can be made on the one machine. This is a valuable way of producing articles which are needed in small quantities, for though the machines are expensive, they are not nearly as expensive as the automated equipment designed for mass production runs. Typical applications are in the aerospace industries and in the manufacture of jigs and dies for general engineering purposes.

A numerically controlled machine tool can also be used for positioning a work piece very accurately prior to relatively simple operations like drilling or jig boring, obviating the need for a highly skilled operator. One other use of a system of this kind is numerical measurement which monitors the dimensions of the job while cutting proceeds, and displays them to the operator, thereby considerably assisting the task of inspection.

Government assistance to firms can obviously act as a stimulus to purchase of machine tools. Investment allowances were made in the first place but these are now investment grants towards the cost of installation (25 per cent normally, but 45 per cent in a Development area). The Ministry of Technology in conjunction with the National Research Development Corporation (see p. 202) has introduced a scheme whereby firms can take delivery of a machine tool of the kind described above on a 'sale or return' basis. The firm can try out the machine tool for up to two years to prove how efficient or otherwise it is for its purpose. This is a good example of the way in which the Government can encourage productivity while at the same time, of course, helping the machine tool industry.

Machine tool manufacturers have in recent times initiated schemes for leasing machine tools to the smaller firm. This is in keeping with the modern attitude to credit and hire purchase. The small firm can offset the effects of inflation by obtaining today's equipment with tomorrow's money, and can avoid using scarce capital or raising extra capital. It is hoped that these schemes will contribute to the ironing out of some of the trade fluctuations.

IMPORTS

Britain imports a significantly greater number of machine tools than some of her chief competitors. Table 8.3 illustrates that West Germany and the USA supply more of their home needs. As with all sophisticated goods, an inter-trade is to be

Table 8.3

Imports of machine tools, 1963

	$ million
Italy	124·3
France	91·2
UK	66·9
Japan	63·6
Germany	53·2
USA	34·6

Source: *UN World Trade Annual*, 1963.

expected, but the trade is not well balanced. West Germany, which has the largest machine tool industry in Europe, exports three times as much as Britain, and many of those exports are machine tools of a more advanced kind than the more standardized types of machinery that Britain tends to continue producing.

The branches of the engineering industry are thus becoming more interdependent as the pace of technology increases. Electrical power and electronic control are becoming so important to the operation of plant and machinery in all manufacturing industry that close liaison is necessary between those who supply the machines and use them and those who devise means of controlling them. The productivity of the engineering industry has become one of the focal points of the economy; the size of the firm in the industry and the nature of government intervention to promote increased productivity have become matters of importance in all branches of the industry because of the direct part they have to play in raising the standards of living in Britain.

9

The motor vehicle industry

The motor vehicle industry is a twentieth-century development. The use of the internal combustion engine for transport purposes coincided with the end of the Victorian era, so that the motor vehicle is essentially the product of the last seventy years. The economic and social changes that it has brought are no less than the changes introduced by the railways in the middle of the nineteenth century and, indeed, the railways themselves have been affected severely by the impact of the motor vehicle.

The shifting emphasis in transport is instructive. First came improvement of the roads, but the advantages offered by the introduction of turnpikes were thwarted by the advent of the railways in the 1830s. The new railway industry grew quickly to impressive proportions, thus making a major contribution to the prosperity and industrial wealth of Victorian Britain. The twentieth century has witnessed a return to the roads. The expansion of the economy has been associated with the motor vehicle and this has necessitated an extensive road building programme. The railways have correspondingly contracted and no longer have a dominant role (see Chapter 12). The demand for road vehicles has increased steadily as the century has progressed and a new industry has emerged upon whose prosperity Britain is now dependent. Should a new mode of surface transport be introduced as revolutionary as was the internal combustion engine in its time, Britain may have to accept that the wealth that the motor vehicle industry has brought will in future have to be found elsewhere. Meanwhile the motor vehicle industry is her largest single exporter; the value of its products in all forms in 1966 accounted for 16 per cent of the value of total British exports. In that year over 2 million vehicles were manufactured in Britain.

Location of the industry

The great centre of the industry used to be the Midlands but diversification has occurred from the 1930s onwards as the causes of location of the industry have become less specific. The original location was due to the combination of factors which established the cycle industry in the Coventry area. The availability of skilled engineering labour was paramount in the days before the production of vehicles in large numbers. The Midlands had an engineering tradition that went back to the 'take-off' period in the eighteenth century, and even before that it had a reputation for the handling of metal. Pig iron was being transported from the furnaces of the Forest of Dean to be worked in Birmingham in the seventeenth century. The making of a motor vehicle calls for the manufacture of very many small components which require skilful assembly. Small metal products had long been the speciality of the Midlands, where traditional skills in metal and engineering lent themselves readily to the manufacture of cycles and subsequently motor vehicles at the beginning of this century. Many of the first firms in the industry were established in or near the Coventry/Birmingham area of the Midlands. Daimler produced the first cars on a commercial basis in Coventry in 1896. Rover, Hillman, Humber and Standard started in Coventry too, with Austins not far away in Birmingham and Morris fifty miles or so away in Oxford. With the onset of flow techniques of production the requirement of skilled engineering labour diminished in importance. Labour was required in increasing quantities but the proportion of unskilled or semiskilled labour was now much higher. When Fords established their new factory at Dagenham in 1932 one of the principal determining factors of location was the availability of a large quantity of unskilled labour from London's East End.

Proximity to the market is not particularly important as a factor determining the location of the industry, but the external economies of scale that can be achieved by concentrating motor vehicle production in one area are very real. The concentration of the American industry that occurred in Detroit is an example which more than matches the early concentration in Britain in the Midlands. A motor vehicle firm is essentially an organization of assembly. It may be concerned with casting, machining and pressing, but it is the assembling of component parts coming from a wide variety of sources that is its ultimate concern. All the firms in Britain rely heavily on external supplies, and the advantages of having the suppliers in close geographical proximity to the assembly plant are obvious. One way to achieve this is vertical integration, which has other advantages which are considered below, but although there has been a steady movement towards such integration over the years, the complexities of supply ensure that progress will never be substantial in that direction. The ordinary car has many thousands of parts. The Vauxhall Victor for example contains 10,000 parts, and the Mini-Minor 14,000.[44] No firm can hope to manufacture and assemble all these itself in one location. Thus Fords, who have carried vertical integration farther than most companies, still buy 65 per cent (in value) of their cars from external suppliers.

The major components of the Jaguar Mark X came from Leeds, Worcester, Cardiff, Ayr, Slough, Plymouth, Manchester, Leicester, Rochester, Derby, Leamington, Chelmsford, Northampton, Stockport and Blackpool.[45] This is a telling example of the extent to which the component suppliers of the industry are diversified. Even so Britain has a geographical advantage compared with its rivals, particularly the USA. The distances involved in transporting component parts are comparatively small. The USA car industry is no longer concentrated to anything like its original extent in Detroit but is spread over a wide area of North America. Transport costs are thus higher.

Fords in transferring from Trafford Park, Manchester to Dagenham in Essex in 1932 not only hoped to achieve greater vertical integration and to take advantage of the supply of labour, but planned to make the import of raw materials (particularly coal from Durham and iron ore from Sweden) more economical. The siting of the Ford works on the Thames Estuary has also helped them with the exporting facilities that have become so important since 1945.

The assembly of motor vehicles as well as the manufacture of component parts became increasingly diversified subsequent to the original concentration in the Midlands. Fords at Dagenham was one pre-1939 example, Vauxhalls at Luton was another. Since 1945 the government has brought pressure to bear on the major companies when they wished to expand, to persuade them to build new plant in areas where there was unemployment and economic slack. This explains the factories of Ford and Vauxhall at Liverpool (Halewood and Ellesmere Port respectively), the Rootes factory at Linwood in the west of Scotland, the BMC factory at Bathgate, West Lothian for production of commercial vehicles and tractors, and the new Rover factory in Cardiff for the production of Land Rovers.

Thus the industry as it has expanded has spread from its point of origin to many parts of the country. This has meant that although the prosperity that a thriving industry brings to an area is still at its greatest, perhaps, in the Midlands area, the whole country can be said to benefit from an industry that now stretches from the west of Scotland to the south-east of England. The high wages paid in the industry have stimulated the economies of the regions where it is located and the direct and indirect demand for labour has done the same thing.

Although the advantages of the external economies of scale have been lost the dangers of a concentrated industry have been avoided. The lessons of Lancashire and cotton have been learnt. If there is a fall in demand for the product of this major industry the effects will not be felt exclusively in one area of the country: the economic consequences will be more evenly spread and will be, therefore, easier to bear.

Expansion since 1945

It has already been observed that until 1939 the British motor vehicle industry was not particularly export oriented, approximately 80 per cent of its exports going to protected markets in the Empire. That situation has been drastically altered since the war. British cars have been sold in large numbers not only in Africa, Asia and Australia but also in the USA. In Europe, even when the tariff barrier of the Common Market countries has militated against them, British firms have gradually increased their sales. The total value of motor vehicles and motor products exported from Britain in 1966 was over £800 million.

The reasons for this tremendous expansion must be examined. In the first place the motor car must be regarded as a consumer good that enjoys an increasing demand as a society raises its standard of living. The number of vehicles per head of the population is sometimes used as a rough guide to the level of wealth in a community. In the USA there is one vehicle for every three people: in Britain there is one vehicle for every six people. As the world becomes wealthier so the market expands for the car-producing countries both at home and abroad. Fears that saturation point would be reached have so far proved groundless especially since the 'two-car family' has become a familiar part of American and then British society. Allowing for cyclical fluctuations the demand for vehicles since 1945 has burgeoned.

Britain was in a privileged position in 1945 and took full advantage of it. The serious loss of production that the Second World War had induced had left a world shortage of vehicles by 1945. The USA and Britain were the only two major producers who were in a position to supply because the European industry had been largely destroyed during the war. The German Opel factory, for example, was actually dismantled by the Russians and removed to the Soviet Union, while the rest of Germany's factories had suffered severely from the fighting and the bombing. The French and Italian industries had suffered similarly. The American market was hungry for cars and this kept the American industry working at top pressure without undue concern for exports. In any case, the acute shortage of dollars throughout the world denied the Americans the opportunity to export. Britain, whose industry had emerged from the war relatively unscathed, found that she was the most important supplier in a sellers' market. The serious dollar shortage in this country and the urgent need to maintain a proper balance of payments compelled successive governments to starve the home market of cars while the greater part of the industry's production was sold abroad to obtain urgently needed currency. In 1950 70 per cent of the total output of motor vehicles was exported. The popularity of the British sports car in the USA was such that only a very small percentage of them appeared on the home market during the late 1940s and early 1950s. The shortage of cars on the home market created a black market in new vehicles. A form of rationing was devised whereby those people with the greatest need were provided with vehicles first, and those who were fortunate enough to obtain a new vehicle were asked to sign a covenant that they would not dispose of it within a year; nonetheless new vehicles were available if the purchaser was prepared to pay several hundred pounds above the list price to an unscrupulous owner.

The concentration of the British industry on the small car in the interwar period held back the opportunities for export, but after 1945 this was the type of vehicle demanded in most parts of the world. The cost of petrol, except in the USA, was high so that the emphasis was upon a vehicle that was economical to run. In the

USA a demand developed for a second family car of a smaller size than the customary big vehicle. Britain was fortunate in that this was just what her industry was geared to supply. What had proved a hindrance to exports before 1939 proved to be a blessing after 1945.

There was hardly a need for a sales force in the British industry at this time, as cars almost sold themselves. The markets that Britain found in the first ten years

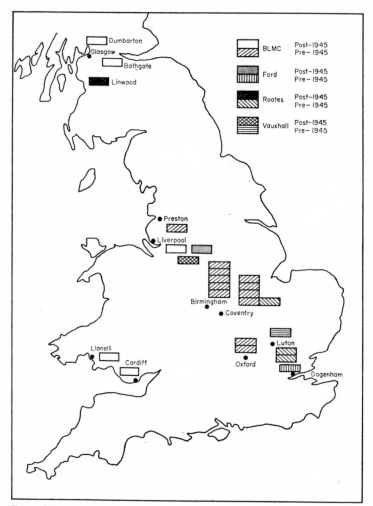

Figure 9.1. Principal factories of the major motor-vehicle producers – post-1945 expansion.

after the war she has clung to ever since. Competition may now be fierce but the position obtained by the British industry when there was little competition from elsewhere has been the making of car exports. Selling was perhaps too easy. In the rush to produce cars to satisfy the enormous demand, insufficient attention was paid

126

to the quality of the product. Too many cars were despatched overseas with defective parts or poorly finished. Nor was there nearly enough effort to establish an after-sales service, especially in those parts of the world where British cars were now being sold for the first time. A car that needs a spare part when there is no spare part to be had, except after a long wait, is in many ways worse than no car at all. The British car industry in neglecting these things damaged its image overseas and thereby made it much easier for the European car firms to make inroads in the 1950s into the markets where Britain had had such a privileged start. One of the major reasons why Volkswagen achieved such startling success in export markets in the 1950s was the first-class after-sales service that was established at the same time as the markets were developed. It has always been the Volkswagen policy to make sure that an agent carries the equivalent of a complete car in spare parts before he is allowed to sell Volkswagen cars. British manufacturers have faced a long battle to convince overseas buyers that the image of the 1950s is not the correct image for the 1960s, but reputations die hard. In all fairness it must be said that in the immediate postwar period there was a shortage of raw materials which sometimes necessitated the substitution of inferior materials for those of orthodox quality, but that did not excuse bad workmanship or lack of after-sales service.

It took the British car industry four years to restore production to the 1939 level. In 1949 it produced 412,000 cars. West Germany did not reach her 1939 figures until 1951. Thus by 1950 Britain was the leading producer of motor vehicles in Europe and the leading world exporter. In that year she exported three times as many cars as the USA and six times as many as West Germany. This was a share of the market that Britain could not expect to hold, but she yielded her position more rapidly than was anticipated. Only six years later West Germany had risen to be the largest European producer and was already selling more vehicles than Britain in Africa, Asia and North America, making her the world's largest exporter. By 1961 France was producing more vehicles than Britain. This was still the situation in 1966. Britain then was only the fourth largest producer of cars in the world, behind the USA, Germany and France, and was also only the fourth largest producer of commercial vehicles, behind America, Germany and Japan. Figures for individual years can be misleading: motor vehicle production is subject to considerable fluctuations, for reasons considered later in the chapter; 1961 and 1966 were poor years in the British industry when demand in the home market was cut back, but the broad picture that the figures give is consistent. Britain has yielded her dominant position and is hanging on to a share of the world market that is roughly 20 per cent of the whole.

Exports

There is no consistent pattern in the direction of exports of motor vehicles from Britain. This fact serves to illustrate the transient nature of Britain's economic security. This major industry has had to face three major changes in the direction of its exports in twenty years or so. In the early days of the post-1945 period the major market was Australia and New Zealand, but by 1956 sales in this market were halved because of the growth of the Australian car industry and a quota restriction imposed to discourage imports. The British industry then turned to the USA where there proved to be a market for the second car. Sales to the USA rose rapidly to reach a peak by 1959 but the Americans countered this British success by producing compact cars which regained much of the market for the home industry. Volkswagen then made great inroads into the British market in the USA, ultimately controlling 60 per cent of the market there for foreign cars. British firms have since turned to European markets and these are currently the most important ones. The removal of trade barriers with the fellow members of EFTA has been beneficial, but sales to the Common Market countries have also substantially increased as well in spite of the external tariff which puts British firms at a disadvantage.

The size of the firm

The motor vehicle industry demonstrates more than most the advantages that accrue from economies of scale. The number of firms in the industry has been systematically reduced as the volume of production has increased, so that by 1967 there are only four firms in Britain producing vehicles in quantity and these have an almost 100 per cent control of the market. Each of these firms is very large by British standards. This conforms to the structural pattern of industrial growth, particularly since 1945, of a few very big firms dominating the major industries.

The experience of the USA seems to show that there is an optimum size for a car assembly plant. The use of flow production techniques brings great efficiency for the production of 60,000 units per annum. 'There are probably further smaller gains at higher volumes, but the significant economies in car assembly appear to be exhausted at about a volume of 100,000 units.'[46] For this reason, American firms have tended to diversify their assembly plant in different areas where each one is capable of producing about 100,000 units. A handsome illustration of the advantages of large scale production is the case of the prewar Ford V8. The Ford plant at Detroit and the new Ford plant at Dagenham both produced the same model, but the Detroit plant made 500,000 and Dagenham made 3,677. The American V8 could be sold in Europe, with transportation costs covered, at 30 per cent below the cost of the Dagenham model.

Thus the small firm has either been squeezed out gradually or has been the subject of a takeover. In the British industry, where concentration of production had already reduced the number of big firms to six by 1939, amalgamation has continued. The most significant merger of the immediate postwar period took place in 1951 when Morris and Austin, faced with the rising challenge of Ford, combined to form the BMC. The merger took several years to become fully effective but it produced the biggest motor vehicle firm in the country. In 1953 the body-making firm of Fisher and Ludlow was acquired by BMC, in 1965 they added the Pressed Steel Company (also body-making) and in 1966 they took over Jaguar which, in spite of a very good postwar reputation for quality cars and its absorption of Daimler in 1960, was fundamentally not big enough to survive. The firm changed its name to B. M. Holdings.

The only other purely British company to survive in the industry was the combination of Standard, Triumph, Leyland, Rover. The dominant firm of these proved to be Leyland. They were predominantly makers of commercial vehicles but entered the car markets by taking over Standard Triumph in 1961. In 1966 they took over Rover, which, like Jaguar, had a reputation for good quality cars, but was not big enough in the postwar world, even though they had previously taken over Alvis. Standard Triumph International Ltd in 1966 secured 7 per cent of the home market in cars.

In 1968 the two separate firms of STI and BMH merged to form a single company, the British Leyland Motor Corporation (BLMC) controlling 40 per cent of the British motor vehicle industry. This was the logical consequence of the challenge of American capital and the need for large scale production and marketing facilities. BLMC is the sixth largest vehicle manufacturer in the world; only Fiat and Volkswagen are bigger in Europe. It has become, incidentally, Britain's largest single exporter, sending £250 million worth of cars and commercial vehicles overseas. In 1967 combined production of cars by the two separate companies amounted to well over 700,000.

The British firm of Rootes survived until 1967. It had produced a wide range of cars and had taken over Singer in 1955, but the annual production of 172,000 vehicles was not enough for them to pay their way. None of the British firms was prepared to provide the capital to resuscitate Rootes so Chrysler, the American firm came to its rescue.

The agreement giving Chrysler control of Rootes placed 50 per cent of the British industry in the control of American capital. This is not surprising. American firms are still very much bigger than any in Europe. There are three major firms only in the USA and one of these, General Motors, controls 50 per cent of the home markets. The American industry, because of the size of the market, is still nearly eight times the size of the British industry and has already reached a stage where expansion in its home market cannot go much further. It is producing replacement units in the USA and is looking to overseas markets for its future expansion. Chrysler have tended, until recent times, to rely on exporting made-up vehicles, but General Motors and Fords have consistently followed a policy of setting up plant in overseas territories, using local labour and component parts but backing the whole venture with American technical expertise and the massive capital of the parent firm. It is the enormous size of the American industry that has ensured the survival of firms such as Vauxhall, Opel and Ford in Europe while indigenous firms have had to give up. Chrysler have now adopted a similar policy to their two big rivals by taking over Simca and Rootes.

The reaction to American participation in the market in Britain has been one of retrenchment. A similar reaction has taken place in Europe. In France the nationalized industry of Renault has merged with Peugeot while Citröen has taken over Panhard. In Germany the firms of Volkswagen, Auto-Union and Daimler Benz

Table 9.1

World motor vehicle production figures

	million vehicles
General Motors	6·7
Ford	4·5
Chrysler	2·1
Fiat	1·4
Volkswagen	1·3
BLMC	0·99
Renault	0·78
Toyota	0·83

Source: *Sunday Times*, 21 Jan. 1968.

have pooled their interest in research and development, servicing and selling in order to compete with Ford and Opel who control 40 per cent of the German market. Italy is the one country left in Europe which has a major company of its own (Fiat) but which has not admitted American capital so far. Elsewhere in the world the Americans own well over half the motor vehicle industry in Australia, Mexico and South Africa, while in Canada they have a complete domination.

There is thus a pattern of world markets where the greatest potential expansion, for the immediate future, is to be found in Europe and where there is room only for the big firm in competition with the spread of American capital. The British industry, narrowed down to one major British firm and three American, is by the late 1960s well placed, though the future would be brighter if Britain were to enter the Common Market.

It has been noted that economies of scale in car assembly became exhausted once a level of 100,000 units is reached. The chances of increasing efficiency in this branch of motor vehicle manufacture are not very great in the British industry because firms have already reached the optimum or are not far from it. The other branches of manufacture are casting, machining and pressing. Casting is done partly in foundries owned by the big firms and partly by outside suppliers. Vauxhalls is the one big firm that has no foundry of its own, There are twenty-four foundries supplying iron castings to the British motor industry which fact indicates that casting is not a process that benefits from the economies of scale.[41] Important economies can be achieved in machining and pressing. These processes can be automated but, for efficient production, require very expensive equipment. Most of the pressing equipment is made particularly for one model. A large number of tools, sometimes several thousand, is needed for a pressed steel body, and the cost is very high.When a model is changed this expenditure recurs, so that it is obviously in the interests of the manufacturer to make as many vehicles as possible of one model. This is the main reason why the American industry is more efficient than any other. Any one model in the USA is likely to sell in numbers much larger than European manufacturers can contemplate. British manufacturers therefore, in common with those of Europe, use very expensive equipment which does not have the full use that the American equipment enjoys. The Americans would therefore seem to have a permanent advantage in pressing. For this reason the American models can be changed, and are changed, every two years or so. British models have to last five years if they are to be economic, but there is no guarantee that the market for any one model will last that long. There has certainly been a marked trend in Britain since 1945 towards keeping a model on the market for as long as possible rather than changing it every year at the time of the Motor Show, as was the practice before the war. The Ford Anglia and the Morris Minor are two cases in point, although the Volkswagen Beetle is the best example of all of a model in production over a very long period. This explains also why a manufacturer will try to alter one part of the design at a time and make only superficial changes from one model to another. The costs of tooling-up for a completely new model are enormous. The risks involved are of a kind that only a very big firm can afford to take. The sad story of the 250 million dollar Ford Edsel is well known. The BMC transverse engine Mini was a venture that hung in the balance for a while before its brilliant success. Similarly had the Hillman Imp been a failure it is unlikely that the Rootes Group would have maintained its independence as long as it did. The cost of tooling for the Imp was £9 million.[42]

An additional problem here is that in spite of the most efficient techniques of production and although enormous costs may have been incurred in modern tooling, there is still no guarantee that a vehicle will be successful. The motor industry is subject to the dictates of fashion that are sometimes more powerful than the dictates of mechanical efficiency or technical innovation. Most firms have experienced at least one calamity of this kind for reasons difficult to analyse.

The machining of component parts is the process in motor vehicle manufacture where the British industry can achieve increasing economies of scale. Automation was introduced in the 1950s when the volume of production rose to a point where the expense of the machinery was justified. Transfer processing machines have greatly speeded up the machining processes while at the same time reducing the number of operatives required for the job. Originally these machines were, like the pressing machinery, used for one model only and then scrapped, but they have now become adaptable so that a transfer line can be used with more than one model. From the point of view of the British industry this makes them particularly efficient. BMC have claimed that the introduction of thirteen station transfer machines in the 1950s proved to be an economy in machine costs per unit and in direct labour costs. It is, then, in machining that the British industry can particularly increase its efficiency, and although this involves heavy capital investment, in this way the American challenge can be met.

Fluctuations in demand

The nature of the product of the motor vehicle industry makes it a costly piece of equipment, in spite of the highly efficient techniques of production commented on above. This makes difficulties for the industry because the elasticity of demand of an expensive commodity is usually high. The motor vehicle is no exception. If there is either an increase in price of the vehicle or a reduction in the income of the consumer, the demand for vehicles shows a marked decline. The motor vehicle industry is thus highly susceptible to fluctuations of the economy. Ever since the postwar shortage was overcome in the early 1950s there has been a succession of booms and recessions in the British industry. These have not always coincided with the fluctuations in Europe and the USA but reflect the peculiar progress of the British economy. Successive governments since the war, in applying deflationary policies, have deliberately affected the demand for vehicles by means of fiscal measures. The tax on petrol (currently 3*s* 11*d* per gallon) has been one method, and purchase tax another. The tax on petrol has not produced the difficulties on the same scale as purchase tax, the changes in which (for cars) are listed below (percentages):

$$\text{Until } 1951 - 31\tfrac{1}{3}$$
$$1951 - 66\tfrac{2}{3}$$
$$1955 - 1959 - 60$$
$$1959 - 1961 - 50$$
$$\text{Late } 1961 - 55$$
$$1962 - 45$$
$$1962 - 25$$
$$1968 - 27\tfrac{1}{2}$$

The fluctuation in prices that these changes have involved has been reflected in the demand for vehicles, creating difficulties for the industry which can upset the most careful planning. It has been argued by Maxey and Silberston that because fixed costs in the industry are not exceptionally high 'a temporary tightening in the home market is not likely to lead to such a ruinous rise in costs that the competitive ability of the industry in export markets will be seriously impaired.'[49] They point out, however, that profits depend very much on output and that if output is cut back too far the low profits which must be the consequence would reduce either the industry's willingness or its ability to expand. Moreover, the industry cannot stockpile its product in any large quantity. Storing surplus production is such a problem that firms very quickly have to lay off workers or introduce short-time working if their vehicles are not being sold. This is an undesirable social consequence and militates against good labour relations.

The long period 1963–68 of no change in purchase tax level indicates that the difficulties that purchase tax changes can cause have been recognized. The restriction of credit, however, is still an orthodox deflationary measure that affects the demand for motor vehicles. Hire purchase restrictions and the difficulty in obtaining bank loans, have an immediate effect on the sale of cars. These restrictions cannot be anticipated sufficiently far ahead. A new model may take five years or more from its original conception to its introduction to the market and may be coming into full production just when credit restrictions are being applied. The result may be very damaging. The normal effects of economic fluctuation produce difficulty enough but these are aggravated, in this instance, by government interference.

Components: buying out

It has been noted that vertical integration can bring economies of scale from geographical location. There are other advantages of vertical integration, yet British firms buy components out much more than the American industry. The American Fords for instance make their own glass and General Motors make their own electrical equipment; but even so the Americans themselves still buy out many of their components. Vertical integration brings control over component manufacture and ensures a steady supply of parts. Why, in that case, is control over component suppliers not taken further?

The answer is to be found in the fact that a component firm supplying several motor assembly firms is thereby a specialist concern that is more specialized than it would be if it supplied only one. Furthermore it has experience and research facilities which would be hard to match, and in any case the assembly firm does not want to be bothered with detailed research for every component part. Firms such as Lucas, Borg and Beck, and Smiths have accordingly developed into large firms prepared to find their own capital for their expansion which has paralleled that of the big car firms. Not all the component firms are big. BMC calls upon the services of no less than 4,000 firms, many of which are very small.

The complexities of car assembly may be imagined. The modern automated plant runs on a highly organized schedule whereby component parts are fed into the production lines in, so far as is possible, just the right quantities. No large stocks of component parts are carried, reliance being put on good transport facilities and carefully timed operations. Turner, in describing production at Rootes says: 'In the assembly of the car itself, the body has six hours in storage, one and a quarter on the premount track, and another fifteen minutes being ferried to the main track. Once there it is only another hour before it emerges, completely assembled.[50] The organization of all this demands a computer. Rootes and Vauxhall have both installed computers that cost £200,000 to keep stock of the supply position. It will be readily understood that such a highly complex affair is fraught with dangers of disruption. Any breakdown of supply from one supplier can completely halt production, the particular supplier in all probability being beyond the control of the assembly firm. This is one of the major drawbacks of buying out. Some firms manage to solve this partially by securing more than one supplier, but the practice of switching from one to another, if there is a shortage, is successful only if the second supplier has surplus stocks or is in a position (which he rarely is) to step up production suddenly.

Industrial relations

The breakdown in supply of any component can throw thousands of people out of work. The failure can be due to shortage of raw materials or labour, or to labour disputes. Industrial relations are not good in the car industry, so it is usually a strike that is responsible if production is halted. In the first half of 1965 for example, there were ninety-nine stoppages in the industry involving the loss of 594,000 working days.[51] The British motor vehicle industry is more prone to labour disputes than the industries in Europe or in the USA for a variety of reasons, although it must be noted that there are inherent difficulties no matter which country is involved. The fluctuations of the economy, because they affect demand for cars more than most goods, create a feeling of insecurity amongst the workers in the industry. Every so often there is an anticipated rundown of production when workers are either laid off or put on short-time working for a period of several months. The workers affected experience a sharp drop in income since wage rates in the industry are normally above the industrial average. When the demand for vehicles is restored and the labour force is again working full-time, it is not surprising that the unions press for the highest return of income while the going is good. A situation of this kind creates an unhealthy working environment. The national shortage of labour in times of full employment has encouraged employers to hoard labour against the time when, with the upswing of demand, they find themselves hard pressed to produce vehicles in sufficient numbers to meet the pressing demand.

There has thus developed in the motor vehicle industry a doubly unfortunate situation where there is a tendency to overemployment coupled with a feeling of insecurity. The union, in these circumstances, sometimes seem to be very touchy, and unofficial strikes are common. The sacking of 12,000 BMC workers in the autumn of 1966 was, perhaps, a laudable attempt to reduce the overemployment in that firm, but it is a further example of how instability is caused, since it must have added to the insecurity amongst those who remained. Ford workers have the added fears, however illfounded, that if things go really badly European production will be transferred exclusively to the Continent.

The past history of the trade union movement and the experiences of the 1930s contribute to the poor industrial relations of the industry. What has been said elsewhere about the attitude of labour to management applies to the motor vehicle industry as much as to any other, although it is a product of the twentieth century. 'A lot of us worked there before the war. Things were shocking. We don't want that position back. The younger ones have heard tales and they aren't going to have it either.'[52] This statement by a Ford worker at Dagenham, quoted by Turner, sums up the attitude very well.

The structure of the unions in the industry does not help. At Fords at Dagenham, for example, twenty-one unions are involved in the negotiations with the management. This contrasts with the situation at the Volkswagen works at Wolfsburg where the German Metal Workers Union is the only important trade union. The virtues of industrial unions are discussed in a later chapter. Here all that needs to be said is that negotiation would be much simpler and quicker if there were fewer unions to consider. Even then, the fact remains that the component suppliers may have poor labour relations and the motor vehicle firms have no control over these.

The relationship between worker and management varies from one firm to another. It would be wrong to suggest that relations are universally bad in the industry. Vauxhalls have a long tradition of good relations that goes back to the time of Sir Charles Bartlett who, in 1925, laid the foundations of a profit-sharing scheme. At Vauxhalls they have a works panel set up by Bartlett in 1941 called the Management Advisory Committee which has considerable power. The committee is made up of five representatives from management and twenty-two representatives from the workers. There are 'constituencies' of workers varying from 800 to 1,500 men, each of which has a representative on the committee. The committee meets once every month to listen to management policy and to question and recommend. In practice its members work almost full-time on committee work because there are several subcommittees appointed to consider many aspects of workers' welfare. It is claimed that through this system any worker can have a grievance taken straight to the department head involved and have it dealt with immediately. Such a system can work well only where there is already a well-established spirit of goodwill.

The common method of determining wages in the British industry is piece-work. This sometimes promotes unrest. While the production lines are running smoothly both workers and management are satisfied with the system but, as we have seen, there are disruptions. A strike anywhere along the line or a hold-up in supplies will reduce workers' earnings. Management may be accused of not carrying large enough stocks of component parts, or it may be alleged that they have laid workers off too soon as a dispute develops. There was even one example of a strike by the bulk of the workers at Morris Bodies because of the constant strikes of the internal transport drivers which were affecting everybody else's earnings. There is much to be said in favour of an annual wage system with a bonus for an annual production rate over an agreed figure. Fords do not have piece-work but rely on time-work with a comprehensive scale of payments for differing types of job.

Labour relations in the industry gave rise to so much concern that in 1965 a Joint Labour Council for the industry was established which was intended to act as an immediate on-the-spot enquiry team to prevent unofficial strikes from damaging production. It consisted of six management representatives and six union leaders under an independent chairman. It remains to be seen if the Joint Labour Council will have a lasting success in an industry where there is a record of stoppages considerably higher than the average.

Certainly, when compared with the European manufacturers the British industry has a poor record of labour relations. The largest French company, Renault, has an enviable record of freedom from labour disputes. It is a nationalized firm which gives its workers direct representation on the board. The company is controlled by a Council of Administration of fifteen of whom six are factory workers. This is very different from the Management Advisory Committee at Vauxhall which does not control the firm but is just a works panel. Volkswagen, who control 50 per cent of the German market, have relied on part-ownership in the form of shares to employees and, because the firm has been developed almost from scratch since 1945, management has been able to concentrate on securing excellent management/employee relationships. Fiat, the one large company in Italy, so big that labour could hold the company and the nation to ransom, and with a Communist element much bigger than in Britain, also has a good record of labour relations. This has been achieved by building up a fabric of welfare facilities and bonus payments that amounts to a benevolence unmatched by any firm in Britain.

Motor vehicles and the Common Market

If European firms have secured an advantage in industrial relations, they have secured another in the Common Market organization. The tariff level between the market countries and Britain is now 22 per cent. This does not mean that British cars in Europe are 22 per cent dearer than their European rivals, because internal taxation tends to even up prices, but it makes selling easier. The great expansion in the European market, in spite of increased sales in Europe by Britain in recent years, has been taken up largely by the European firms themselves. Were Britain to be a member of the Common Market she would benefit not just by producing motor vehicles on the Continent herself, as she does to a small degree now, but by competing on equal terms with her chief European rivals in a market that shows great immediate potential.

136

Japan

In the 1960s Japan has come into the picture as a manufacturer of motor vehicles and an exporter of growing magnitude. Already the American, South African and Australian markets have admitted Japanese vehicles in substantial numbers. This is not a challenge to be ignored, as the history of the cotton textile industry shows. Japan has a large industry based on a thriving home market and one that enjoys a high reputation for mechanical engineering skill. It is arguable that, with the world demand for motor vehicles expanding rapidly, there is room for another major supplier such as Japan; but Britain obviously cannot afford to be complacent, particularly in the light of the resounding success that the Japanese motor cycle industry achieved in the 1960s in Britain's own home markets.[53]

10

Shipbuilding

Britain's insular position has been such an important influence in the country's economic evolution that inevitably shipbuilding has always been a major British industry. As history has shown, no nation that is responsible for a large part of world trade can afford to rely on other nations for its mercantile marine. All the leading trading nations of the world now have a shipbuilding industry, but some of these, the Japanese in particular, are recent compared with the British industry which, with the maritime traditions of the country, goes back many centuries. Britain has a happy combination of geographical situation and worldwide trading interests on a large scale which have promoted the growth of the industry. Not all the leading shipbuilding nations have been so well endowed (although Japan makes an interesting parallel). Sweden for example with a flourishing industry in the twentieth century, has only its geographical situation as a prime factor, its trading interests not being on the same scale. Britain should, therefore, be in a strong position in the world shipbuilding industry. We shall see in this chapter that there are serious problems to be faced.

Shipbuilding, like all transport manufacturing industry is concerned essentially with the assembly into one unit of a tremendous number of component parts supplied by many other industries. As the material of construction has changed from wood to iron and then to steel, so the methods of construction and the component parts have become more and more sophisticated. Advances in methods of propulsion and the transformation of navigational aids have made shipbuilding in the twentieth century a branch of engineering rather than an industry on its own. So much machinery and equipment goes into the making of a modern ship, warships especially, that the basic ship structure is forming a decreasing proportion of the total cost of the ship. Currently there are roughly 140,000 people directly employed in the shipbuilding industry (including marine engine building and ship repairing), but there are four times as many workers involved in the supplying industries. Sometimes as much as two-thirds of the total cost of a ship is accounted for by the work of outside contractors. As an illustration, there were 340 firms involved as subcontractors in the building of Europe's first 100,000 ton tanker, the *British*

Admiral, at Barrow-in-Furness. It is not surprising, therefore, that shipbuilding encounters many problems similar to those of the motor-vehicle industry. These will be considered later but there are some facts concerning the development of the industry in Britain that must be looked at first.

Long before the interwar period the principal shipbuilding centres had become established as the North-East of England (the Tyne, the Wear and the Tees), Clydeside, Belfast, Merseyside and Barrow-in-Furness. The first two of these have been

Table 10.1

Merchant shipping completed in UK yards during 1966

District	Ships	Tons gross
The Clyde	34	292,421
Tyne, including Blyth	22	257,030
Sunderland (Wear)	15	213,896
Tees	3	75,219
Belfast	5	129,107
Mersey	7	95,195
Other districts	125	66,933
	211	1,129,801

Source: The Shipbuilding Conference.

responsible for about 75 per cent of the ships constructed in Britain since 1918 and have tended, therefore, to dominate the British shipbuilding scene (see Table 10.1). Any shipbuilding area in modern times must have a large estuary adjacent to a steel-producing region. The cost of transporting the heavy steel plates and girders would be uneconomic if the shipyards were at any great distance. Belfast is the one area where there is no steel-producing region adjacent to the yards but the sea journey to Belfast Lough from the steel areas of Cumberland and West Scotland is not long and, therefore, not too costly. Barrow became important for shipbuilding when the haematite ores of that area were in great demand before the invention of the Gilchrist-Thomas process in steelmaking in the 1880s. It has since become famous for the construction of submarines. The North-East, Merseyside and Clydeside are all, of course, close to major steel-producing areas, but it is interesting to note that the Clyde, for twelve miles below Glasgow, has had to be dredged to such an extent to allow passage to ships of average size and above that it is virtually an artificial waterway. Ship repairing is carried on not only in the shipbuilding areas but also at the main ports for obvious reasons.

Unlike some foreign industries, notably the American, the marine engineering industry is an integral part of shipbuilding. Almost all the major firms in shipbuilding construct engines. It is sometimes argued that economies could be achieved if the engine construction were left to the major engineering firms that specialize in diesel engines and steam turbines, but the shipbuilding industry maintain that the problems involved in ship engine design are so individual as to require treatment that the shipbuilders are best equipped to provide.[54] Thus there are many firms that are involved in shipbuilding, ship repairing and engine construction while others are concerned with only one sector.

The size of the industry can be gauged from the fact that by 1967 there were about sixty shipyards in the UK capable of building vessels of 100 tons and over, and of these fifteen could build ships in excess of 50,000 tons deadweight. Capacity to build very much bigger ships is now becoming important and will be discussed later. There are approximately 100 ship-repairing establishments and about thirty marine engine-building concerns in Britain.

British shipbuilding since 1945

The long period of world superiority of British shipbuilding and the ultimate malaise of the interwar period have been dealt with in chapter 3. By 1939 Britain had lost much of her share of world markets and the gross tonnage under construction was considerably less than that of the pre-1914 period. The Second World War brought an expansion in the industry which was placed under government control.

Mercantile ships launched rose to an average of well over 1,100,000 tons per year from 1941 to 1944 apart from the increase in naval craft. The number of people employed during the war in shipbuilding and repair was an increase of 51·9 per cent over the 1939 figure[55] so that the industry emerged in 1945 in a position to produce a greater tonnage* than before the war.

Expansion of the basic industries is inevitable in wartime but usually the postwar period is a painful one as the industries are obliged to contract. On this occasion there was no call for contraction. There was a worldwide demand for ships and the yards of Britain's competitors had been largely destroyed during the war. Until 1950 there was a sellers' market, as there was for much of British industry. Unfortunately the British shipbuilders were not in a position to take full advantage of this. The government in recognition of the acute shortage of building materials, operated a licensing scheme for industrial expansion which effectively rationed the supply of new buildings that the British yards required. Apart from this, steel was in short supply. Modernization in the British industry did not really start until the 1950s. Output rose from 1,133,000 gross tons in 1946 to only 1,315,000 in 1950.

---

* *Gross tonnage* is the measurement of the cubic capacity of ship's closed spaces, including holds and deck houses. 1 ton = 100 cu. ft. This measurement is used usually for passenger liners. *Deadweight tonnage* is a measurement of the ship's total carrying capacity in tons weight, including cargo, fuel, passengers and crew when fully loaded down to the permitted line. The size of tankers and cargo ships is usually measured in this way. Tonnage figures in this chapter are gross unless otherwise specified.

After 1950 the reconstructed yards of Britain's competitors were coming into operation and Britain's temporary advantage had been lost. Not only that, the yards of her competitors were now very modern compared with those in Britain itself. The 1950s thus witnessed a growing challenge to Britain's leadership. For the whole of the century, even during the low peak of the interwar depression, Britain had produced more shipping tonnage than any other country in the world. Between 1900 and 1914 she had built 60 per cent of all the merchant vessels launched. Even in the 1920s that figure was 50 per cent. In 1956 Britain had to yield leadership to Japan and since then Sweden and West Germany have produced a greater tonnage per annum than Britain. Although world demand for ships fluctuates, as we shall see, Britain lost her leadership in production at a time when world demand was increasing. The 1950s were years when demand exceeded supply. World launchings were 3,500,000 tons in 1950 but from 1957 to 1964 the gross tonnage of ships launched per annum was 8,500,000 tons. Britain's share of the world market had dwindled to 11 per cent by 1963 of which 30 per cent was exported. Furthermore an unwelcome factor in shipbuilding had become increasingly obtrusive during the 1950s and 1960s. Foreign ships were being imported. In 1962–63 exports were worth £40 million but imports totalled £17 million; this balance of payments for shipbuilding of £23 million was reduced to £11 million in 1964.

Meanwhile a similar transformation was taking place in world shipping. In 1900 one half of the world's merchant fleet sailed under the British flag but by 1965 only 14 per cent of the world's merchant ships were registered in Britain. Greece, Liberia, Panama, Norway, Honduras and the USA all had their own large fleets, even though the British merchant fleet was still the largest active one. This transformation did not necessarily have an adverse effect on British shipbuilding but taken in conjunction with the remarkable fall in Britain's share of world ship construction it demonstrates that during the postwar period Britain has completely lost her domination in the world of ships.

The question that this raises is whether British shipbuilding should be regarded as a growth industry or whether the industry should be classified as one of the old contracting staple industries that should be gradually abandoned to those countries who can, apparently, produce goods more cheaply than Britain. The rest of this chapter is largely taken up with the defence of British shipbuilding as a growth industry.

Problems common to all shipbuilding industries

UNEVEN FLOW OF ORDERS

The number of ships constructed for the shipping companies of the world is dependent in the first instance upon the state of world trade. This is affected by fluctuations which inevitably cause instability in the demand for ships. The long-term trend is for

141

world trade to expand, but in the short term there are almost bound to be periods of depression. No country can escape this. The market is fiercely competitive and the quantity of capital and labour tied up in the production of one ship is frequently very large. It is not possible, as in the car industry for example, to put men on short time and to continue to use the capital equipment at least part time; either there is a ship to be constructed or repaired or the yard is not in use. It is not uncommon for a yard to be shut down for a period, although any prolonged shutdown will obviously put the shipbuilders out of business. There are similar problems when demand increases. The time taken to construct a ship can take well over twelve months, perhaps over three years. If there is a surge of orders by shipowners the more orders that a yard secures the further away is the delivery date likely to be so that the less likely is the shipbuilder ultimately to obtain orders. The ideal is for orders to come in regularly, thus enabling the construction of one ship to be started as soon as the previous one is launched, but the ideal is not often attained. Furthermore it can happen that ships ordered during a period of boom are delivered during an incipient recession, instigating a lowering of freight rates, thereby lowering profits and discouraging owners from placing new orders.

LIFE SPAN OF A SHIP

The length of life of a ship is also of great importance to the shipbuilders since much of their construction is to replace existing vessels. A dry cargo vessel has an average life of thirty years while an oil tanker is designed to last five years less.[56] Even if there is a recession in world trade there will always be a certain amount of replacement construction required, but it is also true that owners are not so keen to replace their vessels when there is not so much trade for them to pursue. It would be wrong in any case to presume that each year brought an even flow of replacement. There are several reasons why there should be a sudden spurt of ship construction followed by a slack period, and this pattern is reflected in the replacement demand.

The trade cycle is one reason, war may be another–the two world wars have both led to a shipbuilding boom. The Liberty ships, built in large numbers during and immediately after the last war by the Americans, are a good example of this. They are now becoming due for replacement, offering great scope to the world shipyards. They are 10,000 ton cargo ships of which between 600 and 700 are still in service but they are expected to be scrapped by the early 1970s. The British shipbuilding industry has made a strong bid for a share in this market.

CHANGE IN CARGOES

Another reason for the uneven pace of shipbuilding is the changing emphasis in cargoes that is a concomitant of expanding world trade. As the pattern of consumption of raw materials, fuels and manufactured goods changes so there is a changing demand for ships specially designed to carry the new commodities. Since the last war there has been a tremendous increase in the demand for oil tankers as oil has been increasingly used as a fuel and source of power, and it is this fact that prevented a serious depression in the industry in the 1950s. The importance of oil tankers to the British industry can be seen by Table 10.2; it has been even more important to foreign

Table 10.2

Merchant shipping completed in UK yards 1957–66 (inclusive)

Types	Ships	Tons gross
Tankers and Coastal Tankers	290	4,834,000
Dry Cargo Ships	539	4,205,000
Passenger and Passenger/Cargo	47	599,000
Ore and Bulk Carriers	127	1,847,000
Coasters and Colliers	146	201,000
Trawlers	421	177,000
Miscellaneous craft	943	449,000
	2,513	12,312,000

Source: The Shipbuilding Conference.

yards, especially Japan. Similarly the expansion in world trade of iron ore (Britain as we have seen is importing an increasing proportion of its iron ore) has created a demand for ore carriers.

SIZE OF SHIPS

The average size of ships also has a bearing on future demand. There has been a marked tendency since the last war for oil tankers and ore carriers to become very large. The political troubles in the Middle East in 1956 and 1967 when the Suez Canal was closed have accentuated the trend towards big ships, particularly tankers, in order to make the longer voyage round the Cape of Good Hope more economic. The Japanese have already launched tankers of over 200,000 tons (deadweight) while iron-ore carriers of 60,000 tons (deadweight) are common enough. Tankers of up to 1 million deadweight tons are envisaged and dry-cargo bulk carriers of up to 100,000 tons deadweight. Ships of this size ensure that there are not so many orders to go round. An order for ten tankers of 10,000 tons can be divided among several yards whereas a tanker of 100,000 tons must be built in one place. Competition thus becomes very fierce and only very big firms can survive unless a smaller firm is engaged in a particular specialization. This is yet another industry where the size of the firm has become of vital importance.

CONTAINER SHIPS

In recent years the 'container concept' has been introduced into shipping with the accompanying demand for specialized container ships. This will increase the short-term prospects for shipbuilding, but it carries a threat in the long term that fewer ships will be required. The container concept arose because of the growing cost of cargo handling and the expense that is involved if a ship is held up in port by a slow turnround. 'In many trades cargo handling in port represents on average over 30 per cent of the net freight which the shipper pays. Looked at in another way . . . a ship is likely to spend 180 days a year in port working cargo.'[54] If a ship is engaged upon short sea voyages the number of days in port is even higher. There has been, therefore, considerable incentive to obtain substantial savings by hastening turn-round procedure. The container ship has standard size containers (8 ft by 8 ft by 20 ft in Europe, but bigger in the USA) which are packed either by the manufacturer or at a container terminal where they are inspected by customs officials. This standardization enables the containers to be mechanically handled from the ter-minal, through the docks at either end of the sea voyage and at the terminal the other end. The port turnround time with this system in operation can be reduced by as much as 90 per cent. If it is combined with ships that travel at 27 knots the efficiency of shipping services is greatly increased. This is, however, another way of saying that not so many ships will be required. The container concept is being referred to in shipping circles as a revolution, a comparison even being made between the change to container ships and the change from sail to steam.[58] The world shipbuilding industry will benefit from the orders for container ships. A deep-sea container ship is likely to cost between £5 million and £6 million whereas a traditional deep-sea cargo liner costs between £1 million and £2 million, so that an order for one of the new ships is a prize particularly worth securing by any shipyard, but fleets of con-tainer ships may ultimately bring about a world surplus of shipping in the same way that the steamship caused a surplus during the Great Depression of the nine-teenth century.

The problems of the British shipbuilding industry

The British industry is caught up with all these problems. It is subject to fluctuations that apply to the world industry, and superimposed on these are the problems peculiar to the British economy; these are common to all British industry but they seem to have had a particularly unfortunate effect on shipbuilding.

BRITISH COMPLACENCY

The British reluctance towards change which springs from the earlier period of supremacy has already been commented on in relation to the general approach to economic progress and to individual industries. Failure to anticipate change in the

1950s was the prime cause of the difficulties of the British shipbuilders in the 1960s. The shipyards of the major overseas competitors were expanding rapidly in the 1950s but the sellers' market disguised the challenge to Britain. The demand for oil tankers was not sufficiently anticipated and the increased size of ships was not taken seriously at first. When the Japanese planned big oil tankers there was a belief in Britain that these would be oversize. Only as the market developed and the success of the big ships became a fact did the British industry take up the challenge. The same can be said about modern techniques of shipbuilding belatedly applied and the allocation of resources to research. There were individual exceptions, and British yards were responsible for some new techniques (e.g. autogenous cutting with photo-electric control) but in general the necessary modernization did not take place until the late 1950s and early 1960s. The capital for investment and research could come from big firms only, but even in 1961 a special subcommittee of the Shipbuilding Advisory Committee was reporting that it did not feel that it 'should positively recommend the amalgamation of firms' although 'managements should bear in mind the possible advantages of amalgamations and should, whenever practicable, cooperate to share effort and the use of expensive equipment.[59]

SUBSIDIES

In other countries the shipbuilding industry was directly or indirectly subsidized by governments after the war. In Japan, apart from government subsidies, there was generous assistance from the World Bank. The French and Italian industries were directly subsidized, while in West Germany and the USA the governments helped in many ways. Of the major shipbuilding powers only Britain and Sweden remained aloof from government aid to the industry. Until 1963 there was no facility in Britain for long-term credit provided by the government for foreign buyers, by which time the industry was going through a very lean period.

INDUSTRIAL RELATIONS

The relations between unions and management in Britain's shipyards were particularly poor. Demarcation disputes, uniquely British, bedevilled construction schemes, giving British yards a reputation for late delivery and unreliability. Several reports on the industry stressed the necessity for improving industrial relations, but little was done. One yard in the North-East closed for nine months while a dispute over drilling holes in metal panels was argued out by the metal workers' and shipwrights' unions. The reason for these poor industrial relations were much the same as in the motor vehicle industry. The fluctuations of the industry caused a feeling of insecurity, the interwar period had left hostility and bitterness, and the general history of the trade union movement militated against successful cooperation between unions and management.

145

INFLATION

The inflation of the postwar period in Britain also affected the shipyards adversely. Contracts for ships were signed by owners and builders usually two or three years in advance of the ships' completion. During the long period of construction prices were likely to rise not just of the component parts and the auxiliary equipment but of the labour involved as well. Most of the prices were beyond the control of the shipbuilding firms because of the fact that it is an assembly industry. In the same way that the motor vehicle manufacturers are dependent on outside firms for supply of many of their component parts and are subject to unexpected price rises and supply bottlenecks, so the shipbuilders were involved with subcontractors. In a period of sustained inflation this proved to be an embarrassment. Promised dates for delivery were not kept and anticipated profits did not materialize, while foreign yards because they did not have a reputation for unfulfilled delivery dates and high prices, obtained an increasing proportion of world orders.

British shipbuilding thus reached the 1960s with order books far from full and an unenviable reputation that deterred not only foreign buyers but home buyers as well. The countries that had overtaken Britain were not all emergent nations. Japan could perhaps be described as such, but not Sweden or West Germany. These last two demonstrated that a country with an advanced economy could maintain a successful shipbuilding industry; shipbuilding was not necessarily an industry, like cotton textiles, that had to be abandoned to the countries with a cheap labour force. There were certain advantages that Britain's competitors enjoyed but they were not impossible to offset.

Japan

Japan demonstrates the advantages that a developing economy can enjoy, but they are not permanent although the inroads into world markets that Japan has made are very considerable. When Japan overtook Britain as the world's leading shipbuilder she launched, in 1956, 1·75 million gross tons or roughly 26 per cent of the world total. Ten years later the Japanese launched 5·36 million tons increasing their share to 44 per cent. During that period 60 per cent of the oceangoing vessels constructed were exported and in the last three of those years that figure rose to 70 per cent. The vessels are of unquestioned high quality and of good operating efficiency.

This impressive record was achieved in the first instance as a result of three advantages over Britain. It has already been observed that Japan was able to reconstruct shipyards from scratch after 1945. Also, in the early postwar years the industry was helped by government subsidies and by the cheapness of the wage bill. It would be wrong to suggest that either of these last two now applies but they were very important in the 1950s. Japanese wage rates are still marginally lower than those in Britain but they are not sufficiently low to make a great difference to the price of a ship. The

146

Japanese have, however, encouraged a strong home market by providing good credit facilities for home shipowners (up to fifteen years at $4\frac{1}{2}$ per cent) and they have imposed a tariff barrier of 15 per cent over a long period.

The home market has been a rapidly expanding one as the Japanese economy has made its remarkable postwar growth. Oil, coal and iron ore all have to be imported to Japan and her swift growth in these industries has meant a constantly increasing demand for tankers and bulk-carriers. It is in these two items that the Japanese yards have particularly specialized, and this has given them the opportunity to secure much of the world market for similar vessels. As the Japanese economy reaches the advanced levels of the Western world so this advantage of a swiftly expanding home market will diminish. The other advantages that Japan possesses are the existence of very big firms which cooperate one with another, and, of course, the absence of demarcation disputes.

Sweden

Sweden has shown that an advanced economy with high wage rates (higher than in Britain) can still make shipbuilding a profitable industry even when there is no very big home market to provide a firm foundation. (Sweden exports 70–80 per cent of its output.) This has been done by use of capital to offset the high labour cost. Swedish yards have been modernized at great cost but with remarkable gains in efficiency. The Arendal yard of A. B. Götaverken near Gothenburg (Fig. 10.1) has become almost a byword for shipbuilding efficiency although it was completed only in 1963. The principle of the Arendal yard is not unlike that of a car assembly plant. There is a straight flow production line for steel plates and profiles which travel on a long roller conveyor belt through a number of indoor working sections where they undergo the necessary treatment and prefabrication. Mechanized handling is used wherever possible. About fifty men work in the mechanized plate shop, for example, compared with 180 in an equivalent modern but conventional yard. The finished plates reach an assembly point upon which converges another flow of component parts and equipment. The hull sections are then erected under cover and progressively pushed out into the open building dock while new sections are added under cover. Practically all the work takes place indoors, which means better conditions for the workers as well as a higher standard of work, but of course the main advantage of the yard is that there is an improved utilization of plant by a well-balanced sequence of operations. This method of ship construction is radically different from conventional methods. There is no need for a slipway or the traditional launching (an expensive procedure) which requires the extra waterway length for pulling up the ship; this removes one of the limiting factors determining the siting of a shipyard. Furthermore the building dock technique does away with the need to lift component parts of the ship to a great height over the ship; in fact most of the parts have to be lowered.[60]

147

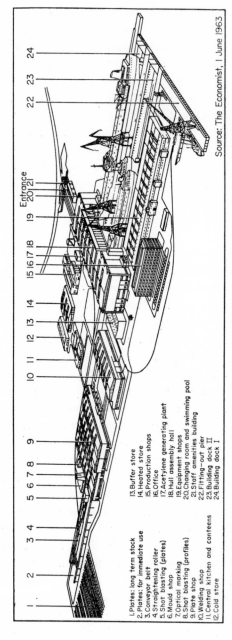

1. Plates: long term stock
2. Plates: for immediate use
3. Conveyor belt
4. Straightening roller
5. Shot blasting (plates)
6. Mould shop
7. Optical marking
8. Shot blasting (profiles)
9. Plate shop
10. Welding shop
11. Central kitchen and conteens
12. Cold store
13. Buffer store
14. Heated store
15. Production shops
16. Office
17. Acetylene generating plant
18. Hull assembly hall
19. Equipment shops
20. Changing room and swimming pool
21. Staff amenities building
22. Fitting–out pier
23. Building dock II
24. Building dock I

Entrance

Source: The Economist, 1 June 1963

Figure 10.1. Building ships on car assembly principles. The Arendal Yard of A. B. Götaverken near Gothenburg.

The Arendal yard cost £14 million but it has cut down the construction time of a 50,000 ton tanker from 40 weeks to 19–20 weeks. The Japanese are now using the Arendal technique and the Americans are using some of the methods under patent. Not all the Swedish yards are as modern in design and technique as Arendal, but they demonstrate what can be achieved by lavish use of capital.

Even so the Götaverken company proved to be not big enough to bring a satisfactory return on the capital outlay and was taken over in 1967 by a Swedish group of shipbuilding companies (Brostrom) which controls between 8 and 10 per cent of the world's new shipbuilding capacity. The size of the firm is increasingly important to the shipbuilding industry, as with so many of the modern industries of the world.

The Swedish industry has the added advantage of good industrial relations. There are only three trade unions involved in the Swedish shipbuilding industry compared with twenty-two in Britain, and the relationship between unions and management reflects the spirit of cooperation which is a feature common to the whole of Swedish industry.

The place of the British industry

There is a place, therefore, in world shipbuilding for the industry of developing and advanced economies. Britain has a tradition of shipbuilding that is second to none and has built up over the centuries an enviable fund of knowledge and experience, now backed by advanced technology, that should help to keep her well to the fore even if she cannot take the lead. In the latter sixties there is evidence that a determined effort is being made to overcome the obstacles to improving efficiency in the whole British industry so as to make it really competitive. There is nothing so fundamentally wrong with the industry that it must be looked upon as a spent force.

Changes in the 1960s

GOVERNMENT CREDIT SCHEMES

The vexed question of credit for shipowners has now been resolved in that the government have recognized that as a matter of principle the industry must be in a position to offer the same credit terms as its overseas rivals. The government made available in 1963 facilities for 80 per cent loans for periods up to ten years at an interest rate of $5\frac{1}{2}$ per cent. This was for foreign buyers and helped the export sales figures. Meanwhile British shipowners were obliged to seek the best credit terms that they could on the open market if they were intending to place an order with a British shipyard. Sometimes this meant paying 9 per cent interest. Inevitably the superior terms available in foreign yards induced British owners to place orders abroad. In the first nine months of 1966 71 per cent of new tonnage booked by British owners was placed overseas.[61] In 1967 the government passed the Shipbuilding Industry Act which made credit available at $5\frac{1}{2}$ per cent interest to British shipowners, but only on condition that the shipyards that benefited from the orders satisfied the

11

government via the Shipbuilding Industry Board that satisfactory progress was being made with reorganization and modernization.

GEDDES REPORT 1966

The Shipbuilding Industry Board was established as a result of the report into the industry made by a government appointed committee led by Dr Ray Geddes. The report proposed many changes aimed at reorganizing the structure of the industry, improving the efficiency of the shipyards, cutting the cost of supplies, improving research design and selling activities and promoting cooperation between management and unions. The function of the Shipbuilding Industry Board, which was recommended to have a life of five years, was to control government help to the industry. The first chairman was, significantly, Sir William Swallow who had an outstanding record of successful management of Vauxhall Motors, following in the footsteps there of Sir Charles Bartlett. The government have provided help not only through underwriting credit facilities but by making £32½ million available in grants and loans to encourage the grouping of the major firms into a select few groups. The Geddes Report recommended five regional groupings, two in the North-East, two in Scotland on the Clyde, and one in Belfast. Before the end of 1967 some mergers had already taken place in consequence. In the North-East, the firms of Swan Hunter, Vickers, Hawthorn Leslie and John Redhead have formed a group that will be able to take advantage of the combined capital of the firms and the total manpower of 10,000 workers. Phasing the finishing of ships is much easier with a big firm because the fitting-out trade (e.g. electricians and carpenters) can move steadily from ship to ship instead of being out of work one week and doing overtime the next. On Lower Clydeside Scotts of Greenock and Lithgows of Port Glasgow made a similar merger thus providing a labour force of 7,000 with similar advantages to the North-East. On the Upper Clyde John Brown have agreed to merge with Fairfield, Alexander Stephen and Connels thus forming a group employing 11,000 workers.

MERGERS AND MODERNIZATION

Mergers on this scale make possible the sort of modernization that has taken place abroad. Although there has been substantial modernization to British shipyards since the war, the cramped sites of the existing yards and the comparative scarcity of capital due to the size of the firm, have caused the improvement to be somewhat piecemeal. Formation of a big firm involving several yards makes it possible to scrap one yard completely and to rebuild it, perhaps, on Arendal lines while the firm continues its everyday business in the remaining yards. Also it becomes possible to establish yards that can construct very big ships. Swan Hunter have announced that they are capable, if necessary, of building tankers of 1 million tons. Only big firms are likely to be able to afford the use of computers to the extent that these will be required. Transmission and interpretation of all measurement data between office and works and between detailed planning and processing of materials is bound to become more and more the province of the computer. There is also the possibility of integrated schemes for the overall computer control of steelwork production. In other words the economies of scale achieved by sophisticated techniques of production and associated with the big firm, are, in common with so much of British industry, becoming vitally important.

SLIPWAY V BUILDING DOCK IN BRITAIN

The efficiency of the Arendal type of yard is so impressive that the building dock is likely to have preference in any layout for a future shipyard in Britain. Some of its advantages have already been mentioned. Another advantage is that the dock can be used for repair work when building orders are not plentiful. There are, however, some difficulties in introducing building docks to Britain. The Baltic, where the existing building docks are to be found, enjoys a very small rise and fall of tide (at Arendal it is 1 ft). For a ship drawing 28 ft a dock would require to be only 34 ft from coping to floor level in the Baltic, but in Britain it would have to be 10 ft greater to allow for the variations of the tide.[62] Also, most British shipyards have a long waterfront but have little depth, whereas the nature of the construction of the building dock method demands exactly the opposite, considerable depth with a long waterfront being unnecessary. The Arendal yard was built on a completely new site and this is, perhaps, what British firms would have to do. A building dock would be at its most efficient if it were in continuous use; in fact the capital at risk would be much too large for a firm to contemplate anything else.

STANDARD SHIPS

The new techniques of shipbuilding, as they become more and more an engineering process lend themselves to repetitive production. British shipowners have stood out against any suggestion of a standard ship, claiming that their requirements are too individual to admit of any standardization, but attitudes are starting to change. Ships produced in a range of computer-optimized standard designs will be at an attractive price to owners. The American Liberty ships were of a standard design and the British industry's bid to share some of the replacement market also involves a standard design. A 14,200 ton deadweight ship, the SD 14, has been designed and constructed by Austen and Pickersgill Ltd, but it is being constructed also in another Sunderland yard and a number of other British yards are ready to build to the same design as the market develops. The modernization that is now possible in the British yards will undoubtedly increase this trend.

LABOUR IN BRITISH SHIPYARDS

The traditional methods of shipbuilding, which are still largely the rule in the British industry, involve unit construction. The units are made by craftsmen in workshops scattered all over the yard and are then brought together at the berth for assembly. Unit construction is, however, giving way to flow production as the machines involved in construction become more sophisticated and costly. The man is brought to the job rather than the job to the man; fewer craftsmen are needed, but more engineers and machine operators. This change in the constituency of the labour force is taking place while the old labour structure remains intact, and the traditional suspicion and mistrust between unions and management are still there.

THE FAIRFIELDS EXPERIMENT

The poor level of industrial relations in the shipbuilding industry is its worst handicap and, as has been noted, sets the industry at a disadvantage in a competitive market. For this reason the experiment at the Fairfield yard is important because it may well indicate a way of resolving this very serious industrial problem. The Fairfield yard on the Clyde went into liquidation in 1965 and a bold experiment was decided upon to keep the yard going. The government, private enterprise and trade unions all combined to put up the necessary capital to restart the yard on completely different lines. The union, having subscribed some of the capital have a say on policy decisions and they, in turn, have yielded ground on the old bugbears of demarcation disputes and wage agreements. National wage agreements have been replaced by wages negotiated on the basis of actual productivity. The men pledged that there would be no strikes for at least three years. On the management side, 300 or so new staff were gathered together from outside the industry or by means of promotion from within. The Fairfields approach to the industrial relations problem had many features similar to the Esso Fawley agreement. Since the yard has resumed with this brand new organization there have been strikes, but so far not crucial ones. Wages at the yard are high but it remains to be seen how productivity has risen. Fairfields is one of the yards involved in the merger (mentioned above) of yards on the Upper Clyde. Success there has obvious farreaching repercussions.

Shipbuilding and the British economy

The success of the shipbuilding industry in Britain ultimately depends upon price alone. If British yards can promise delivery of ships at the right price, orders will come their way. With the fresh approach to government aid, mergers, and cooperation between management and unions, there is no reason why British yards should yield ground to other countries. They have to overcome a bad reputation for high price and poor delivery time, but if this can be done the industry can hope to take advantage of the fact that the Geddes report described shipbuilding as a growth industry and one in which Britain could take a fair share. Fluctuations are bound to occur for the reasons outlined early in this chapter, and the industry will go through lean times. Several major industries suffer from time to time from world surplus capacity: steel, plastics, motor-vehicles have all suffered from a similar dilemma in the postwar years and shipbuilding in the 1960s is therefore not alone in its troubles, but it is too important in the country's economy to be allowed to contract. It is not a question simply of the value of its exports and the balance of payments, although these are of course very important; Britain relies on overseas trade to a degree that makes her vitally dependent on the ships that ply to and from her ports. If they are not built at home Britain becomes dependent upon other countries for a vital means of communication. There is thus a political reason to add to the economic one for sustaining the belief that shipbuilding is an industry with a future of growth in Britain.

11

The chemical industry

Whereas the steel, coal and motor vehicle industries are so simple to define as to need no formal definition in this volume, the chemical industry, because of the variety of its products and the widely differing details of processes and problems of manufacturing must be defined more precisely. The borders between it and other industries are blurred. When, for example, does nylon cease to be a chemical and become an artificial fibre? Should the distillation of crude oil, a chemical process, be considered as an activity of the chemical industry?

There are well over 2,000 firms making chemicals whose products are based on the science of chemistry (excluding all those making products the manufacture of which involves chemical change, e.g. steel), but a list of their products would be far too long to consider here. The Central Statistical Office has made definition easier by giving Minimum List Headings in its Standard Industrial Classification; the commonly accepted definition of the British Chemical Industry, used by the Chemical Industries Association Limited and also for the National Plan for 1970 is based on these (nos 271–7) and is the one used in this book. It includes not only acids, alkalis and bleaches, but also dyestuffs, fertilizers, pharmaceuticals, explosives, paints, the manufacture of plastics, synthetic resins, synthetic rubber, polishes, glue, oils and fats, and the grinding of gums and natural resins. This is not comprehensive and does not correspond exactly with definitions of the chemical industries of other countries, but it is a reasonable basis for achieving some measurement of the size and growth of the industry. Statistical comparison with other countries should, however, be taken only as a guide because a much wider definition is frequently used overseas.

It is commonplace to state that the chemical industry is one of Britain's basic industries. Although it is its own best customer it is also a supplier of materials to virtually every other industry in the country, including agriculture. The tardy realization of its importance in 1914 was, as we have seen, instrumental in the expansion of the industry during and after the First World War. In 1921 it was recognized as a key industry and fine chemicals were given a protective duty of $33\frac{1}{3}$ per cent. This had the effect of trebling the capital employed in fine chemicals between 1920 and 1938 and of nearly quadrupling the number of research chemists and the amount spent on research during that period.[63] Thus Britain was not caught napping in 1939 as she was in 1914; the synthetic organic chemical industry was much more prepared for the tremendous pressure put upon it by six years of hostilities. The production of dyestuffs had been similarly affected by protective legislation so that whereas in 1914 the United Kingdom imported 90 per cent by weight of the internal consumption of dyes, this figure was down to 10 per cent by 1939.

It had already become apparent by 1939 that there were particularly important advantages in organizing the chemical industry in large units. ICI, as has been noted, had been formed in 1926, but in the other major industries of the world large units were already in existence. In Germany I.G.Farbenindustrie had been formed in 1925, in America the du Pont Company and the Allied Chemical and Dye Corporation were well advanced, while in France and Italy the units were also large. The British industry was thus in a position to compete with foreign industries with no such marked deficiency in structural organization as affected coal, steel, textiles and even motor vehicles before 1939. It would be wrong, incidentally, to look upon ICI then or now as constituting nearly all of the British chemical industry. It employs about one-third of the workers in the industry and its net output is roughly 40 per cent of the total, which gives it an exceptional position, but not one of almost complete domination, which is an impression that is commonly held.[64] Nonetheless the size of ICI, with a capital of £65 million on formation, from the outset allowed the British industry to enjoy, along with its rivals, the economies of scale.

The Second World War made great demands on the chemical industry. Chemicals were required specifically for war purposes and other industries had to be supplied with raw materials or substitutes. For example, carbide was not made in Britain before 1939, but during the war two plants were erected which were capable of satisfying the whole of the country's needs by 1945.

Unusual pressure was exerted for new materials, which meant intensive research. The most outstanding new products of the war or just before were the plastic materials polyethylene, polymethyl methacrylate (Perspex) and polyvinyl chloride. Other discoveries were made (e.g. Terylene) but could not be developed until resources became available after the war. Synthetic resin adhesives were developed that were used in the production of Mosquito aircraft and plywood pontoons. In the field of medicinal chemicals the introduction on a large scale of antibiotics and sulphonamides is well known. DDT was used in quantity during the war to deal with lice and so control typhus amongst troops. These are a few, perhaps the best known, of the many chemical products produced in quantity for the first time during the war.

New chemical plants were designed and constructed and new factories were built. 'The volume of capital constructional work (apart from metal and ammunition plants) undertaken by the chemical industry for the Government during the war and the preceding rearmament period exceeded £50 million. In addition some 2,500 senior staff and key men were seconded for Government service in either the Ministries or the new Government factories.'[65]

By 1945 the chemical industry was poised for great expansion. Unlike the old staples for which there was a declining demand combined with undercapitalization, chemicals were to be in increasing demand from an industry reasonably equipped to meet it and able to take advantage of improved techniques of production. Thus since 1945 the chemical industry has proved to have one of the highest rates of growth (roughly double the average for all industries). In terms of output the industry is now 'second only to the construction industry; it is 15 per cent larger than mechanical engineering, twice as big as electrical engineering, 72 per cent larger than vehicles, including aircraft and almost ten times the size of shipbuilding.'[66] In terms of value of exports it has reached the position of the third most important British industry, behind engineering and motor vehicles (including aircraft). The great surge forward in new products promoted by the war has been maintained, the impetus being given by the rising standard of living at home and abroad, and the increase in population. It has been estimated that of all the materials now being produced by the chemical industry, well over 25 per cent were not commercially available at the end of the war.

Petrochemicals

The greatest expansion in the industry since 1945 has been in the use of petrochemicals. It is sometimes said that petrochemicals constitute an industry in its own right that has outgrown its parent. The growth rate of organic chemicals (which is what most petrochemicals are), has steadily outstripped that of inorganic chemicals. In recent years the rate has been on average 15 per cent per annum.

The reason for the advance of petrochemicals at this stage needs some explanation. It is essentially a case of logical progress in scientific discovery. There are four chemical elements out of the 103 elements known that are of primary importance to the industrial organic chemist: carbon, oxygen, hydrogen and nitrogen. Of these two are freely available in the air around us (oxygen and nitrogen) and two (oxygen and hydrogen) are available in water. Scientists in the late nineteenth century and early twentieth century devised ways of liquefying air and of combining atmospheric nitrogen with other elements as well as isolating the hydrogen in water by using coke to take up the oxygen. Carbon was obtained in various forms from coke or from distilled coal tar. Because of its availability in Britain coal was looked upon as the obvious source of carbon. In the 1920s, however, the Americans discovered that petroleum oil and natural gas are an even cheaper source of carbon which is already combined with hydrogen. The petrochemical industry thus originated in the USA where, of course, supplies of petroleum and natural gas were plentiful; by 1939 the Americans held a substantial lead. The first production of petrochemicals outside the USA was in 1942 when the Shell company put their plant at Stanlow into operation. Courtaulds built the first catalytic cracking plant in Britain in the same year.

There are two stages in the conversion of crude oil into chemicals. Distillation takes place first of all in order to separate the various carbon-hydrogen molecules. This process in itself provides some chemicals directly, but for most of the chemicals required the second process of catalytic cracking is necessary. This involves breaking down the complex mixtures of hydrocarbons by heat and pressure to give simpler combinations. One of these is hydrocarbon ethylene which is used in the making of antifreeze and Terylene, while ethylene itself is used for making polythene. Careful control of both pressure and temperature in the cracking process provides the particular chemicals required. The oil industry does much the same with its products but does not have to refine the crude oil to the same degree because petroleum and fuel oil consist of a combination of constituents and therefore do not have to be broken down so far.

The very close connection between the two industries, oil and chemicals, is evident. This has been a post-1945 development and thus involves a very considerable change in industrial structure. Four of the producers of petrochemicals are primarily chemical manufacturers (ICI, Courtaulds, Monsanto Chemicals and Union Carbide) while each of the major oil refining companies is represented in the field, though not perhaps directly in each case. ICI has even taken the step of entering the petroleum business in order to enter the oil-refining field to secure feed-stock for heavy organic chemicals. The chief centres of the petrochemical industry are to be found adjacent to oil refineries at Stanlow, Fawley, Isle of Grain, Grangemouth and Tees-side. The structure of the petrochemical industry is thus one where it is difficult to disentangle the oil firms from the chemical ones. BP for instance recently (1967) proposed that they should take over the chemical and plastics operations of the Distillers Company Ltd (DCL). Already the two firms under the name of British Hydrocarbon Chemicals were joint partners in the production of ethylene, polyethylene and a wide range of other basic petrochemicals. In addition each owned a third of Border Chemicals, Forth Chemicals and Grange Chemicals, the other partners being ICI, Monsanto and Standard Oil of California respectively. The interrelationship between the two industries is also demonstrated by the pooling of resources, British and American, in the prospecting for North Sea gas and oil.

This connection between oil and chemicals is perhaps obvious but another common link is the size of the firm. It has already been observed that the manufacture of chemicals is best achieved by large units and this is particularly so with petrochemicals. The assets employed per man run at about £10,000 in petrochemicals. ICI's quoted figure of £7,000 of assets per man reflects the increasing proportion of petrochemicals in its industrial base. The capital involved is so vast that the combined resources of the chemical firms are necessary if the highly sophisticated techniques of production are to be applied. The oil refinery at Tees-side, for example, opened in 1966, was part of a £10 million capital development which included the building of a new road and rail distribution terminal two miles away, storage tanks and a riverside jetty big enough to take tankers of up to 60,000 tons and capable of extension to take tankers even larger. The capital was provided by ICI and the Phillip's Petroleum Company of Oklahoma. Automation is a prime characteristic in the production of petrochemicals, which is one reason why such large capital investment is required. Continuous processing is one form of manufacture which lends itself to automated control.

The cost of petrochemical plant is so substantial that the British industry can never hope itself to provide all the chemicals that are demanded even on the home

Table 11.1

Capital expenditure in chemical and allied industries (1958 prices)

	£ million
1958	197
1959	169
1960	150
1961	186
1962	178
1963	152
1964	182
1965	220

Source: *Board of Trade Journal.*

market. The range of chemicals is so wide and the plant so specific that the capital required would be too great if the whole range were to be covered. This applies to the whole of the chemical industry and for this reason the industry is becoming more and more international in its outlook. The industry, more than most, is demonstrating the advantages of the international division of labour, and is one where there is almost universal approval of the British intention to enter the Common Market. Table 11.1 illustrates the size of investment in the industry. The changes in technology are so rapid and the plant is so specific that the firms involved must rely on big markets in order to sell their products in large quantities in a short space of time. The only firms that can provide the capital and run the risks involved are big ones.

The extraction of chemicals from oil and gas has several economic advantages over the use of coal as a base. There are no chemicals obtainable from coal that cannot be derived from other sources, so that the source that is used depends upon economic extraction. Broadly speaking the British economy benefits considerably from the expansion of petrochemicals. Only 2 per cent of the crude oil imported to Britain is used in their manufacture. The policy of the major oil companies to build oil refineries on the British coast rather than rely on refineries on the oil fields themselves has meant that the facilities for the provision of the raw materials for petrochemicals have been set up, as it were, by an external agency; the petrochemical industry has been able to take advantage of raw materials brought in primarily for another purpose. For this reason the value of the finished product of the industry is high in relation to the cost of the raw materials.[67] Furthermore, the world supply of oil being pentiful, the price of the raw material has remained remarkably stable–in contrast with coal which tends to become more and more expensive. A gallon of petrol cost 1*s* 4*d* in 1912 without tax; well over fifty years later the price has risen to only 2*s* per gallon. Taxation has risen, of course! Furthermore oil is easy to handle and the cracking process produces materials of a high degree of purity. The economies to be achieved by using oil rather than coal are thus evident and are demonstrated by the fact that 61 per cent of organic chemicals produced in this country were derived from oil in 1962, whereas the equivalent figure as recently as 1957 was only 45 per cent.

Now that natural gas has been discovered under the North Sea, the industry has another potential source of chemicals. The principal use for natural gas would be to replace naphtha, which is currently imported. The naphtha used for chemical synthesis is 2·6 million tons per annum which puts £20 million on to the British import bill. Also, 'the use of cheap natural gas would put the UK ammonia and fertilizer industry on a closer footing with its foreign competitors. Currently the Chemical Industry is largely dependent on imported naphtha for feedstock purposes. While £7/ton naphtha is equivalent to natural gas at about $3\frac{1}{2}d$/therm, equivalence of price is irrelevant. In order to compete successfully in export markets and to be competitive in home markets, the Chemical Industry needs access to cheap feedstock. Natural gas is available at low prices to many petrochemical producers–in Holland at about $3\frac{1}{2}d$/therm, and lower prices are being negotiated, on the US Gulf Coast at less than 2*d*/therm, in Trinidad at about $\frac{1}{2}d$/therm and in Kuwait at about ·02*d*/therm. If natural gas were available to the British Chemical Industry at the right price this would make a considerable contribution to the balance of payments by facilitating a reduction in imports and an increase in exports of fertilizers and ammonia products.'[68]

Petrochemicals are being used more and more for new purposes which can often mean significant savings in the nation's import bill. The use of synthetic rubber, for example, was saving Britain $30 million worth of natural rubber imports per year by 1960.[69]

Plastics

A major use of petrochemicals is as a base for plastics which deserve some special consideration here.

The chemistry of plastics has evolved from the steady improvement in chemical techniques which has been going on since the eighteenth century. The great landmark

159

in chemical theory then was Dalton's idea of the formula with a definite number of atoms in each molecule. In the nineteenth century compounds were discovered (polymers) whose formulae were the exact multiple of the formulae of similar compounds; but only when techniques of dealing with single unit molecules had been mastered was it possible, in the 1920s, to tackle polymers with molecules containing hundreds, perhaps thousands, of basic units.

It was discovered that if compounds were enlarged by the application of heat, light, pressure or initiator chemicals, new polymers would be formed by a sort of chain reaction. The relationship between the physical properties of structural materials and the inner chemical structure of the large molecules composing them is still the subject of research, but from the results already achieved have come the plastics that have produced what is virtually a new industry and a new technology.

The very fast rate of annual growth of the plastics industry has thus depended on the development of new materials and the use of existing plastics as alternatives to traditional materials. This is obviously where the future of the industry lies, and it is one which seems limitless. An estimate puts the cost of research and development in plastics at between 4 and 5 per cent of turnover,[70] necessary expenditure for an industry that is so very much based on science and technology.

The fastest growing sector of the plastics industry is that which is providing materials for engineering. Plastics are now used in pumps, gears, valves and tubing, and have increasing application in the products of electrical, aircraft and motor vehicle firms. A sports car has already been produced which has a vacuum-formed plastic body (this is admittedly only a testbed for plastics), and one British car in mass production has a plastic timing gear-wheel as well as the plastic upholstery and fittings now almost traditional. The building industry has already made use of plastics for insulation and plumbing, and there is probably a much greater usage possible here. Plastics tend to become cheaper as more usages are found, which makes them increasingly attractive as a raw material. They have impinged on everyday life to such an extent that there is no need to stress their use in consumer goods. A word of caution is necessary here. Plastics are not necessarily cheap materials when compared with traditional materials like timber, or steel. Even though a ton of plastics is in bulk much greater than a ton of say steel, because of the difference in specific gravity plastics are still much higher priced. Plastics will be used only if there is some real advantage over other materials. The advantages are to be found in the costs of manufacture of what may be a complicated shape but one that can be easily moulded, and in the fact that plastics are damp-proof and provide good insulation.

The British production of plastics reached 1·02 million tons in 1966, the first time it has ever passed the million tons mark; 320,000 tons of this were exported.

Chemicals for Agriculture
Chemicals have become increasingly important in agriculture. Since 1945 there has

been a marked increase in the use of fertilizers and in chemicals for weed-killers, fungicides and pest control. Agricultural productivity has risen impressively (Britain produces 143 per cent more grain, 90 per cent more fruit than in 1940, for example), and much of this increase must be attributed to chemicals, though increased mechanization and the successes of agricultural research have obviously played their part. As with the rest of the chemical industry growth depends very much on costly research. There is much that can be achieved in agriculture in the way of chemical ploughing and safe but highly specific pest control for growing and stored crops, so that not only would yields be improved but some of the annual loss of crops could be avoided. The annual world loss in crop yields has been estimated at 30 per cent,[71] a serious proportion, especially in the context of expanding world population. This represents a challenge to the chemical industry and an opportunity for exports.

Paints

The importance of chemical research is also evident in the impressive progress made since the war in paints and dyes. The paint trade has a government-subsidized communal research centre. The nature of paints used for domestic and industrial purposes is increasingly making them more like a fine coating of plastic with the hard wearing and resistant properties that plastic possesses. Apart from experimenting with the constantly widening range of new materials that are becoming available from the chemical industry in general, the paint manufacturers are studying new ways of applying paint and the means of making paints dry even faster than at present. It has long been recognized that it is uneconomic (but hitherto unavoidable) to mix paint with costly solvents in order to make the paint transportable from the factory to the job; the solvents evaporate during the drying and are lost. Research has therefore concentrated on water-thinned paints, dry powder paint and techniques of applying the paint hot. Also the technique of roller coating to sheet and coil metal has become well established as an industrial process, along with electrolytic deposition of liquid paints and fluidized bed and electrostatic spraying of powder coatings.

Dyestuffs

Similarly with dyestuffs there has been a remarkable increase in the quality and range of dyes on the market. Not only have the dyes for traditional materials been made much more resistant to fading but methods have been found for colouring or dyeing the new materials of the chemical industry. Manmade fibres require dyes of a different type from the traditional textiles, and ways had to be devised for colouring plastics. New synthetic pigments have been made for the paint trade and the motor industry has been provided with new finishes for its products. This is one part of the chemical industry where plant has become less specific as it has increased in size. Modern plant tends to be multiproduct and of high versatility in comparison with the

161

old less flexible unit. Total production of dyestuffs in 1964 is shown in Table 11.2 and indicates the competitive nature of the trade in synthetic dyes.

Table 11.2

Production and trade in dyestuffs

	1964 (metric tons)		
	Total Production	Imports	Exports
West Germany	72,230	6,317	41,475
Switzerland	29,840	5,360	29,194
United Kingdom	42,700	5,090	20,449

Source: O.E.C.D., *The Chemical Industry* 1964–65.

Pharmaceuticals

The other branch of the chemical industry that has developed enormously in recent times is the production of pharmaceuticals. It is probable that three-quarters of the drugs and medicines on the market today were not known before 1945. The discovery in 1935 of prontosil, the first sulphonamide, has led to dramatic developments in chemotherapy. In 1935 the United Kingdom production of pharmaceuticals totalled £19 million. By 1950 this had risen to £100 million and by 1965 had reached £250 million. Exports have expanded proportionately.

Table 11.3

Trade in pharmaceuticals, 1935–66

	Exports £m	Imports £m
1935	3·3	1·7
1966	75·0	14·6

Research expenditure has been heavy as befits a branch of the chemical industry where it is necessary to run to keep in the same position. £11·6 million was spent on pharmaceutical research in 1965, over four times what was spent in the early 1950s.[72]

Apart from the production of heavy chemicals the manufacture of pharmaceuticals demands the highest proportion of labour in the industry, much of it very highly skilled and much of it female. Pharmaceuticals involve, of course, a very large number of products, most of which by comparison with the other branches of the industry, are produced in small quantities. Thus there is not the same opportunity to introduce the highly productive large-scale methods as elsewhere, and there is a high labour content in manufacture.

Research

In a way, all industry is science based, but the chemical industry is the industry which, par excellence, depends upon scientific research. It should be evident from what has been said above concerning its rapid change and development that it is the one industry more than any other that employs a very high number of very skilled men. There are roughly 6,000 people engaged in industrial research in the industry (pure research is of course done in the universities and colleges of technology), and the current annual rate of expenditure on research is about £50 million. One of the problems of the industry is to recruit graduates in sufficient numbers, particularly the most able of the Ph.D. students leaving the universities. There is a tendency in this country for industrial research to be looked upon by the academic world as a pursuit inferior to pure research. For that reason there is not the same close liaison between the universities and industry as exists elsewhere, particularly in Germany. So much research and development is going on in the chemical industries of the world that no one nation can hope to avoid purchasing the results of another nation's research. In this way the chemical industry is becoming more international. Technological developments are exchanged, commodities are produced under licence, and plant and research centres are set up in foreign centres. Britain is no exception. National boundaries are becoming less important. We have noticed this trend in reference to petrochemicals and it can be said to apply to the whole of the industry –indeed it is one of the industry's distinguishing features.

Exports

As standards of living increase on a worldwide scale, so the demand for chemicals must increase. We have seen that chemical manufacture demands very expensive, highly sophisticated plant backed by a highly skilled labour force. Britain, as one of the advanced economies of the modern world, is in an advantageous position because she has the capital and the skilled labour force to provide chemicals for herself and also for the developing countries who possess neither the capital in sufficient quantity nor a highly skilled labour force. Further, as was noted with petrochemicals, there is an increasing tendency for countries to specialize in particular chemicals, because plant is specific as well as being costly. Chemicals offer, therefore, an excellent prospect for exports. The best export markets are, at the present time, the Commonwealth, Western Europe and the USA, but this pattern is likely to change as the developing countries increase their demand. British exports in 1966 reached £469 million compared with imports of £295 million.

Productivity

In comparison with other major industries in Britain the chemical industry is highly capital intensive and, as would be expected, highly productive. Encouraging as this is, the industry does not come out so well in comparison with the industries of

163

competitor countries. As Tables 11.4 and 11.5 show, not only have Germany and Japan enjoyed a very fast rate of growth they have also now overtaken Britain in the size of their industries. France and Italy, both coming up fast, may soon catch up. A report by the NEDC on the productivity of the USA industry, published in

Table 11.4

Comparative size of chemical industries in 1964 (by numbers employed)

	Value added £m	Nos. employed (thousands)
USA	5,600	850·0
Germany	1,347	452·7
Japan	652	411·0
UK	955	400·0
France	724	267·0
Italy	716	195·0

Source: C.I.A.

1967, revealed that the American chemical industry is three times more productive than its British counterpart.

Does this imply that the British industry is inefficient? It would be disturbing to find that the most highly productive of British industries was inefficient compared with its major competitors overseas. Although inefficiency does exist (no industry is 100 per cent efficient) the most important reasons for lower production lie elsewhere. Part of the reason is to be found in the overall rate of expansion in the economy. Experience shows that in a modern economy the chemical industry expands at

Table 11.5

Comparative rates of growth of chemical industries from 1958 to 1964

	Production index for 1964 (1958 = 100)
Japan	243
Italy	226
Germany	193
France	177
USA	160
UK	155

Source: CIA.

somewhere between one and a half and twice the rate of overall growth of the economy. Britain is no exception to this. In recent years the rate of economic growth in other countries has been faster than in Britain and this has been reflected in chemical output. The reasons for the faster overall growth are discussed in Chapter 14; the point here is that the discrepancy is not necessarily an indication of inefficiency in the British chemical industry.

The report on the American industry pinpointed the size of production units as the biggest single factor to explain the difference in productivity rates between Britain and the USA. This is, of course, no reflection on efficiency. The report accepted, however, that changing the scale of the industry would take time, and recommended that improvements in the efficiency of manpower utilization be effected which, it was estimated, could reduce the total work force by about one-fifth, or, alternatively increase the average output per head by one-quarter. This is where the inefficiency in the industry lies, as in much of British industry. One important factor in the US industry, noted in the report, for example, was the complete absence of 'mates'. In Britain the fear of redundancy and the memories of the interwar period have tended to prolong a system whereby a craftsman has a 'mate' to hold the tools, run messages and make cups of tea. This was one of the inefficiencies of labour ironed out in the Fawley agreement (see p. 194). The US industry has no such problem because any assistance required by craftsmen is supplied by other craftsmen, craftsmen trainees, or operators. There is thus greater flexibility in the industry in America. Another feature of British industry was included in the report in the context of inefficiency: the familiar problem of a multiplicity of unions. The American situation is that all the work people on the payroll at any one works are likely to be members of one union, regardless of whether they are general workers or craftsmen. This makes plant contracts possible, usually of two or three years duration. There are firm agreements which prohibit strikes or lockouts; if there is disagreement during the period of the contract a plant grievance committee deals with it.

This is not to suggest that in Britain industrial relations in the chemical industry are poor. The British chemical industry is, in fact, proud of its labour relations; it is not strike prone. In 1954 a comprehensive productivity structure was developed in which the representatives of management and union are equal partners and share the chairmanship of the Area Productive Committee of the industry. The manufacturers have themselves come together to form the Chemical Industries Association Ltd, in order to coordinate the activities of the individual firms in the interests of the industry and the nation.

We thus have a picture of a chemical industry in Britain, greatly expanded since the last war, dependent very much upon new materials, enormous sums of capital and a highly skilled labour force backed by research. Although Billingham is the biggest chemical complex in the world, the plant size in the British industry is not big enough yet, and further investment on a big scale will be necessary in conjunction with increased amalgamation at home, perhaps overseas, before it can compete in efficiency with the USA, Japan or, indeed with its major European competitors.

Manmade fibres

The chemical industry has overflowed into the world of fibres to such an extent that no survey of its activities can afford to omit manmade fibres. Growth of the manmade fibre industry has been spectacular in the twentieth century and all the manmade fibres owe their origin to the modern chemical industry. They have been discovered as a result of organized research and their manufacture involves chemical processes; although the finished product cannot fairly be called a chemical, the chemical industry is in no small way responsible for it.

The old distinctions between one industry and another are becoming increasingly blurred. It was possible at the beginning of the century to talk of the textile industry as one comparatively well defined unit of the economy because its raw materials (principally cotton and wool) were natural fibres and used almost with a single purpose. Now we have a situation where many textiles cannot be described simply as a product of one manufacturing industry nor are the raw materials used exclusively for textiles. Nylon, for instance, is made by a chemical firm and supplied as a yarn to the textile manufacturer or as a raw material to a whole variety of industries; rayon is used for clothing and also to make car tyres. 'Raw materials' is not an apt phrase to describe manmade fibres because they are the product of highly sophisticated processes. To complicate matters still further there are now many blends in textile manufacture that involve a mixture of natural and manmade fibres. Even the meaning of the word fibre has thus changed. Originally it meant the unit into which cotton, wool, silk or flax could be divided, but now it means any chemical material formed with fibrous properties and dimensions: some metals, metal oxides, glasses and so on, are now available in fibre form. Thus although the textile industry still

Table 11.6

UK Consumption of fibres

	1937–38	1950	1960	1966	1966
		percentage shares			*million lb.*
Cotton	58	52	45	36	620
Wool (incl. re-used)	33	30	25	21	360
Manmade fibres	9	18	30	43	750
	100	100	100	100	1,730

Source: *Financial Times*, 24 July 1967.

exists it has become part of a wider industry that applies processes to fibres of all kinds to produce domestic, industrial and consumer goods. The chemical industry is involved directly or indirectly with all of these.

In order to make clear the reasons for growth of manmade fibres, and to explain their importance in the economy, something must be said about the different varieties and their method of manufacture. There are two main groups.

RAYONS

Rayons are made from natural fibrous materials, i.e. they are based on vegetable raw material, usually some form of cellulose (cellulose is the main constituent of dry vegetable matter). There are two kinds of rayon: (*a*) viscose, made by treating cellulose, usually wood pulp, with caustic soda; (*b*) acetate, made by using acetic anhydride with cotton linters to form a cellulose acetate which is then dissolved in acetone. The former involves a wet-spinning process, the latter a dry-spinning process, both involving extrusion through a spineret. Rayon can take the form of continuous filament yarn, which consists of several hundred extruded threads twisted together, or staple fibre which consists of similar filaments cut into short lengths which can then be spun like wool or cotton. In Britain production is divided almost equally between the two. Almost all rayon staple fibre is viscose, and a large proportion of filament yarn is viscose as well–in fact three times as much viscose is made as acetate. This is explained by the fact that viscose rayon is cheaper to make and more durable. The attraction of acetate rayon is that it comes closest of all to the look and feel of natural silk but it does not pleat well and has to be washed with great care. A comparatively new market for acetate is in the form of tow for cigarette filters. Viscose rayon is used for car tyres and in the last ten years or so viscose carpet staple has secured about 40 per cent of the UK consumption of all carpet fibres (Evlan is a viscose rayon) but it has lost ground considerably in the domestic apparel market. The future for viscose rayons is linked with the development of Polynosic fibres which, though manmade, closely resemble cotton. In America these new fibres already account for some 30 per cent of all viscose rayon used for apparel. Total British production of rayon in 1966 was over 430 million lb, which was over 100 million lb more than all the other manmade fibres made in Britain.

SYNTHETICS

The other group of manmade fibres consists of synthetics based on minerals. These are synthesized from simple chemical substances which were originally obtained from coal but are nowadays extracted mainly from oil. Nylon, still the most important synthetic fibre, is a polyamide; terylene is a polyester; both are manufactured by condensation polymerization. A second group of synthetics is made by addition polymerization, the most important of these being the acrylic fibres which include Courtelle, Acrilan and Orlon.[67] The synthetic fibres are mainly a post-1945

167

phenomenon and are closely associated with the growth of the petrochemical industry. Each fibre has been developed because it offered characteristics superior in one way or another to those of natural fibres while retaining most of their desirable qualities. Each synthetic has its disadvantages too, and there is fierce competition in an expanding market.

TWENTIETH-CENTURY DEVELOPMENT

The first manmade fibre was cellulose nitrate, invented in 1882 by Chardonnet in France. This was explosive and inflammable but paved the way for viscose rayon, invented in 1892 by the British chemists, Cross, Bevan and Beadle. Courtaulds took out the British patent rights and built the first factory for artificial silk, as it was then called, in 1906 at Coventry. The Dreyfus brothers developed the acetate process after the First World War, marketing their produce under the brand name of Celanese. So far as Britain was concerned rayon was the only manmade fibre before 1939 and, indeed this was so until 1950. Production continued to grow rapidly until 1960 since when growth has tailed off and over 80 per cent of the volume of growth has been in synthetics.

Nylon was an American development, the result of a Du Pont research programme; the patents were published in 1938. ICI obtained the sole manufacturing rights in Britain and in association with Courtaulds formed the British Nylon Spinners Ltd, establishing a large factory at Pontypool, South Wales, near to coal from which the necessary benzene could be obtained. Both companies are now producing nylon independently. Nylon is still the most important synthetic fibre (see Table 11.7). Its markets are increasing in variety and size; apart from those already mentioned it is challenging rayon in the car tyre and carpet markets.

Terylene was invented by the British chemists Whinfield and Dixon in 1941, but because of war and postwar difficulties it was not put into large-scale production until 1955. ICI acquired world rights for this fibre outside the USA and have a large plant for producing it at Wilton. The polyester fibres with a base of ethylene (a petrochemical) have made very rapid growth since 1960 and, if world performance is anything to go by, will ultimately overhaul nylon's rate of growth. In Japan for example, polyester already holds one-third of the synthetic fibre market.

COMPETITION WITH NATURAL FIBRES

Acrylic fibres were first manufactured in Britain in 1957. They have made a rapid advance in the apparel market and now have penetrated the carpet market as well. The pace of growth is illustrated in Table 11.7.

It will be seen from Table 11.6 that the consumption of cotton and wool fibres has declined in Britain since the war. On a world basis the production of synthetic fibres has already doubled that of wool. Cotton production is still markedly larger than synthetics or rayon, but there is an undeniable trend towards a growing share of

168

world markets by manmade fibres. The reasons for this are threefold. The superior characteristics of the fibres have already been mentioned. Coupled with this is the fact that manmade fibres can be controlled in both volume of production and quality more easily than the natural fibres. Thirdly they have a price advantage.

Table 11.7

UK synthetic fibre consumption (estimated)

	1960	1966
	Million lb	
Nylon	72	174
Polyester	26	57
Acrylic	20	85

Source: *Financial Times*, 24 July 1967.

From 1925 to 1940 viscose yarn prices fell more than half as did the price of nylon from 1952 to 1967. Prices of acrylic fibres, which as we have seen, have been in production in Britain only since 1957 had dropped by one-quarter by 1967.

The growth of the manmade fibre industry is of especial value to the economy because the import content of the manufactured article is either low or cheap. Petrochemicals, as we have seen, take a very low percentage of oil imports: wood pulp is cheap and accounts for not much more than one-third of the final value of the cheapest rayon staple fibre and very much less than that in filament yarns. This means a saving on imports which the natural fibre textiles cannot match.

In common with so many of the products of the chemical industry manmade fibres are of the twentieth century. A very large percentage of them are new since 1945. This has given the industry something of a pioneer spirit which has enabled it to keep abreast of its competitors. Because the industry is so new there are no old traditions to hinder development and Britain, not having had a head start, is keenly aware of its foreign rivals in this field. It is an industry that demonstrates the advantages of the economies of scale in the manufacture of fibre; the more it produces the lower are its costs and the greater the opportunities to obtain an increasing share of the fibre market. The need for production in volume has reduced the number of firms in the industry to two very big ones, Courtaulds and ICI, each backed by huge capital reserves and employing highly skilled labour. Dutch and American firms have subsidiary firms manufacturing in the United Kingdom, but their share of the market is small. Comment on monopolies is made in the last chapter of this book, but here we may note that although these two firms dominate the British market, competition exists between one manmade fibre and another, and there is always the challenge of the natural fibres which must not be underrated.

Here at least is one branch of British industry that can be held up as an example of rapid economic growth achieved by modern sophisticated techniques made possible by concentration of production in very large economic units. In other words the manmade fibre industry matches the criteria that are necessary for British industry if Britain is to achieve the pace of economic growth that is expected of an advanced economy.

12

Transport

The transport of goods from one place to another becomes increasingly important as the economy of a country develops. Greater distances are involved as a growing variety of goods has to be carried in quantities that are constantly expanding in volume. In many parts of the world, geographical barriers have held up economic development because of the difficulty of transporting goods over rough terrain or in adverse climatic conditions, but Britain has always been fortunate that geography has not hindered economic growth this way. The nature of the terrain, the climate and the compactness of the country have, from earliest times, favoured the building of lines of communication and transport and must be counted as factors promoting Britain's early economic development. Her insular position provided good trade routes for overseas trade, but major problems have arisen in the internal transport system, which is the subject of this chapter.

The economic pressures that brought about the industrial revolution eventually transformed the transport system of Britain from a number of navigable rivers and sadly neglected roads in execrable condition, to the system of canals, roads and railways necessary for carrying the greatly expanded volume of freight and passenger traffic of the nineteenth century.

Parallel with this development fundamental problems appeared that have remained unresolved ever since but have increased in size in proportion with the size of the transport system. Should there be unrestricted competition between one form of transport and another? Should there be a monopoly within any one type of transport to avoid excess capacity and duplication? Should the system be solely a competitive profit-seeking enterprise or should it be a system that maintains standards of public service which, in some instances, would be unremunerative? Finally, should the state control the system and, if so, to what extent?

Transport, like so much of British industry, has evolved piecemeal, leaving a legacy for the twentieth century that has compelled the state to intensify its interest, a national authority being the only one capable of dealing with a confused, irrational, complex but vital part of the economy.

171

Roads

For centuries the roads received relatively little maintenance; rather like the sea which provided the external routes, roads had always been there for everyone's use but their upkeep was neglected and increasing traffic brought embarrassing problems of maintenance.

The parish was the first unit of government to be given the responsibility of maintaining the roads. The Highway Act of 1555 instructed all parishes to elect a surveyor of highways whose task it was to enlist the aid of all inhabitants in the work of road maintenance; the wealthy provided the implements and the materials, the poor provided the labour. The Parish was, however, too small a unit for this scheme to be successful; compulsory, unpaid assistance by all was hardly likely to provide efficient road repairing. The minimum of effort was applied, no attention was paid to the needs of the long distance traveller and because the roads had not been constructed in the first instance with wheeled vehicular traffic in mind, the conditions of the roads steadily deteriorated until they were so bad that something had to be done.

Delegation of responsibility to the parish had demonstrated at an early stage that the state accepted that road maintenance was the ultimate responsibility of the central authority. There were no funds for the task, so the expedient of unpaid labour was a convenient means of dispensing with an awkward dilemma. The inadequacy of these measures was evident by the eighteenth century; travellers frequently took to the fields, travelling by coach was hazardous and the transport of fragile goods over land was not considered worthwhile.

Parliament's reaction to these conditions was to attempt to determine the type of vehicle and the size of load by Acts of Parliament but this was Canute-like action against an economic flood tide. Growth of industry demanded an improved transport system and because the government was evading its responsibility, private enterprise took over. Turnpike trusts appeared in numbers to maintain stretches of road; they had to obtain the permission of Parliament to operate, but this was easy enough to obtain from a Parliament which would otherwise have had to take the responsibility itself. New techniques in road construction were devised during this period (this was the period of McAdam, Telford and Metcalf) and road conditions were measurably improved, but only where the turnpike trusts existed. A long-distance traveller would find that very good stretches of road alternated with very poor ones, while in areas where trade was not developed to any great extent turnpike trusts, which existed purely as profit-making organizations, did not exist at all. The road system was, therefore, a patchwork and not a network.

The turnpike trusts were virtually eclipsed by the railways in the 1830s. The railways had obvious advantages over horse-drawn coaches and the turnpike trusts themselves effectively outlawed the steam coaches that appeared by raising tolls so high that running steam coaches was an uneconomic proposition. The objection to steam coaches was that their weight would have meant great expense in road maintenance. The 1865 Act (the man with a flag) limiting the speed of mechanically propelled vehicles to a maximum of 4 m.p.h. was passed with steam coaches in mind.

The decline of the turnpike trusts meant a deterioration in road conditions and a return to parish compulsory labour. This was replaced by a system of highway rates in 1835, but this so greatly strained the parish rates that ultimately the government made a grant to parishes to cover part of the expense. In 1888 the Local Government Act transferred the responsibility for all main roads to the county councils. Even so, there was no suggestion of a national policy for highways. For example, the Great North Road, from London to Carlisle, was controlled by seventy-two separate local authorities.[74]

The advent of the internal combustion engine made it necessary to create a Road Board in 1909 with powers to make grants to highway authorities for new construction or improvements, or even to construct new roads on its own account. At the same time, the Road Improvement Fund came into being, supplied by the revenue from road licences and from the tax on petrol (threepence a gallon). The intention was to use the Fund, later known simply as the Road Fund, exclusively for road development. In this way, by 1914 the central government had adopted considerable powers with regard to the roads and the vehicles that used them. The principle had been established that road users should contribute to the cost of roads by payment of taxes to a central authority, and that the central authority was responsible for ensuring that the development of vehicles went hand in hand with the development of roads.

Meanwhile, the county authorities were footing the main part of the bill through the ratepayer. This situation was not altered in 1919 when the Road Board was superseded by the new Ministry of Transport (created ostensibly to coordinate transport development). The collection of motor taxes was transferred from the customs and excise authorities to the county and county borough councils. Receipts of the Road Fund grew rapidly in the 1920s, though expenditure on the roads by central and local authorities exceeded the receipts. In 1926 Churchill, as Chancellor of the Exchequer, made use of the fact that Road Fund expenditure alone did not match receipts and diverted £7 million of the Fund to the Exchequer. He thereby introduced a new principle, which has subsequently become established practice, that motor taxation is a source of revenue no different from any other revenue-raising taxation and is, therefore, not destined for expenditure in any particular part of the public sector of the economy. Since the 1930s the revenue from motor taxation has greatly exceeded the expenditure by all authorities on roads. The Road Fund was abolished in 1956.

The need for central government authority over trunk roads was recognized in 1936. Under the Trunk Roads Act of that year 4,505 miles of main roads became the responsibility of the Ministry of Transport.

173

During the 1930s, even so, total expenditure on roads did not rise in spite of the increase in the number of vehicles using the roads. No motorways were built and the road improvements that were made were not ambitious enough nor in sufficient numbers to prevent growing traffic congestions and an alarming road accident problem. Central government expenditure on roads rose to a peak in 1932 of £29·9 million which was not exceeded during the rest of that decade. The tremendous expansion in road traffic of the post-1945 era was not easily foreseen but certainly little preparation was made for it in the 1930s. The result was not so much a deterioration of the existing roads, as had happened in previous centuries, but the decline in efficiency of the system because of its inadequate size.

Railways

Before any reference is made to railway development in Britain, brief mention must first be made of canals. During the early stages of the industrial revolution, while road improvements were being slowly effected, and before the steam locomotive had been developed, canals proved to be the most efficient agency for bulk transport. There was a period of canal construction mania between 1760 and 1830 which demonstrated the dangers of allowing a monopoly to those who operated the lines of economic communication. The limited supply of water prevented duplication of canal construction so that canal companies were in a position to charge high rates and make large profits at the expense of the traders and society in general.

The abuse of monopoly power in transport had, therefore, already been so well demonstrated by the time that railway expansion started that the government was prepared to take the necessary steps to prevent a recurrence of the same sort of thing. The canal period left its mark. Suspicion of monopoly was at an early stage written into government legislation on railways and lasted well into the twentieth century. In particular, railway charging was limited by the obligation not to show 'undue preference'; this had been written into an Act of 1854 designed to restrict discrimination by railway companies between one consignor and another. The effect of this was to limit the commercial freedom and the flexibility of the railways until the 1950s.

Between 1830 and 1850 the railways experienced a construction mania similar to that of the canals. Private capital was invested in very large quantities in the construction of a railway network that was far from cheap. There was strong opposition to the railways by many people who had to be bought over if they could not be won over. Those who were in any way able to charge the new companies dearly for the privilege of laying track over privately owned land mostly did so and the costs of actual construction were frequently high. The railway companies inevitably schemed to achieve a monopoly in their individual areas, if necessary by buying up the canal companies that might constitute a challenge, and then resorted to devious methods of raising charges.

Parliamentary control was exercised through Railway and Traffic Acts and also by the incorporation of the companies as joint stock companies by special Acts of Parliament. Such special Acts could be passed on condition that special clauses were adhered to. The general policy was to avoid unnecessary waste and duplication by preventing any line from being constructed too close to another, although this meant granting a form of monopoly; there was never any attempt to consider a national railway network. Only in 1846 was a standard railway gauge prescribed.

There were attempts to protect the user. An Act of 1844 required all companies to provide at least one train a day consisting of third class accommodation travelling at not less than 12 m.h.p., for which the rate was not to exceed one penny per mile. This same Act also limited the dividends of any new company to a maximum of 10 per cent per annum, any surplus to be used to reduce rates. The government reserved the right to purchase these companies once they had been in operation for twenty-five years, although this option was never taken up.

As the nineteenth century developed, so the railway companies themselves took steps to improve their efficiency. The most effective method was amalgamation. End-on amalgamations were generally approved by Parliament because they offered the chance of through routes, but other mergers were resisted on the ground that the monopoly danger was too great. Towards the end of the century, Parliament was compelled to amend its views on railway monopoly because so many companies were making little or no profit and many had gone out of business. By 1914 there were still 124 separate railway companies in Britain but only a dozen or so of these were big companies. Parliamentary suspicions were still serious enough in 1909 to turn down a proposed amalgamation of the Great Northern, Great Central and Great Eastern railways.

During the First World War the railways were taken over by the government and run by a Railway Executive Committee composed of managers of the existing companies. The government guaranteed the companies their 1913 revenue but did not increase freight charges. Wage levels rose to a stage where in 1918 the wage bill was three times higher than before the war. Maintenance and investment fell behind and the companies were faced with deficits unless adequate compensation was offered by the government. One hundred per cent increases in rates were authorized and compensation was paid for deterioration of assets during the war but this did not put the railway finances on a firm footing by the time the railways were handed back to private enterprise in 1921.

The Railways Act of 1921 recognized the need for changes. It provided for the amalgamation of the railway companies into four regional companies, each with a monopoly in its own region (London, Midland and Scottish; Great Western; London and North-Eastern; and Southern Railways). Wages, hours of work and conditions of service were placed in the hands of a wages board, while the classification and schedule of standard rates was put in the charge of the Railway Rates

Tribunal. Railway charging, even so, was still made difficult because of the loss of flexibility mentioned earlier. The Act of 1854 still in force did not encourage special rates to be quoted to obtain traffic for fear that all similar rates would have to be reduced accordingly. This system made profit-making difficult. The inflation of the First World War had reduced the capital reserves of the railways so that a low revenue combined with these low reserves provided insufficient basis for the modernization schemes that the railways required. Only the Southern Railway made real progress by converting from steam to electric traction. The LNER paid no ordinary dividend between 1925 and 1938.

Competition between roads and railways in the interwar period

The fears of monopoly abuse, still evident in the 1921 Railways Act, did not take into account the challenge of the roads. The interwar period witnessed the growth of road haulage firms. There was no legislation to compel these firms to become common carriers as there had been with the railways. They could pick and choose their loads, accepting profitable business and leaving awkward loads to the railways. The convenience of door to door or factory to customer service was something the railways could not always offer. There was no scheme by the Ministry of Transport to integrate services. During the interwar period the railways lost one-third of their general merchandise traffic. This was perhaps inevitable, but the railway owners, not unjustifiably, complained that they were fighting with one hand behind their backs.

The Ministry of Transport's principal restrictions upon the road hauliers were through a licensing scheme. The licences were to be granted at the discretion of Licensing Authorities who were to decide if there was a need for the service. There were three categories.

A licences, by which a vehicle could carry only other people's goods;
B licences, by which a vehicle could carry its own firm's goods and, with some limitations, those of other people;
C licences, by which a vehicle could carry only its own firm's goods.

A and B licences were, not surprisingly, more difficult to obtain than C licences. The railways made one challenge in that, permitted to own road vehicles of their own, they ultimately bought out and operated the two largest parcel carrier firms in the country.

At the start of the Second World War there was much that was wrong with Britain's transport system. The roads and the railways had both been starved of the necessary investment to keep them up-to-date with the changing but growing need for transport. There was a Ministry of Transport but, by and large, the different sectors of the transport system were engaged in a 'free-for-all' within the limits of parliamentary legislation that was not in keeping with the changed situation.

Nationalization

The Second World War strained the railways to the limit. The intensive use to which they were put, the damage inflicted by aerial bombardment and the inevitable lack of capital investment, brought them to the stage where drastic action had to be taken to restore them to a sound condition. The Labour government of 1945 nationalized not only the railways but also road transport and Inland Waterways in an effort to devise a public service.

The 1947 Transport Act did little, however, to provide an integrated transport system. It centralized control in the British Transport Commission and created five separate executives, including one each for railways and road transport, but did nothing to diminish the competition between railways and roads. In the crucial matter of charges, the railways were still not able to fix charges in relation to costs, but were still treated as if they were a dangerous monopoly. They were obliged to publish their charges and had to justify them before a Transport Tribunal. This often meant that the increases applied for were so long in being granted that increasing costs had swallowed up the advantage before the charges came into operation. Furthermore, the railways were expected to run unremunerative services when it was thought that to do so was in the public interest.

The operation of long-distance road haulage vehicles (41,000) was placed in the hands of the new Road Transport Executive. A and B licence carriers were allowed to operate within a radius of twenty-five miles. C licence traders still had complete freedom to provide transport on their own account. Competition from C licence holders grew rapidly but the railways had no chance to compete successfully because of the unrealistic charging system which they were obliged to operate.

Competition between roads and railways in the 1950s

There was insufficient time to assess whether the Transport Act of 1947 was a success before, on the return of a Conservative government, road transport was denationalized in 1953. Most of the lorries were sold back to private firms but the British Transport Commission retained about 7,000 lorries which it found difficulty in selling: these have been operated as British Road Services ever since. The full element of competition between road and rail was then restored.

The railways were operating with rapidly depreciating capital equipment. There had been so many demands on government capital expenditure in the immediate postwar period that the railways had received lean treatment. They had been deprived of adequate capital expenditure for twenty years. In 1955 the British Transport Commission announced a modernization plan which proposed the spending of £1,200 million on the railways. Diesel locomotives were to be introduced and electrification was to be extended beyond the Southern Region in a vast modernization plan that was to last fifteen years. Only at this stage was it decided that profit should be a major criterion in determining the future of the railway system; branch line services were to be closed where fares bore no relation to economic costs.

The size of the growing British Railways deficit made the issue of whether the government should provide a public service with no direct relation to cost, or whether the railways should be made to pay their way, one of increasing public and political debate. The nationalized railways had made a working profit up to 1955 even if, with central charges taken into account,* there was an overall deficit from the start. After 1955 there was not even a working profit and by 1961 the cumulative total of all railway deficits amounted to £737 million.

Beeching plan

At this juncture, the government appointed Dr Beeching, an industrialist from the board of ICI, to reorganize the whole railway system with a view to making the railways ultimately pay their way. The Transport Act of 1962 replaced the British Transport Commission by Boards each responsible for a sector of nationalized transport. Dr Beeching was made the first Chairman of the Railway Board. The Act stated that it would not be reasonable to leave the railways subject to out-of-date restrictions on their commercial activities, that is it freed the railways at long last from the irksome controls that had hampered railway charging since the nineteenth century. The Beeching Plan published in 1965 treated the railways in isolation. It planned to reduce the 7,500 miles of line in existence in 1962 to 5,000. The number of passenger stations was to be reduced from 4,293 to 2,363 and an extra £250 million was to be spent on diesels. The number of railway employees was to be reduced by 70,000.

The effect of this was bound to intensify the use of road transport, but the capital invested in the road system could not match the demands made upon it. If the belief was that the free play of the forces of the market should determine the ultimate structure of the transport system, the government responsible for a modern but contracted nationalized railway system and also for the provision of an adequate road network was bound to be involved in massive capital outlay which it could hardly afford. The government was already committed to a very large outlay on the railways yet, in spite of the proposed reductions in services, the gap between expenditure and income was to increase for some years to come. Meanwhile road transport was increasing so fast that, in order to cope with it, the road building programme needed to be greatly accelerated. Road construction, maintenance and improvement is not the only aspect of increased road usage that involves expenditure. The cost of the roads also involves ancillary services such as police, traffic control, lighting and road signs which are not usually taken into account but should certainly be part of the reckoning if road costs are to be compared with railway costs.

* Payments (a) of interest to previous owners (b) to a sinking fund for ultimately reducing the government stock.

Table 12.1 shows the great increase in road traffic since the nationalization of the railways. The significant expansion in goods vehicles was not amongst the long distance hauliers with A or B licences but among the C licence holders who were

Table 12.1

Vehicle licences issued in UK (in thousands)

	Goods vehicles	Private cars
1948	788	2,003
1956	1,206	3,981
1966	1,635	9,190

Source: *Key Statistics*, 1900–1966.

using vehicles for the carriage of their own goods and could obtain licences easily. By the end of 1965 only one-tenth of the money spent on moving freight was going to the railways.

Motorways

Work on Britain's first motorway had begun in 1956 with a promise of a thousand miles of motorway by the early 1970s. The plan lagged behind the reality; the motorways were needed years before construction was started and the volume of traffic was increasing much faster than the motorways planned, even after the programme had begun. By 1966 there were over 400 miles open to traffic, but the promised one thousand miles seemed an over-optimistic target. Since 1958 motorways have been constructed at less than sixty miles per year; they are now needed at ninety miles per year if the promise of 1,000 miles is to be met by 1972. The road building programme has suffered from more than one cut in public expenditure because of recurring economic crises. Both roads and railways have thus suffered from too little capital development.

Attempted integration

The Labour government elected in 1964 adopted the idea of an integrated transport system, with the dominant philosophy that transport should be a public service. Lack of general mobility was said to be a new form of poverty. For the first time ever, a scheme was evolved which looked at all the transport services in Britain with a view to organizing them as a whole. While the plan was being drawn up, the Beeching Plan was slowed down, although much of it had already been implemented. A National Freight Corporation (NFC) was to be formed which was to amalgamate all the publicly-owned freight transport institutions (in particular British Railways and the Transport Holding Company*). It was intended that all freight being carried by the NFC should be sent by road or rail according to the decision of the operator (the NFC) not of the customer. The introduction of the 'container concept' on the roads and railways encouraged organization of this kind.

The government's intentions for an integrated transport system became clearer when a succession of White Papers was issued in 1967. For the railways the aim was to be rid of the annual deficit by 'about 1971' by means of drastic capital reorganization. Reductions of route miles were to stop at 11,000 miles (there were still 13,200 miles in 1967), but the government intended 'that this basic network shall be adapted and developed to meet present and future needs, and the necessary finance will be provided for new worthwhile investment, including the modernization of traction, rolling stock, track and signalling that can be justified on a proper economic basis'.

Payment for unprofitable passenger services, retained for social reasons, was no longer to be accounted for as part of the railway deficit. The social cost of the lines was to be assessed and the Railways Board would receive Exchequer Grants to cover the cost. Subsidies of this kind were expected to cost £50–55 million per annum. For the first time since the beginning of the railways, formal recognition was given by a government that it accepted responsibility for specific parts of the railway system which were to be run, not as a profit-making enterprise, but as a social amenity. This was very different from paying deficit grants to the railways on a non-discriminatory basis as had been done before.

A further subsidy was to be paid to cover the cost of eliminating surplus track capacity and a large part of the British Railways capital debt was to be written off, so that the railways had a chance of breaking even by 1971. These proposals thus involved substantial government financial aid for the railways.

The White Paper on *The Transport of Freight* (Cmnd 3470) proposed a reorganization of publicly owned road and rail freight services and introduced a new road carrier licensing system designed as a matter of policy, to attract freight traffic away from the roads back to the railways. The A, B and C licences were to be scrapped and replaced by a quantity and quality control system.

All vehicles under 30 cwt unladen weight were to be free of licensing altogether (this involved 900,000 vehicles), while the other 600,000 vehicles were to be subject to a quality control where licences would be granted on evidence of professional competence and standing. Vehicles over 16 tons gross weight engaged on hauls over 100 miles or carrying bulk traffic would be subject also to a quantity control where licences would be granted only if the loads concerned could not be carried economically by rail.

Supporting the new licensing scheme was an additional tax, ranging from £50 to £190 a year, on all goods vehicles over 3 tons unladen weight, the heaviest tax

---

* The Transport Holding Company groups together the various boards for British Road Services and the publicly owned bus, shipping and freight companies.

falling upon vehicles of over 8 tons unladen weight. In addition, it was intended to make a charge on operators of goods vehicles carrying abnormally large or over-hanging loads; the charge would range from a shilling a mile up to £15 a mile.

An important step towards integration proposed in the White Paper was the decision that the NFC should take over from the Transport Holding Company all its general and specialist road haulage services while British Railways should hand over the assets (excluding trains) employed in the freightlines and sundries (parcels) services and British Railways cartage vehicles. Thus NFC would take commercial responsibility for all traffic originating by road, leaving British Railways responsible for everything originating by rail. The government's plans, set out in the White Paper, were incorporated in the Transport Bill placed before Parliament in 1968.

Although the Transport Bill of 1968 envisaged an integration of the publicly owned transport system, it must not be forgotten that much of the traffic on the roads is still commercially or privately owned. The transport system is like many other parts of the economy, a mixture of state control and private enterprise, where the private sector is indirectly controlled by taxation and (in this case) a licensing system as well. The transport industry is one where the need for state control was recognized at a very early stage and has been implemented to an even greater degree as the pace of economic growth has increased. But central control means that deci-sions have to be taken that involve anticipating future changes a long way ahead. Enormous sums of money are at risk in decisions that are made on a national scale; if the decisions are wrong, the result must be calamitous, but the alternative is the almost certain calamity of confusion, inefficiency, waste and frustration that follow when the public, through the medium of demand and supply, determine the transport system they want. The roads were neglected in Britain when the railways were developing; then the railways suffered while the motor vehicle secured much of the share of the nation's traffic. The road system continued to suffer from neglect while the railways declined. This was the consequence of failure to exercise firm central control when it was needed. At no time since the First World War has Britain ever had an adequate transport system.

Successive governments since 1945 have tried to grapple with the problem. None has found a satisfactory solution; each has made a contribution; all have been obliged to initiate or expand capital programmes that are intended to make up for some of the neglect and lack of foresight in the past. The plans of the Labour govern-ment in the 1960s involve heavy expenditure and a belief that there is a need for a substantial railway system for some time to come. Government control over trans-port, however, is not total and the needs of market forces can still greatly affect future development. The transport problem in Britain in many ways resembles the fuel and power problem. In both instances there has been a long history of neglect; the state has been obliged to take over the ailing sectors of both industries while

13

private enterprise has expanded other sectors rapidly. The government's plans for the coal industry have accepted the need to allow the industry in its contracted form to face competition on its own by the 1970s; the railways, in contrast, have been given government protection and substantial financial aid, though at the same time a contraction in the extent of the railways has been accepted.

It remains to be seen whether these decisions were the right ones, but at least no charges of lack of forethought or starvation of capital can now be laid, and it was these two factors that were mainly responsible for the difficulties until 1945. Perhaps the next generation will be laying similar charges about urban traffic congestion, a problem not within the scope of this volume but, nonetheless, part of the transport problem and woefully neglected in our own time.[75]

13

The trade unions

History

The relationship between employer and employee in the British economy, of vital importance in conditions of private enterprise, depends very much on the past; indeed, a knowledge of trade union history is essential if modern industrial relations are to be properly understood. The facts of trade union development help to explain the attitudes adopted by employer and employee in present times. This is not to suggest that the rank and file of the trade union movement or all the employers are themselves fully conversant with the historical facts, but they are all involved in the attitudes that stem from them. The structure of the trade unions in Britain is unique and has been brought about by a long evolutionary process lasting over 200 years; the unions play such an important part in the functioning of the British economy that their origins must be known if the policies of the unions are not to be seriously misinterpreted.

Essentially the history of the trade union movement is one of a long struggle for legal recognition in an effort to establish a fair basis for bargaining with employers. The struggle has been not simply between the trade unions and employers but one between the unions and the judiciary and Parliament as well. The latter struggle has now been concluded, but the spirit of conflict rather than cooperation still exists between the unions and the employers. The system of free collective bargaining that has flowered fully since 1945 and the espousal of the socialist ethic by many trade unionists have produced a situation where universal cooperation between employer and employee cannot easily be achieved.

The most convenient starting point in trade union history is the beginning of the nineteenth century, when industrialization in Britain was well under way. The times when a worker could hope to become a master of his trade had gone and the working class, destined to be so very much a feature of the Victorian era, was emerging. At first the unions of tradesmen that were formed were tolerated or even welcomed, but the violent excesses of the French Revolution led to a fear in Parliament that organized groups of the working classes might similarly resort to violence in Britain. The Combination Acts of 1799 and 1800, therefore, made all combinations (the word union was not used until later) illegal, and made provision for the summary trial of offenders. The punishments laid out in the Acts were not particularly severe and there is no evidence that the Acts were invoked very often, while unions continued to exist and be formed, but, technically from the outset unions were not legally permitted at all. For the succeeding hundred years the Unions were to have to struggle from this illegal status step by step towards the full legal recognition that they enjoy in present times.

The repeal of the Combination Acts is associated with the name of Francis Place. He and influential friends, particularly an MP, Joseph Hume, argued that because trade unions were illegal there was suspicion between the employers and their men. It was their contention that, given the free interplay of supply and demand, wage prices would find their own level and that combination to secure high wage rates was, therefore, unlikely. The repeal took place in 1824 and made the act of combining legal, but a subsequent Act in 1825 tightened the law against the use of violence or intimidation by unionists and defined the purpose of combination as one of concern with hours of work and wages. The immunity from prosecutions under law of conspiracy was withdrawn.

This was the period of economic development when the worst effects of the factory system were to be observed and when scant attention was paid either to working or to living standards in the urban centres of industry. Child labour was commonplace; the first really effective Factory Act, forbidding the employment of children under nine years of age in textile mills was not passed until 1833. Once the Combination Acts had been repealed there was scope for the growth of unions to counter the undoubted exploitation of workers by some (though by no means all) employers. At the same time, at a higher level, arguments were being put forward for the reform of the franchise, which culminated in the Reform Act of 1832. It was a time in history when, by virtue of the changing economic scene, many new ideas and ambitious schemes were being put forward passionately on the political and social fronts. The climax of these schemes as far as the unions were concerned was the formation in 1834 of the Grand National Consolidated Trades Union, inspired by Robert Owen who, far in advance of his time, envisaged a general strike which would achieve radical alterations in the political structure of the country.

Owen's union was a failure largely because its members had too many local and sectional interests that were considered to have a higher priority than the concept of national union, and, not unnaturally, there was some public alarm at the spread of unionist ideas. The whole structure collapsed with the affair of the 'Tolpuddle Martyrs'. This was a legal decision, the first of several, that undermined the ostensible legitimacy of the unions. The six labourers concerned were found guilty of administering a secret oath to new recruits to the branch of the union, and under an Act of 1797 designed for an altogether different purpose, were sentenced to transportation and seven years penal servitude in Botany Bay, Australia. The Home Secretary of that time was wishing to make an example of a few in order to discourage the zealousness of the many interested in the new-found strength of trade unionism. The public outcry at the excessive nature of the punishment resulted in the early return of the labourers from Australia and their subsequent rehabilitation, but, not surprisingly, the ardour left the trade union movement for a while.

The period that followed is generally described as the period of the new model unions. It lasted from the late 1840s until the later 1860s thus roughly coinciding with the period of mid-Victorian prosperity. The unions that developed during this time were not designed to challenge authority but were run more on the lines of friendly societies. They were national in scope and aimed to provide financial and other help for members in times of need. Assistance was given to members if they were ill or unemployed, widows were helped, tools were bought, and so on, the money coming from members' weekly subscriptions. Because of the considerable benefits accorded to members subscriptions were high; thus, only well-paid workers, i.e. craft workers, could afford them. The new model unions were, therefore, unions of skilled men. The Amalgamated Society of Engineers was the most famous of these. The unskilled workers' unions were not formed until later in the century and this division between the craft and unskilled unions has remained ever since. Except for one or two important exceptions the unions in Britain have never been organized as industrial unions. The image that the new model unions created of themselves was one of peaceful, law-abiding organizations and was a great contrast to the hot headed challenge of the 1830 period. The Trades Union Congress was formed at the end of this period, 1868, to act as a forum for trade union ideas. The TUC has never been anything other than a voluntary organization with no power to order any union to do anything it does not wish, even to not being a member of the TUC unless it so desires.

This peaceful development was rudely disturbed by another legal decision (Hornby *v*. Close) in 1867 which threatened to undermine the financial status of the unions, and, hence, struck again at the security of the union movement. The treasurer of the Bradford branch of the Boilermakers' Society had embezzled £24 of union money. He was sued by his union but the courts decided that trade unions, although permitted to exist, did not constitute organizations which had authority to sue in a court of law. The union had imagined that because it had deposited a copy of its rules with the Registrar of Friendly Societies it would be treated in law as a friendly society; this judgment meant that trade unions were still outside the law and that union funds were unprotected. The trade union movement obviously regarded this as a major threat to its continued existence.

The place of unions in society had been made a matter of national interest at about the same time because of a series of violent acts in Sheffield inspired by disagreements amongst the cutlers over the closed shop principle. A long series of outrages had culminated in the blowing up of a workman's house and the public interest which incidents of this kind aroused had led to the formation of a Royal Commission to consider the whole question of trade unions. The situation brought about by the Hornby *v*. Close affair came within the purview of the Commission as well.

The leaders of the union movement were able to demonstrate that the 'Sheffield Outrages' were the exception not the rule, and that unions were peaceful, law-abiding bodies. The mildness of the unions in the mid-Victorian period now stood them in good stead. Public opinion was on their side once the report of the Commission had been published. The result was the Trade Union Act of 1871, followed by further Acts in 1875 which attempted to clear up previous anomalies in the legislation and make the legal standing of the unions quite clear. A major problem was the satisfactory legal protection of trade union funds. If the unions were given merely the same protection as commercial companies (incorporation) it meant that not only could they sue officials, but, and this was the drawback, they could be sued themselves. This would have involved a danger of being sued by employers for damages in the event of strike action. Thus the Act of 1871 did not mention incorporation which was generally taken to mean that unions still had no legal status and could, therefore, sue in regard to their property but could not be sued themselves. The Acts of 1875 freed trade disputes from the law of conspiracy and legalized peaceful picketing. Thus it was reckoned that the trade unions were now fully legally recognized and safeguarded, and the way was clear for a great expansion of the movement.

The expansion of the trade Unions coincided with the Great Depression when British industry was to feel the effects of overseas competition for the first time. The threat of lowered wages or unemployment gave impetus to the combination of the workers, particularly the unskilled who felt that the opportunity had arrived for militant unionism. The old-established unions were cautious because of the need to protect the not inconsiderable funds they had built up over a long period, but the unions that were now formed, and which demanded only a small subscription from members, had little to lose. A division appeared between the craft unions and the new unions of unskilled workers. The threat of unemployment not only engendered fierce demarcation disputes, but also made the craft unions anxious that no work should be allocated to the less skilled. Dockers, farm labourers, gas workers, firemen and merchant sailors all formed unions, along with many other unskilled workers, but they were not interested in protecting skills or union funds; they were concerned primarily with a challenge to employers over higher pay. The craft unions tended to be exclusive while the new unions were willing to recruit workers irrespective of their type of employment. In fact it was a group of skilled workers, thrown out of work by the Great Depression, who organized many of the unskilled workers. John Burns, later to become a Liberal cabinet minister, and Thomas Mann were two of the most effective. They travelled up and down the country demanding a new union policy and receiving support from those who were now advocating the new socialist ideas. It was at this period that trade unionism and socialism started to draw together.

The older unions had been in the practice of negotiating wage scales tied to the price of the commodity produced, thereby admitting the respectability of the profit motive. An agreement of this kind implied that an employer should be prepared to share increased profits with the workers. The new unions, affected by socialist ideas, rejected commodity-price related wage agrements. The Great Depression had demonstrated that prices go down sometimes as well as up, but now, significantly, the new unions campaigned for wage scales related to the cost of living. They argued that any firm may pay its workers a living wage and if it could not do so then, rather than it should underpay the workers, it should go out of business. Any firm which did not pay a living wage was regarded as parasitic.

One of the aims of the new unions was to secure political power, which they could do only by enlisting the aid of a political party in the House of Commons. The Conservatives and the Liberals, however, both included many employers within their ranks so that a new party was called for. The Independent Labour Party came into existence in 1893 and was devoted to the interests of the working class. Its leading personality was Keir Hardie, a Scottish miners' leader and an ardent socialist, but it represented only the new trade unions and socialist sympathizers. By 1900 the older unions were won round to the idea that representation in Parliament could be achieved only if all those sympathetic to the workers' cause were to come together and form a united front. The resultant party was formed in 1900 and was called the Labour Representation Committee; it included the Independent Labour Party, the whole of the trade union movement and the intellectual socialist groups, the Fabian Society and the Social Democratic Federation. In 1906, after twenty-nine of its candidates had been elected to Parliament, it changed its name to the Labour Party. Thus it can be said that the Labour Party sprang from the trade union movement and was formed specifically to further the interests of the working class. It has subsequently broadened its interests and its representations, but its origins are important in the context of present day industrial relations.

The support for trade union representation in Parliament was given a considerable boost by an unfavourable decision in the law courts which once again threatened to undermine the hard earned legal status that the trade unions considered was by now firmly established. In 1901 the Taff Vale Railway Company in South Wales sued the Amalgamated Society of Railway Servants for damages incurred in an eleven-day strike that had taken place in the summer of the previous year. Picketing to prevent the use of blackleg labour had taken place, but the union leaders were confident that their action, which was in support of a signalman who, they alleged, had been victimized for leading a movement for increased pay, was within the limits of the legislation of the 1870s. The decision of the House of Lords was that 'if the legislature has created a thing which can inflict injury it must be taken to have impliedly given the power to make it suable in a court of law.' Damages of £23,000 were awarded to the Company and the Union was instructed to pay the costs which amounted to another £7,000. The unions saw this as a major setback; the right to strike, which they regarded as fundamental, was now swept away because no union would want to risk a court action of this kind every time a strike took place. The Taff Vale decision rallied many unionists to the side of the Labour Representation Committee. By 1903 the unions and trades councils affiliated to it represented nearly 850,000 members. The annual conference of the Committee in that year voted to raise a fund for the payment of MPs supporting the cause of Labour by means of a compulsory levy on the unions.

The general election of 1906, which returned, as we have seen, 29 Labour MPs, gave a sweeping majority to the Liberals many of whom were sympathetic to the aims of their Labour colleagues. Almost immediately an Act was passed which established beyond question that a union could not be sued for any action of its servants or agents in pursuit of a trade dispute. Once again the unions believed that their legal status was firmly established.

In 1909, however, the Walthamstow branch secretary of the Amalgamated Society of Railway Servants, W. V. Osborne, who was a Liberal, claimed that the union had no right to pass on part of his union subscription to the upkeep of the Labour Party, that is he objected to the political levy established in 1903. His argument was that such a levy was *ultra vires* for a trade union. As with the previous legal decisions, the case was taken through the High Court, the Court of Appeal and to the House of Lords. The Lords judgment was that because the right to make a political levy was not specifically mentioned in the Acts of 1871 and 1876 (an amending Act) an action of this kind was, as Osborne claimed, *ultra vires.*

The Osborne Judgment caused almost as much resentment as the Taff Vale decision. It appeared to many trade unionists as if the judiciary were consistently and deliberately set against trade unions. The Labour Party, which had come into being largely in consequence of the trade union movement, could not survive if its major source of income was taken away.

The remedy to the Osborne Judgment came firstly with the Act of 1911 instituting payment for members of Parliament and then in an Act of 1913 which made political levies legal but made provision for anyone who objected to his subscription being used partly for political purposes to 'contract out'. Contracting out involved the filling in of a form, and it was recognized that form-filling was an unpopular activity so that only the most conscientious objectors would contract out.

It must be said that although the legal decisions affecting the trade unions were made in strict accordance with the British legal tradition of impartiality they were not always seen to be so. It did not escape the notice of the trade unions that the House of Lords was Conservative dominated. Lord Halsbury who was one of the Law Lords responsible for the Taff Vale and Osborne decisions was well known for his hostility to the trade union movement. The feeling had thus gained ground that before the unions could be comfortably assured of what they considered to be their rightful place in an industrial society, Parliament itself, the House of Commons and the House of Lords would have to be sympathetic to the workers' cause, since Parliament made the laws that the judiciary interpreted. The syndicalist views of some of the trade union personalities before 1914 were never universally adopted, the great majority of trade unionists remaining faithful to the concept of British democracy, but there was a popular conviction which remains to the present day that the Conservative Party was hostile to unionism. The Conservatives did nothing to diminish this conviction when, as the government of the day, dealing with the aftermath of the General Strike of 1926, they passed the Trade Union Act of 1927 which made sympathetic strikes illegal and changed contracting out to 'contracting in'. This seemed to be a deliberately hostile act because the proverbial dislike of form-filling would now operate against unions funds. The Labour government of 1945 repealed the 1927 Act and 'contracting out' has remained the practice ever since.

Rookes v. Barnard

Even since 1945 there has been one further legal decision which, although it did not create anything like the disturbance of the Taff Vale and Osborne judgments, has perpetuated the popular trade union belief in the hostility of the judiciary. It concerned a draughtsman Rookes, employed by BOAC at London Airport, who, as a result of a disagreement with branch officials of his union, the Draughtsmen's and Allied Technicians Association, resigned from the union. BOAC, however, had an arrangement with the union that if a department had 100 per cent union membership they would not introduce non-union labour. The union had registered with the management a 100 per cent membership in the design office where Rookes worked, so they claimed that unless Rookes was withdrawn from the design office they would consider the agreement broken and threatened a strike. BOAC dismissed Rookes who took legal action for damages, not against the union but against two representatives of DATA working at London Airport and against a full-time official of the Association. The decision of the House of Lords (1963) was that a threat to take strike action had been made in breach of a collective agreement and that this constituted an unlawful threat. Rookes was awarded damages. It had been thought that the 1906 legislation had made this sort of decision impossible but the Law Lords drew a distinction between the illegality of suing a union and the acceptability of an action against union officials. The Labour government in 1965 passed a Trade Disputes Act which gives protection to officials who, in the course of trade dispute induce others to break a contract of employment. The unions thus have at last a status fully recognized by law, with all the necessary safeguards for funds, officials, members and strike action.

Industrial unrest before and after the First World War

The achievement of virtual full legal status by the trade unions early in the twentieth century gave them the opportunity to challenge the power of the employers and the government. The years before and after the First World War were years of consider-able industrial unrest, hostility and, in some instances, violence. This was occa-sioned, at least in part, by the changing economic pattern. The coal industry, for example, was already facing a challenge from industries abroad that were more productive by this time than the British industry. It must also be remembered that this was a time in British economic evolution when there was a good deal of poverty and when there was a wide disparity between rich and poor (see Chapter 5). Some of the bitterest industrial disputes in British history took place in the coal industry in the earlier part of the twentieth century. In 1910 the Durham and Northumberland miners struck for three months, in vain, against the introduction of a three shift system which would upset their home life. In the same year the Welsh miners struck for ten months over a pay award during which police and troops were sent to South Wales and one miner was killed in rioting at Tonypandy. In 1912 there was a national coal strike when thirty million working days were lost. The story was the same in the 1920s in the coal industry, culminating as we have seen in the General Strike called

Table 13.1

Trade union membership–selected years

Year	Members (in 000's)
1900	2,022
1902	2,013 (after Taff Vale)
1907	2,513 (Taff Vale rectified)
1913	4,135 (Osborne judgment rectified)
1920	8,348 (Postwar militancy)
1927	4,919 (Aftermath of General Strike)
1933	4,392 (Depth of interwar slump)
1939	6,298 (Recovery from slump)
1946	8,803 ⎤
1955	9,726 ⎟ Postwar affluence
1960	9,883 ⎟
1965	9,928 ⎦

Source: *Annual Abstract*, 1900–1966.

to support the miners. In other industries too there was considerable unrest. Dockers and seamen went on strike in 1911, and the dockers again in 1912 as well as the railwaymen.

A feature of the period before and after the First World War was the appearance of a few very large unions. The National Union of Railwaymen was formed in 1913 from several unions, the National Union of Distributive and Allied Workers was created in 1921, and the Transport and General Workers (including the dockers and vehicle workers) came into being in 1922. The other big union that appeared at this time (1924) was the National Union of General and Municipal Workers which included the gasworkers, general labourers and municipal employees. The miners' union (not called the National Union of Mineworkers until 1945) was already large, as was the Amalgamated Engineering Union, renamed as such in 1920 but one of the earliest unions. Although some of these unions were industrial, others straddled several industries, thus giving the trade unions a complicated structure. Many craft unions remained alongside the new big general unions and the few industrial unions. In 1925 there were 1,176 unions in Britain. But, if there were many unions there was a movement towards coordinated action. The railwaymen, the miners and the transport workers formed the Triple Alliance in 1915 with the intention of combined action if one of the three was involved in strike action. Robert Owen's ideas were revived and there was much talk once more of syndicalism.

The climax to this period came in 1926 with the General Strike. This proved to be a fiasco for the unions largely because public opinion was not on their side, but also because the majority of union leaders were themselves not anxious to challenge the democratic system. The unions in any case lacked strength because the economy of the country was at a low ebb. Once the failure of the General Strike was evident support for the unions fell away and it continued to do so through the severe economic depression of the early 1930s, although much bitterness remained. The mass unemployment of the interwar period proved to be something about which the unions were able to do very little although membership increased again with the slow recovery from the slump up to 1939.

Unions and postwar affluence

1945 saw the election of a Labour government with a large majority and the application of economic policies that secured full employment. This placed the unions for the first time in a position of great strength particularly because they considered that the government was favourably disposed towards them, and also because labour became a scarce commodity. The unions were able to push up wage levels systematically without undue militancy by pursuing moderate policies. Strikes occurred but with nothing like the frequency nor intensity of the prewar or pre-1914 periods. In fact there was no major industrial dispute during the period of the Labour government 1945–51. On the other hand the unions had cause to be more satisfied with the increased share of the national income enjoyed by their members. In the period 1939 to 1949 wage earners received a 25 per cent increase in share of GNP whilst salary earners suffered a 2 per cent decrease and profits, investments, rents and fees a 23 per cent decrease. During the thirteen years of the succeeding Conservative governments although there was increased industrial unrest the unions continued their moderate policies and secured a steady improvement in the relative income of their members. The increasing wealth of the nation and the rapid expansion of the consumer goods industries provided a much higher standard of living for everyone, while the success of union policies combined with the redistribution of wealth through government taxation policies blurred the erstwhile clear distinction between the working and middle classes. Gradually it became evident that the unions had largely won the long drawn-out struggle that had started with the Combination Acts of 1799 and 1800.

Size and number of unions

Since the industrial unrest of the 1920s the number of trade unions has been drastically reduced, while the membership has similarly increased. In 1920, the peak year, there were 1,384 unions compared with 591 in 1964. This has been achieved largely by amalgamation. There are now eighteen unions each with over 100,000 membership which together account for 68·3 per cent of total union membership. The very big union is thus part of the industrial scene. These unions, organized on a national scale, have produced problems which have emerged particularly since 1945 but have their origins with the growth of big organization.

Shop Stewards

The shop steward was originally a trade union member whose duty was to collect subscriptions at workshop level and act as a go-between for union officials and the workers. As the unions grew in size so the union officials tended to become more remote from the workers and the shop steward assumed a growing importance. The basic organizational unit of a union is a branch which may be centred on the place of work or on the geographical area of members. Full-time officials will normally oversee a whole district, but the spokesman for the members at the place of work is usually the shop steward. Where the branch is based upon a place of work the shop steward fits into the pattern very well, but if the branch is geographically sited a difficult situation arises. Interpretation of wage agreements and settlement of disputes are more easily dealt with through the man on the spot rather than bringing in a branch official from another factory. Shop stewards in a factory are quite likely to come together to consider common grievances and policies, and it is only a short step from there for shop stewards from several factories to get together to form an organization that is multi-union in membership and outside formal union organization and control. The consequence of this development is the unofficial strike and (if the shop stewards in an area are militant) the establishment of local power in the hands of men who are not necessarily committed to official union policy.

The unofficial strike has been prevalent in the period since 1945. A Court of Inquiry investigating labour relations at Briggs Motor Bodies Ltd, in 1957 found that there had been over 500 stoppages in just over two years. This is an extreme case and is an example taken from the one industry that is perhaps most afflicted with 'wild-cat' strikes, but serves to illustrate the problem that is inherent in trade union organization. If communications in unions are poor, if shop stewards are not trained to accept their function within the trade union and if employers and union officials do not give the right lead, then by virtue of the organization of the unions, unofficial strikes are almost inevitable.

Industrial unions

A possible solution to the problem of union structure is the industrial union. Management have for long argued that negotiations when several unions are involved are very cumbersome and union discipline of its members would be much easier if one union covered a whole industry. Unfortunately the deeply rooted traditions of the craft unions and the jealously guarded privileges of many other unions have precluded much progress in this direction so far, though there have been several attempts. The general workers' unions are both big and strong, and their membership covers many industries. Many members of craft unions feel that if they joined an industrial union the craftsmen's interests would be swamped by the semi-skilled and unskilled workers. The two industries, coal and railways, that have evolved an industrial union structure have not succeeded in recruiting all their workers to a single union. The railwaymen are divided between the National Union of Railwaymen and the Associated Society of Locomotive Engineers and Firemen, while in the railway workshops and in the coalmines many of the craftsmen belong to the engineering unions. The trade union movement thus seems to suffer from its past. Its structural pattern, although irrational, seems to have ossified. Industrial union structure would provide very big unions which would give all the workers in each industry a sense of unity and would provide the research, education and legal facilities that can come only from a big organization.

The Trades Union Congress

In one way, British trade unions are at an advantage compared with those in Europe. The Trades Union Congress, although it has little controlling power over the unions, is at least a single organization which in size and influence is much bigger than any in Europe. Political and religious differences have divided trade union organizations on the Continent. In France and Italy there are three national union organizations based on the Communists, the Roman Catholics and the Social Democrats. In Germany and Sweden there are separate organizations for manual and non-manual workers. In the USA there were two central organizations from the 1930s to the 1950s, one based on the craft unions and the other (a breakaway organization led by John L. Lewis) based on industrial unions, but they have now come together to form the American Federation of Labour and Congress of Industrial Organizations.

The British Trades Union Congress, founded in 1868, is by comparison long established and enjoys a status whereby it is consulted by the government and its views are regarded with respect.

Trade unions and politics

The close association of the trade union movement with the Labour Party had led to the unions' being deeply involved in British politics. The majority of unions are affiliated to the Labour Party. Two active union leaders in their book on the trade unions[76] say: 'Most of them (active British trade unionists) would, however, subscribe to the general view that fairly substantial changes are needed in the structure of our existing society if workers' interests are to be properly protected. There are very few of them, if any, who would deny that political action is necessary for the full attainment of trade union objectives'. This close association has militated against close cooperation between the unions and the Conservative governments which have been in office for much of the period since 1918. In 1951 with the advent of the first postwar Conservative government the General Council of the Trades Union Congress issued a statement which claimed: 'It is our long-standing practice to seek to work amicably with whatever government is in power and through consultation with Ministers and the other side of industry to find practical solutions to the social and economic problems facing this country'.[77] The years that followed witnessed an uneasy truce between the two sides when it was evident that neither the unions nor the Conservative government wished to return to the more direct confrontation of the interwar period, but the political differences remain. Industrial conflict is inevitable in a society where the distribution of wealth is challenged and where the unions seek to secure for their members not just a constant share of a steadily increasing national wealth, but a greater share of that wealth.

Productivity agreements

The most hopeful sign that new attitudes are being adopted is the appearance of productivity agreements in the 1960s. The forerunner of these (and there are not very many so far), was the agreement signed between the Esso Company and relevant trade unions at the oil refinery at Fawley. In return for the abolition of restrictive practices by the unions and the drastic reduction of overtime working, the company granted pay increases of about 40 per cent. This agreement was made only after very close and detailed discussion between both sides of the industry concerned, when the full picture of the benefit to the workers was put before the workers' representatives and adequate compensation was guaranteed for those workers made redundant. A similar agreement was signed in 1966 between the Esso Company and the Transport and General Workers Union on behalf of the transport drivers and distribution workers. The number of workers' grades was reduced from twenty or more to five, and although it was accepted that each worker would specialize in

194

one main function he would be allowed by the unions to do other jobs connected with his special work: restrictive practices were abolished. Overtime was reduced to two hours per week, bonuses and special payments were incorporated in the basic rates of pay. A truck driver found that by accepting these rationalizations his working week was reduced by one hour but his basic pay went up from £13 6s 3d to £21. Productivity agreements such as these indicate an important step forward in employer/union cooperation and indicate that in some parts of industry at least, the bitterness and hostility of the past are being forgotten. It would be wrong, however, to suggest that productivity agreements are as yet an established pattern of procedure. Professor Blackett has pointed out that[78] 'the number of work-days lost in Britain by strikes in manufacturing industries is much lower than in France, Italy or the USA. The average working week is a little longer than in Germany and markedly longer than in the USA, and British workers work to a later age'. This is, at least in part, an indication of the damage to productivity that restrictive practices are causing in British industry as opposed to the strikes that usually make the news.

The role of trade unions in a modern economy is now a subject of national debate. The need for controlled increases in national productivity and the control of inflation is paramount in economic policy and the traditional activity of free collective bargaining is being brought into question. The ability of the trade unions to modify their structure and amend their policies to suit the changing economic scene will depend upon the extent to which their past history has developed deeply ingrained attitudes that are resistant to change. It is certain that no policy for change will have any chance of success if it does not accept the influence of the past.

The question that still has to be decided is whether the change that is bound to come in the unions in the light of increasing affluence will involve greater centralization of power in the Trades Union Congress or the abrogation of that power in favour of a central government control.

14

Problems of the modern economy

So far in this book, we have dealt with the broad factors influencing the evolution of the British economy and the main features and problems of the major industries. Now the time has come to look at the British economy as a whole and to consider the mould into which it has been cast by its industrial evolution.

Modern Britain has evolved as a nation of over fifty-four million people concentrated in a comparatively small area dependent on the rest of the world for much of its food and many of the raw materials that it needs. Trade with the rest of the world is thus necessary for survival and economic growth. Since the importance of her natural resources has declined Britain has come to rely on highly sophisticated industries, the products of which can be used both to help cover the balance of payments and to increase the nation's standard of living. The lead which Britain held, but has now lost, has given her a place among the world's wealthiest nations with a correspondingly huge supply of capital to promote future increases in wealth. Standards of living are high and full employment has been achieved by the exploitation of economic policies and circumstances outlined in Chapter 5. The wealth of Britain is such that it can afford to employ a high proportion of the labour force in providing those services which are a hallmark of a sophisticated economy.

The problems of Britain's economy are thus not concerned with how to become wealthy but how to achieve the fastest pace of economic growth in conditions of affluence. Keynesian economics were designed to bring the idle factors of production into use in order to promote an increase in the national income through increased investment. Keynes was writing and campaigning in times of mass unemployment and low levels of investment: these problems have been overcome and new ones have emerged. Now that the bogey of unemployment has been successfully laid, and now that the pattern of modern industry has been established, two major problems stand out, productivity and inflation. The two are closely interrelated. In conditions of full employment there is inevitably a strong pressure on all the factors of production; there is an inherent tendency for the competition for labour and capital to push up prices because labour and raw materials in particular are in short supply. Firms, in their anxiety to make sure they have an adequate labour force will offer high wages; the ordinary forces of supply and demand ensure that the cost of materials is rising. This is what the economist calls cost-push inflation. This is combined with demand inflation brought about by the rising demand induced by high incomes. Inflation thus seems to be a concomitant of full employment. Apart from the distress that it can cause to people on fixed incomes, inflation, if allowed to occur at a pace faster than that of Britain's principal rivals in world markets, will make it very difficult for Britain to sell her exports. This is a fact of life which is now commonly recognized in this country, because inflation has existed for nearly thirty years. Certainly the control of inflation has been central to economic policy in Britain since the end of the Second World War. The all too familiar policy of stop–go represents the only answer, albeit an unsatisfactory one, that economists have so far found to the control of inflation.

The most important weapon in the fight against inflation is, undoubtedly, the increase of productivity: the increase in production per head of the working population. This is another way of describing a more efficient use of capital and a more economic use of the existing labour force and it is in the attempted achievement of these two fundamentals that Britain is affected by her economic evolution. Increased productivity can be achieved only by cooperation between the management of industry, the trade unions and the government but the approach to this cooperation in Britain is coloured by the relationship of all three over a long period of time. The nature of the problem can be seen if we look at productivity and inflation in turn.

Productivity

THE SIZE OF THE FIRM

One fact stands out from a review of Britain's major industries in modern times; the prosperous industries involve very big firms. All the industries reviewed in this book (and the industries selected are those of greatest importance to the economy) demonstrate the economies of scale that are being or can be obtained from amalagamation and merger. The motor vehicle industry is reduced to four big firms, three American owned or controlled challenged by one British owned and managed. The electrical engineering industry is dominated by giants as are the petrochemical industry, chemicals themselves, and steel. Coal, electricity supply and gas, being nationalized, are very big economic units. The oil industry has managed to keep the price of oil stable by the application of large capital sums in oil refining. The capital cost per ton of annual throughput of a refinery with an annual capacity of 5 million tons is only half that of a refinery with an annual capacity of 1 million tons. Oil firms are therefore big. BP and the Royal Dutch/Shell Group together account for about one-third of the international trade in crude oil and its products.

This is the age of the very big firm because the market is available for consumer goods in superabundance, which makes the production of goods in enormous quantities a sensible economic proposition. In a way the system perpetuates itself. The larger the firm the greater the economies of scale and, hence, the lower the price of the commodity produced. The low prices bring more and more people within the range of the manufacturers. The supply of motor vehicles is a good example. The price of the motor car has not changed significantly over the last twenty years or so. The cost of a popular family saloon is much the same today as it was not long after the war. If the depreciation of the currency is brought into account this means that the real price of a car has dropped substantially over twenty years because of the greatly improved techniques of production (automation in particular) that have been introduced over this time. More people can afford a car; this means an increased demand which brings even cheaper production costs.

Professor Galbraith has described the modern big firm as a basic planning unit which 'can effectively fix minimum prices. It can manage consumer wants. In conjunction with other corporations, it can control prices of production requirements and arrange supplies at these prices. And it can extract from revenues the savings it needs for growth and expansion'.[79] The big firm has thus secured for itself a control of the home market in the commodities with which it is concerned, which gives it an advantage that a smaller firm, relying much more on the forces of supply and demand, cannot possibly match.

British industry has required some jostling to persuade firms to merge their interests after what were, in many cases, very long histories as independent units. Lack of competition from abroad in the early days minimized the inducement to amalgamate. Independence is attractive to a firm provided it is competing on equal terms with its rivals. Even when competition came in overseas markets, especially after 1914, there was still reluctance to lose independence because there was not the same urgency over exports as there was to be after 1945. Tardiness over amalgamation in the coal industry, as we have seen, led to nationalization. The steel industry was engaging in last minute mergers before it too was taken over in 1967. In shipbuilding the Geddes Report pinpointed the size of the firm as a major cause of the failure of the industry to compete favourably in world markets. Amalgamation, as we have seen, was recommended. The aircraft industry was obliged to bring about substantial mergers in order to survive, and even then the Concorde project had to be shared with France because the capital costs were so enormous. The governments concerned have underwritten the cost. Only in the chemical industry was there an early acceptance of the need for the big firm. Reluctance to change has been overcome in almost all the major industries by now either because nationalization has taken place, or the government has compelled amalgamation (using a carrot or a stick) or because firms have been obliged to merge for sheer economic survival.

Economists argue over the optimum level of production. In practice there is no evidence that British industry has reached optimum level. The competition with

US industry particularly shows the advantages of American bigness. The report on the productivity of the chemical industry referred to in Chapter 11 shows that even firms as big as ICI cannot match the productivity of the big American firms. Dupont, the biggest American chemical firm has a turnover almost half as big again as the turnover of ICI (Dupont $3,021 million, ICI $2,285 million).[80]

INTERNATIONAL FIRMS

For Britain internal amalgamation of industry is not the whole answer. Efficient production for the home market is only part of the problem in an economy which is so dependent upon successful exports. If a large company controlling the home market is not as productive as a major company overseas the result will be evident in export performance. The pursuit of increased productivity has thus now passed the stage in the key export industries where the big British firms are adequate. The next stage is becoming evident. Industries are becoming international in scope and size because of the size of the international market.

Here again the Americans with their much bigger home market as a basis for large scale production, are showing how the big firms can compete successfully overseas even with tariff barriers to surmount. Britain in the nineteenth century took advantage of her economic superiority to invest overseas and reap a rich reward. The USA is doing the same thing in our times from a similar position of superiority. From 1945 to 1965 USA invested $13,894 million in Europe ($5,119 million in Britain), which constituted 6 per cent of industry.[81]

No matter how efficient any British firm may be it is now evident that in straight competition with the USA in the major industries, the USA has the advantage. We have noted earlier in this book how Britain is well advanced in the higher technologies. Britain spends nearly 3 per cent of her national income each year on research and development, which is nearly the same percentage as the Americans and considerably more than France or Germany, but Britain's efforts are still small, in actual value, compared with the Americans. Britain, for example, is well in advance of other European countries in the computer industry, but her share of the market in Europe is only 15 per cent, the USA taking the lion's share. The conclusion to be drawn from this is that a concentration of the higher technologies is being formed largely in the USA and that the resulting overflow of investment capital is swamping not only British but European investment in the new industries which are likely to be the predominant industries of the next few decades. *Time Magazine* claimed in 1968 (January), that US companies owned half of all modern industry in Britain. This may have been an exaggeration but 75 per cent of US capital invested in this country has been in the growth industries reviewed in this book: electronics, motor vehicles, computers, pharmaceuticals, petroleum and office machinery.

These American sales in Europe increase the number of units over which the research and development costs have to spread; this in turn makes the Americans more competitive and by the same token makes it more difficult for British firms to make headway with their higher prices. Britain has attracted far more capital from America than any other European country has done, twice the investment in Germany and three times that in France. In this way Britain has, perhaps, affected its chances of growth more than elsewhere.

THE COMMON MARKET AND INCREASED PRODUCTIVITY

An argument that emerges clearly from a study of Britain's past and its application to the present situation is that it is important to keep ahead in the most modern technologies. Failure to do this will place Britain once again in a dangerous situation where developing countries with the benefit of cheap labour will be able to challenge staple industries, with the resultant threat to Britain's standard of living. The challenge of American economic advance emphasizes these dangers but also stresses the advantages that would accrue to Britain from membership of an economically united Europe. If the industries of Europe (including Britain) were to have a common home market it would be one of 240 million people. This would give European industry the same impetus as that of the Americans, while the size of the firm could rise to that of the largest US firms.

The size of the firm is thus vital, particularly because Britain exports such a high proportion of the gross national product. The greatest market potential for Britain is to be found in those countries where high income has created a demand for sophisticated consumer goods. These countries are also Britain's competitors. If they were to group together to form one unit in Europe with Britain outside, no matter how efficient British industry might be it would not compete effectively with either Europe or the USA. This is the prime economic argument that has persuaded all the major political parties to support entry into the Common Market. The argument was so strong by the late 1960s that political objections to union with Europe were overcome. This is in keeping with the lesson of history that economic motive frequently determines political change.

The second economic argument to support Britain's participation in the Common Market is also concerned with increased productivity. Adam Smith set out the advantages of free trade in the late eighteenth century and these have never been disputed since. The Law of Comparative Costs is still basic in the economics of international trade. We have noted that because of the disparity in wealth of the nations of Europe free trade was not a success in the past, but now that the main countries of Europe are on a reasonably equal footing the way is clear for international division of labour to become a working proposition. The removal of tariff barriers promotes the maximum volume of international trade; this means greater competition but a bigger market. In theory this should produce bigger and more efficient firms. For Britain it means that there is increasing emphasis upon productivity.

MONOPOLY LAWS

The growth of the big firms, although a feature of the economy from the beginning of the century, has accelerated in pace since 1945. This has produced a suspicion of monopolies and restrictive practices that has crystallized in the Monopolies Commission and the Restrictive Practices Court. The former was set up in 1948; it is empowered to investigate industries in which one-third of the final output or the processing or the export of a good is in the hands of a single firm. The Restrictive Practices Court was established in 1956 to consider whether any agreement between two or more parties which limits freedom in respect of prices, sales or production is in the public interest. All such agreements have to be registered with the Registrar of Restrictive Practices, and the onus is upon the parties concerned to demonstrate that the agreements are positively in the public interest. The court consists of five judges and up to ten laymen.

It is ironic that these two should have come into being at a time when the economic mergers that give quasimonopoly power are seen to be necessary if Britain is to meet the challenge from overseas. A double standard of monopoly seems to have evolved in consequence. If a firm is supplying the home market and exporting little, it and its fellow firms in the trade are liable to come under the close scrutiny of the law. If, on the other hand, a firm is engaged in considerable export trade then competition is deemed to be supplied from overseas rivals. In this way the major British car firm, although it controls 40 per cent of the British market has not been the subject of an enquiry by the Monopolies Commission, whereas Lucas, the electrical component manufacturers to the industry have so been. The government of the day is likely to find itself in something of a dilemma. In 1966 for example, a merger was tentatively proposed between ICI and Courtaulds which would have placed over 90 per cent of the production of manmade fibres in the hands of one very big firm. The negotiations broke down, thus obviating the need for action by the Monopolies Commission, but the decision on the matter would have been an interesting one. Should the firm be allowed to become very big in order to compete more successfully with the American and European competition, or should a merger be forbidden on the grounds of possible abuse?

The Labour government in 1965 created the Industrial Reorganization Corporation (IRC) with a view to bringing about regroupings and amalgamations in industry at a pace faster than would otherwise occur if firms were left to their own devices. The IRC has the right to draw up to £150 million from the Treasury to help oil the wheels of rationalization where this will obviously improve productivity. Also in 1965 the government passed the Monopolies and Mergers Act which gives power to the government to hold up proposed mergers while their rivals are investigated by the Monopolies Commission.

Britain is thus at the crossroads in this respect. The Americans made their decision in the matter at the time of their Anti-Trust Laws but they were not being challenged by any overseas country which could undercut their sales abroad. Monopoly is still frowned upon in the USA, but because the individual firms are enormous in any case, due to the size of the markets, there is not the same conflict over monopoly.

GOVERNMENT AND THE USE OF CAPITAL

The more efficient use of capital as a means of increasing productivity is not now left exclusively to private enterprise firms, big though they may be. The importance to the national economy of employing sophisticated techniques of production and developing new products and inventions has been recognized as the province also of the state.

This is an example, of which there is an increasing number, of the complementary functions of private enterprise and the state. The small firm still exists in industry and has an important part to play in a mixed economy, but sometimes lacks the capital and the marketing facilities for new products. The National Research Development Corporation (NRDC) was set up by the Development of Inventions Act 1948 to examine new inventions and to consider their value for development and commercial exploitation. It does not initiate research projects but investigates inventions submitted to it by the public and small firms; in suitable cases, with loans from the government, it arranges further technical and commercial development. The Hovercraft is a good example of an invention that it has helped to promote. It is also concerned with promoting new production techniques, particularly the use of automation in manufacturing industry. There is sometimes small incentive to instal automation in a private firm because of the disruption to existing production flow and the experimental nature of the work; automated systems are notoriously prone to breakdown in their early stages. The NRDC has initiated a scheme whereby firms are invited to submit schemes involving the automation of manufacturing processes; development and installation costs will be paid for by the corporation in suitable cases, but any participating firm must agree to act as guinea pig and pass on the full details of the experiment for the benefit of others, which it would not wish to do were it paying for the whole installation itself. Up to 1967 eight projects had been accepted, mainly in the plastics industry, printing and food.

The Ministry of Technology, established in late 1964 to coordinate and promote efforts to increase productivity in industry, has become very much involved with the application of automation. It has for example, provided £3 for very £1 provided by industry towards research specifically into industrial instrumentation, up to a maximum government contribution of £1 million.

AUTOMATION

Automation is one aspect of production that promises significant increases in productivity. The four types of automation have been defined in the chapter on postwar affluence where the contribution of automation to postwar increases in productivity was commented upon. It is estimated[82] that British industry and the government between them will have spent £1,600 million to £2,500 million on automation by 1980. This, it is thought, will lead to a 3 to 5 per cent reduction in costs and an equivalent increase in output and rise in productivity. We have noted how automation has been successfully applied to the chemical and steel industries for continuous processing. The airlines and the commercial banks have been the big spenders on computers. Many smaller firms have, however, purchased computers for office accounting and process control equipment for assembly lines. In general automation has gone ahead much faster in offices, banks, hire purchase firms, insurance companies etc. because introduction of an automated process causes far less disruption in these spheres than in industry. For that reason NRDC introduced its scheme (noted above) for encouraging industrial automation. The fact remains that the big firm in industry has the capital to involve itself in risk and is, therefore, the big spender in automation. Peach and Tozer, for example (part of United Steel) have six 110 ton arc furnaces controlled by a computer which is designed to dovetail production requirements with an off-peak tariff agreed with the CEGB. The installation is now working well, but broke down thirty times in its first year. The smaller firms in industry cannot afford disruption of that nature.

EDUCATION, TRAINING AND PRODUCTIVITY

Another feature evident from a survey of Britain's modern industries is that they are all science-based. The rapid advance of technology has transformed productivity rates through greatly improved machinery, computer control, the use of newly discovered materials, and so on. The twentieth century has, therefore, created a demand for scientists and technologists which is so great that the education and training of labour is of paramount importance to the nation's economy. A high degree of specialization is required from people who work for a big firm. The bigger the firm, the narrower the specialization. The term 'electrical engineer', for example, is now only a very broad description of what was at one time looked upon as a specialist occupation. An electrical engineer these days is a specialist in one only of a long list of specializations – transformers, switchgear, electronics, telecommunications, transmission, control, application and so on. The electrical industry is itself divided into heavy engineering, consumer appliances, electronics and control with a considerable overlap into mechanical engineering. Originally men could be trained for the crafts involved by the firm employing them, but twentieth-century technology demands a long expensive training with considerable academic background. Education has thus been caught up in the economic whirlpool and the incessant demand for increased productivity.

No firm can itself expect to provide training for all the specialists it requires so that in a modern economy the state is expected to provide the facilities within its education scheme for much of these high level skills. A partnership has grown up between the state and the institutions of further and higher education whereby the necessary supply of highly educated labour is reasonably assured. Galbraith has pointed out[83] that when the state of the economy demanded that the majority of workers should be unskilled or semiskilled, the education system, private or state run, provided comparatively little in the higher levels of education. It is not a cynical statement to suggest that the education system is motivated by economic pressures, it is a fact. When there is a demand for a large number of skilled scientists and engineers the education system provides the basic training. There is, however a time lag because the state is supplying the training for an economy which is largely run by private enterprise, and there is no system of coordinated planning. Furthermore, the cost of the education system is met by the taxpayer. The willingness of the taxpayer to finance an expansion of the higher education system has to be set against the taxpayer's desire to spend his income on consumer goods. Britain does not come out of this very well. Politics enter this too. Increased productivity in the future has to be shown to be the desirable alternative to immediate consumption. There is keen competition, anyway, for the funds available for public investment – we have seen how investment in the nationalized industries has involved enormous expenditure since 1945. The pressing demands on government expenditure are well enough known. The education system thus has to compete with other claimants for money to enable it to expand. Yet the increased productivity of industry depends more and more upon the supply of highly skilled labour.

Much of the cost of the lower levels of education is still covered by local authority rates (about 50 per cent of the rate bill). The level of rates has now become a national issue. Payment of rates is a painful affair for the householder because it is, unlike most income tax, not deducted at source. There is thus a logical connection between the need for spending more as a nation on education and the national debate on how that money should be raised.

There has been a remarkable expansion in recent times of the further and higher education system in Britain. Twenty-one new universities have been founded or named since 1960 to augment the twenty-four that already existed. From 1956 to 1966 the number of university places has doubled while government spending has tripled over the same period. In addition there are thirty polytechnics being developed from existing colleges of technology, all contributing to the supply of engineers and scientists for research, design and the practical requirements of industry. Nor must the increasing emphasis on efficient management be overlooked in the establishment of business courses and business colleges, the Schools of Business Studies at London and Manchester being set up in 1963 specifically with close government support to give the lead in this field. Harvard Business School was established in 1905.

How does Britain compare in this respect with her chief competitors? The situation today is much better than it was in the 1950s and early 1960s. The time lag then produced alarming discrepancies, particularly between Britain and the USA and USSR.[84]

In 1958 in Britain there were 19·9 per 1,000 of the population at university. In Holland, West Germany, Italy, Belgium, Switzerland, Sweden and Austria there were over 30 per 1,000.[85] Any comparison between one country and another can be only a rough guide. It is possible to assess the percentage of GNP devoted to education and to quote the number of scientists and engineers trained in a given period but these statistics do not consider quality of training or use of skilled labour once that training has taken place. However, it seems that Britain has been slow in developing the potential of her skilled manpower.

The reasons for this are to be found in part, in Britain's particular evolution. During the period of Britain's economic supremacy the emphasis in education lay in the need for initiative and enterprise in administration and trade. The engineer and the scientist were not considered to be so important because of the limited place that their work was seen to have in the community. A classical education was thus felt to be right for the leaders of industry and the Empire. The ancient Greeks, in particular, were greatly admired and they, it will be remembered, were prone to scorn the applications of science. The advent of state schemes of compulsory education in the 1870s brought no significant change. Only when the need for technologists became really pressing did the emphasis on applied mathematics and science in the secondary schools occur. There are many commentators who now suggest that the pendulum has swung too far and that in pursuit of the advantages of a technological age we have lost sight of the prime purpose of education. That is not a subject to be disputed here; we are simply noting that the pendulum has swung in Britain although it was a little late in swinging.

THE BRAIN DRAIN

One consequence of the training of so many more highly skilled personnel in Britain has been the so-called brain drain. Apparently the demand for skill has outpaced the supply even in the USA where the output of graduates has been so much greater for so long. Britain, because of the language link, is the most attractive source of labour. The USA, because of its great wealth, can offer a higher standard of living and superior research facilities; these are advantages that cannot be countered. In the short term Britain stands to lose because public money is spent in Britain on costly training which is exported to the USA free of charge. In the long term the results of research in the USA will benefit all, even if the commercial exploitation of the research will be controlled by the Americans in the first instance. In any case there can be no effective legislation to stop emigration, nor is it desirable. Britain stopped trying to ban the emigration of skilled artisans in the nineteenth century.

205

THE EFFICIENCY OF LABOUR

We have considered how the size of the firm and the education and training of the labour force affect productivity. Now we come to the third aspect of the economy that is similarly concerned with productivity–the efficiency of labour.

TRADE UNIONS

In her trade union system Britain is at a marked disadvantage. Germany and Japan, the two competitors who have achieved spectacular growth rates have an industrial structure that has improved since 1945. Britain's industrial structure has been improved by rule of thumb over a period of over 200 years. In Chapter 13 the evolution of the trade union movement was briefly outlined. When a movement struggles for recognition over a very long period of time it is not surprising to find that it clings tenaciously to its hard won gains, but in doing so it is bound to appear old fashioned as time goes by. In the period of full employment since 1945 the unions in Britain have not kept pace with the fast-changing economic conditions. Apart from the modern need for industrial unions (see Chapter 13) there has been a need for the unions to promote increased industrial productivity. In the USA the unions have accepted much more readily than in Britain that increased mechanization and automation will bring increased prosperity to union members and society in general. The unions in Britain in times of full-employment have been able to bring pressure to bear on employers: skilled labour has been scarce and in order to retain it management has yielded ground to the unions and passed the cost on to the consumer. The yielding of ground has not always been over wages; frequently it has been over the use of labour. Jobs have been protected and employment has been guaranteed at the expense of efficiency. Restrictive practices have grown up which have had an almost measurable effect upon productivity. The Fawley productivity agreement was the forerunner of what, it is to be hoped, will be many productivity agreements whereby overmanning of industry is replaced by the efficient use of labour. Overmanning has also occurred because of the readiness of the management to hoard labour against the time when during boom periods orders are flowing in and the demand for labour is high.

MANAGEMENT

We have, therefore, a picture of a strong but old-fashioned Trade Union movement in Britain persuading a none-too-strong management to pass on the cost of low productivity to the consumer. There are many British firms with forceful, dynamic management but the broad picture portrays a British weakness in management that is reflected by the unprofessional labour relations policies that are pursued. A comparison with American management shows the deficiencies of the British technique. The Harvard Business School and others in the USA have long pointed the way to the need for professional standards in management. It has been realized in the USA that productivity levels are determined more by management than by the unions. Business schools have now been established in Britain and far greater attention is now paid to management training, but the USA has a long lead. It is only fair to add that the attitude towards management in the USA has been helped all the time by the attitude of all sides of industry in America that the profit motive is a respectable one, and that management has a right to manage. In Britain the prolonged emphasis on class conflict has challenged the right of ownership and questioned the right to manage, thereby making management more difficult. The difference between the two reflects the different heritages of the two countries.

LOCATION OF INDUSTRY

The efficiency of labour is also affected by the changes in location of industry that have taken place over the long period of Britain's industrial evolution. The migration of population to the north of England in the nineteenth century followed by the movement to the south in the twentieth century has presented a twofold problem. Industry has been run down in the areas of earlier development thereby creating a problem of unemployment and of under-used social and fixed capital. The growth of the Midlands, London and the South-East has presented the difficulties, exactly opposite, of overfull employment and over-use of social and fixed capital. The problems are not exclusive to Britain. France, for example, is troubled by the slow development of the outlying agricultural areas of Brittany and the south-west, while Germany is faced with the decline of the coal industry in the Ruhr. Holland is concerned with the growth of a conurbation that threatens to make the Hague, Rotterdam and Amsterdam one continuous built-up area. There is common concern, particularly now that the scheme to build a Channel tunnel has been officially sponsored, that there will be an enormous concentration of population in Europe (including Britain) in a triangle roughly bounded by Birmingham, Paris and Ham in Germany while other areas decline. The development of the Common Market is bound to accentuate this problem. The danger is of an imbalance, naturally induced, that will engender economic inefficiency, to say nothing of a decline in social amenities that would be overcome utlimately only by a redispersal of industry. It remains to be seen whether this redispersal will be achieved by government intervention before the imbalance goes too far.

In Britain the aid given to the areas of earlier industrialization has been part of government policy since the 1930s. The change in emphasis of government aid can be seen by the succession of titles these areas have been given. In the first instance they were labelled depressed areas, then growth areas and now development areas. Government aid is substantial and has become increasingly so as the social and economic arguments for aid become more pressing. The social injustice of the existence of areas of slow development in an otherwise booming economy is self-evident but the point to be emphasized here is that in times of full employment and a

207

national shortage of labour, one obvious way of overcoming that shortage of labour is to use to the full the existing supply. Government aid to the development areas has always been of the same kind. Industry has been attracted to the area by means of financial inducement. The Board of Trade has built factories for lease or sale at attractive prices or firms have been offered substantial assistance towards the cost of building their own. Furthermore firms have been allowed very considerable tax allowance to set against the cost of machinery and plant installed in these factories. In the Development Area of Scotland, Wales, the North, Merseyside and the South West the present grants cover 45 per cent of the cost of plant and machinery and up to 35 per cent of the cost of new buildings. Government retraining centres have been set up to assist with the labour problem, and loans have been made available for working capital. Meanwhile firms outside the Development Areas have found it increasingly difficult to secure an industrial development certificate for any factory or extension of over 5,000 square feet.

The more recent thinking behind government aid to these areas has recognized that their economic and social amenities must be improved in order to make firms anxious to move there. If an area declines because of a contracting industry the road system, housing and public facilities tend, at the best, to stagnate while in the more prosperous parts of the country constant improvement is likely to be taking place. A gap opens up which militates against the reintroduction of industry. Particular attention is now being paid to these amenities in the Development Areas and regions are being developed as a whole rather than as many disconnected communities.

There has been some concern about the continuation of these schemes if Britain enters the Common Market. It is felt by some that the Market rules about subsidizing industry will conflict with state help for the Development Areas. The preamble to the Treaty of Rome, however, refers to 'reducing the gaps between the different regions and the backwardness of the least favoured' as one of the Market's principal aims. The EEC Commission is specifically empowered to authorize exception to the rules on state aid and in addition, the Community has an Investment Bank (EIB) and a Social Fund both of which may make contributions to solving regional problems. In this way Britain's efforts to improve the overall efficiency of her labour force by overcoming regional unemployment will be partly safeguarded. There is a danger, however, that rather than transfer to a Development Area a long way from the prosperous markets, firms will go across the Channel and still be close to London and the South-East.

The alternative to promoting growth in the Development Areas is to encourage the movement of labour to those areas where labour is in short supply. The need for government action on this has been recognized ever since the introduction of labour exchanges by Churchill in 1909. Government retraining centres have been established not just for the Development Areas but also to train labour for industry elsewhere. There are now thirty-eight training centres providing 8,000 places for training in forty different trades, the majority being in the engineering and construction industries. There has been resistance by the unions to the employment of such retrained labour at the same rate of pay as for craftsmen trained by the orthodox apprentice scheme but the number of training centres has increased in spite of this. The increasing use of automation makes it certain that the need for retraining will increase.

A picture thus emerges of increases in productivity in British industry made possible by the efforts of the industrial firms (particularly the big ones) themselves,

Table 14.1

The number required to produce the same output as one man in the USA

	Steel	Chemicals	Metal products	Electrical machinery	Transport equipment	Non-electrical machinery
USA	1·0	1·0	1·0	1·0	1·0	1·0
Britain	2·3	3·4	2·2	4·2	3·2	3·5
West Germany	1·7	2·6	3·2	3·8	2·4	3·2
France	1·6	3·0	3·1	2·6	2·0	2·3
Sweden	n/a	2·5	2·6	2·3	1·4	1·9
Italy	1·2	2·5	4·2	2·3	2·1	2·4

Source: *The Economist*, 1 Oct., 1966.

the trade unions in cooperation with the firms, and the government supplementing the work of both. The need for all three to work harmoniously is becoming increasingly apparent although the old traditions of laissez-faire are still, in one form or another, militating against the smooth working of the economy. Table 14.1 shows the leeway that Britain still has to make up in comparison with other nations.

Inflation

If increases in productivity are achieved there still remains the problem of controlling inflation, which we look at next. Productivity increases themselves help to combat a rise in prices but experience has shown that they are not effective on their own. The imperfections of the economy that we have already noted have produced since 1945 a chronic inflation which is constantly working against the steady pace of economic growth. The rôle of government has become accepted in this context without question. Keynesian policies have secured full employment and the government is expected to ensure that inflation does not extend beyond reasonable limits.

The policies applied to the problem of inflation have reached the same stage by the late sixties as had the policies to cope with unemployment between the wars. In both instances the thinking of the time was that cure was a necessary but temporary expedient, while prevention, if it could be found, was the real answer. Since 1945 a succession of governments has had to come to grips with inflation and it has been dealt with by a variety of monetary and fiscal policies, but none of these has succeeded in getting at the root cause of rising prices.

The Labour government of the immediate postwar period was, of course, engaged in implementing full employment policies in a period when the shortage of raw materials of all kinds resulting from the war greatly aggravated the inflation problem. Furthermore there was the difficult problem of an excess of purchasing power that had been built up over the war period but which had been held in check by wartime control of prices and physical restrictions. In any case, with the memory of the prewar mass unemployment so acute, it was some time before there was agreement that the disinflationary policies necessary in times of full employment should be followed. The six or seven years following the war must be looked upon as a period of acute problems caused by the war and a time when the policy of full employment was implemented and accepted. The government of the day found itself in an embarrassing dilemma. There was a pressing need to increase output particularly in the export industries, but there was an alarming shortage of capital. Investment could come only from increased savings, but savings were low and would be made lower by the policies for redistribution of wealth to which the government was committed and the high level of taxation which was necessary to siphon off the excess of purchasing power. The policies that were pursued were, therefore, contradictory. Initially taxation was reduced, but subsequently it was substantially increased. On the other hand the cheap money policy of the 1930s was continued in contradiction to the Keynesian doctrine that low interest rates were to be applied in a recession and not in a period of inflation. Like all attempts since 1945 these contradictory policies were a mixture of success and failure. Government expenditure was heavy and full employment was achieved, but inflation was not checked sufficiently while unpopular controls had to be retained in order to hold back demand for limited capital resources.

Since 1951, as it has become clear that the prime consequence of full employment is inflation, so policies have been applied to cope with it. Fiscal and monetary policies which are designed to control the movements of the economy in many directions have been increasingly applied to deal with rising prices and excessive rises in income. Cheap money has been dispensed with and manipulation of the bank rate to control demand for capital resources has become very familiar. The credit squeeze combined with a policy of high taxation has become the orthodox technique for siphoning off excess spending power creating inflationary pressure. At regular intervals, coinciding inevitably with an adverse balance of payments, successive governments have 'taken the steam' out of the economy by using these methods, but in so doing have damaged the pace of economic growth by applying methods that constitute a temporary cure rather than prevention. Each time the credit squeeze has been applied the rate of investment has been cut back because a climate has been created that has discouraged the necessary investment for growth. Taxation is not effective if incomes rise to counter its effects; price control is not possible if, except in the public sector, the government has been given no power to intervene. All that any government can do in these circumstances is to exhort and cajole, but the level of incomes and prices remains firmly in the hands of the employers and the unions.

There have been attempts to control the level of incomes. In 1949 the unions were persuaded by Sir Stafford Cripps to accept a wage freeze because of the obvious economic dilemma in which Britain found itself, but the 'freeze' lasted no longer than twelve months and there was no attempt to regulate incomes in any way. Similarly in 1961 Selwyn Lloyd imposed a wages pause which was not very successful and incurred the hostility of the unions who objected to the absence of control on any other form of income. The Labour government of 1964 established a Prices and Incomes Board which is intended to decide whether increases in income and prices are necessary or in the interests of the national economy but the Board has been operating in the climate of a severely adverse balance of payments when the serious nature of the economic imbalance has been obvious to all. The government adopted temporary powers to impose another incomes freeze followed by a period of severe restraint, when the temporary powers were yielded.

The trade unions have reacted to attempts to centralize control over incomes by advocating a control over incomes by the TUC which would investigate all claims for increased wages in preference to the Prices and Incomes Board; the Board would continue, under their scheme, but only to vet increases in other forms of income and prices. The unions, ironically enough after their long struggle for legal recognition and a brief period of great strength in times of full employment, are being pressed to yield the central pivot of their sovereignty–control over wages.

Government, trade unions and industrialists

This is the stage of economic evolution that Britain has now reached. The relationship between those who control industry, the trade unions and the government are determined by the way in which each has secured its share in the control of the economy. In the early stages the owners of industry were predominant, labour was not properly organized and the government saw little reason to interfere. Labour ultimately became strongly organized only when the need for government intervention in economic affairs had become accepted by all political parties. The postwar era has seen a substantial strengthening of the rôle of government while the unions and those who control industry have yielded ground. It is becoming apparent that independent policies on the part of all three are no longer a satisfactory solution to the problem of achieving steady economic growth, but the exact rôle of government is ill-defined. The influence of politics cannot be ignored. The Labour Party had its origins in the trade union movement so that when in office the Labour Party has been able to achieve greater cooperation from the trade unions than has the Conservative Party. This does not mean that union leaders slavishly follow Labour Party directions nor even accept their policies, but there is mutual respect for each other's views. The Conservative Party on the other hand, though not commanding the same support from the trade unions, relies on the support of those (particularly industrialists) who are not anxious for the traditional virtues of private enterprise to be extinguished too rapidly by encroaching government control. Mr Edward Heath has stressed that Conservative policies are based on 'free enterprise, individual responsibilities, high wages, low costs and greater profits for firms'.[86] There are, of course, many examples of Conservative support amongst trade unions and of Labour support among industrialists, but the broad division holds true. The popular image of the two parties, though it has become blurred considerably since 1945, is still one of 'the working man' and 'the bosses'.

In fact the greatly increased influence of government in economic affairs demands that it should be independent of either side of industry. Here again the history of the major parties hinders the implementation of policies that are genuinely intended to be in the interests of the national economy because they are regarded with suspicion that is rooted far back, even as far as the nineteenth century. The control of inflation is now however so important to the concept of economic growth in Britain that it is taking precedence over the claims of both sides of industry to maintain themselves in entrenched positions of long standing. Throughout the 1960s the debate over government control of prices and incomes has intensified, particularly with the advent of a Labour government in 1964 and the possibility of active cooperation on the part of the unions. The issues involved are complex and farreaching. The difficulties are so numerous and daunting that any success in implementing a control of income through this means must be very gradual. A successful prices and incomes policy would mean a very significant step forward in government control and, hence, another big step away from laissez-faire convictions of the capitalism with which Britain began her industrial evolution. No small part of the difficulties in achieving this radical change will be the overcoming of the prejudices, hostilities and suspicions that Britain's earlier history has created.

The rôle of state

The rôle of government in promoting productivity and in controlling inflation is thus one of increasing importance. The part played by the state in managing the economy in the interests of economic growth has become more and more significant as Britain has increased her wealth. Indeed, this has been one of the main themes of this book.

Britain's economy is subject to the control of the state partly through state ownership and partly through government economic policies. No precise measurement of this is possible because policies and their effect are not measurable. The only assessment of state control possible is the value of the nationalized industries. By 1967 their net assets with steel were valued at nearly £12,000 million and their annual investment of £1,700 million was equivalent to the whole of that for private manufacturing industry. They contributed about 11 per cent of the gross domestic product and employed about 8 per cent of the total labour force.

A comparison with the other advanced economies is of interest here. France is the European country most like Britain in the extent of its public sector. Her railways were nationalized in 1936, and coal mines, electricity, gas, the Bank of France and some other banks were all nationalized immediately after the war. Also, the Renault motor firm is publicly owned and about half the French insurance business. In West Germany there is less public ownership. Railways have been nationalized and gas and electricity but apart from these and the Volkswagen motor firm German industry has remained in private hands. Private enterprise in Germany is, however, subject to laws relating either to supervisory councils or works councils which limit a company's independence. Italy, apart from nationalized railways and gas, has two publicly owned holding companies with shares in many firms that sometimes amount to a controlling interest. In Austria, as has been noted, the steel industry has been nationalized. The degree of public ownership in Scandinavia and Holland and Belgium is less than in Britain, so that Britain, with steel now in public ownership, must be regarded as one of the advanced capitalist economies with almost the highest level of public ownership. The USA has nothing like the same level of public ownership. Airlines, telephones, railways, radio and television are all still in private hands in the USA but nevertheless there is considerable intervention in the running of the economy by the Federal Government and independent regulatory agencies. All the countries mentioned are, of course, subject to the application of government economic policies which are governed by Keynesian economics and varying degrees of planning.

The conclusion must be drawn that the rôle of government has assumed a greater importance in Britain, partly because of the wide gap that has developed between the two sides of industry from earliest times. With the owners of industry actuated by a profit motive which the unions have found in many ways unacceptable, the gap has had to be met by government measures that compel both sides to yield ground. Although a similar gap does exist in the USA (the economy that offers the greatest contrast) it is not nearly so wide and the need for government measures has, accordingly, not been so strongly felt or acted upon.

15

Sterling as an international currency

The control that the government exerts over the economy is made more difficult by the fact that sterling has for so long been recognized as a major world currency. No other European country has this complication although the USA has a similar responsibility through the dollar. The sterling area came into being in the nineteenth century (see p. 15) at a time when Britain was the dominant nation in world trade. The role of sterling in international trade was emphasized in the 1930s when the gold standard was generally abandoned and exchange control took its place. An area emerged consisting of most of the British Empire, that part of the Middle East that was under British influence, the Scandinavian countries, and certain other countries inside and beyond Europe where the governments concerned preferred to align themselves with the pound. These were all countries that traded extensively with Britain and found mutual interest in maintaining exchange stability with Britain. Although there were no formal 'club rules' the members of the sterling area pooled their foreign reserves in London, holding their reserves in the form of sterling balances but reserving the right to exchange these reserves for other currencies if they thought it necessary. The number of countries in the sterling area has since diminished, but it still involves most of the ex-Empire countries, excluding Canada. Use of the currency of an individual state as an international currency produces a conflict of interest. The government of Britain in controlling the economy through fiscal and monetary measures has to consider not just what the internal repercussions of these measures will be, but also what the effect will be on the pound sterling in the world arena. The pound must be kept strong as far as possible, not just for the sake of the British economy but because of the threat that would otherwise arise to the sterling reserves of other countries. Devaluation thus becomes a very serious matter. There is a tendency in times of an adverse balance of payments, for governments to take extra-strong measures to control inflation in order to impress external creditors that the economy of the country is being kept on an even keel and that there is, in consequence, no danger of devaluation. This can mean that the stop part of stop–go is successful in persuading sterling investors that their sterling deposits are safe, but it can also have the effect of slowing down unnecessarily the pace of investment that is necessary to maintain a steady economic growth. This is another example of how Britain's past economic supremacy has made matters more difficult in the present.

Balance of payments

A characteristic of Britain's economy since 1945 has been the recurring crises over an adverse balance of payments. A protracted adverse balance in an advanced economy is always a sign of a maladjustment that must be tackled by serious measures, but such a difficulty was almost unknown before the war in Britain. The balance of payments problem had first appeared in 1931 when there was a very marked fall in invisible export earnings due to the world recession in trade and the corresponding fall in demand for shipping and other services provided by Britain. This was an exceptional circumstance. Britain, as we know, had long since been used to a wide trade gap which had to be covered by income from foreign investments, but until 1931 there had not been a deficit on current account. In the years that followed until 1939 only in one (1935) was there a favourable balance, but we do not associate these years with balance of payments crises. In fact Britain was able to sell assets overseas and borrow money in order to make up the difference, and in any case net invisible income was still sufficient to pay for one-third of the import of goods. The Second World War made the problem acute. A substantial proportion of British overseas assets were sold to help pay for the war and, with the export level being very low in 1945 Britain faced for the first time since the Industrial Revolution the prospect of great difficulty in paying its way. Britain had, in fact, been transformed into a manufacturing economy dependent vitally upon overseas trade but had lost the comfortable margin of safety built up during the period of economic supremacy. The only solution was an export drive to produce income that would replace the lost invisible income.

Net invisible income has never been restored to its prewar position of supplying the cost of one-third of imported goods. Since the war it has not exceeded 9 per cent of the cost of imports. The emphasis has thus been much more on exports and because these have fluctuated in relation to imports, there has been since 1945 a series of crises that has reflected these fluctuations. These crises must not be allowed to obscure the real situation. The success in developing exports has been remarkable. Whereas estimates immediately after the war suggested that exports would have to be 75 per cent above the prewar level in order to achieve a balance of payments equilibrium, in fact exports have risen to no less than 140 per cent while imports have increased by 40 per cent only since before the war. Furthermore, the crises occur only when an unfavourable balance shows signs of worsening. For much of the period since 1945 the balance of payments on current account has been favourable.

The nature of Britain's dependence upon exports in modern times will thus be seen. Britain has moved from an economy that exported goods in quantity in order to supplement existing income, to an economy that must export in quantity in order to maintain and expand the existing standards of living. In this context, control of inflation is very necessary. If inflation is not controlled exports become difficult to sell and a balance of payments crisis will be threatened.

The pace of economic growth

There can be no denying that Britain has become a very wealthy country and that standards of living have greatly increased since the war. The reasons for the remarkable economic growth in Britain since 1945 have been analysed in Chapter 5. The wealthier the country becomes the faster is the pace of economic growth because a small percentage rise in the national income each year means an increasing rise in income year by year even if the percentage growth remains the same. A 2 per cent rise in the USA can mean much more in terms of actual wealth than a 3 per cent rise in Britain or a 10 per cent rise in Japan. In spite of postwar affluence there are, however, criticisms of Britain's economic growth in comparison with other major world economies. In the world league table of economic growth (measured by assess-

Table 14.2

Gross national product – percentage change on previous year

	1961	1962	1963	1964	1965	1966	1967 (estimate)
Britain	3·3	−0·3	3·0	4·9	2·3	1·2	1·0
USA	1·8	5·4	3·9	5·0	5·9	5·4	3·0
Canada	0·2	6·2	4·0	5·9	6·9	5·9	4·0
Japan	16·1	5·7	7·5	13·8	3·2	9·0	10·0
France	4·5	5·8	4·7	5·5	3·4	5·0	4·5
West Germany	5·5	4·4	3·2	6·5	4·8	2·6	0·5
Italy	8·3	6·0	5·0	2·9	3·5	5·5	5·5

Source: National Institute of Economic and Social Research.

ing the percentage growth of GNP) Britain always seems to come out badly (see Table 14.2). Does this mean that Britain is slipping behind and if so what are the reasons for this?

In terms of its own wealth, Britain is steadily forging ahead, but it does seem that the chief rivals are able to maintain an overall faster pace of growth. There is no single factor that explains this simply. The European countries were all devastated by the war to a greater extent than Britain and have been able to build up industries with modern capital equipment and techniques, obviously to Britain's detriment, but this argument is becoming a little thin by the late 1960s.

A fair comparison is difficult in any case because the countries concerned have not started off from an equal base, nor are they, necessarily, at an equivalent stage of economic growth. Japan, for instance, started a long way behind and still has leeway to make up before living standards compare with those in Britain. Italy, similarly, has ground to make up.

It is to be expected that a developing country will devote a higher proportion of its GNP to investment to secure the rapid growth of its major industries at the expense of the living standards of its people. The Soviet Union has demonstrated this forcibly by investing 25 to 30 per cent of its GNP over a long period of time, thereby achieving spectacular growth but limiting personal income in the process. In the early stages of development the direction of investment is easy to determine, but as an economy reaches a sophisticated stage the task of allocating investment becomes much more difficult. There is much capital equipment to replace because it is either worn out or obsolete, and the choice of investment in new fields of development becomes an involved one. We have noted this in relation to fuel and power, and to steel in particular, in Britain. Thus the percentage of GNP devoted to investment declines in importance in a modern economy while the quality of investment becomes of much

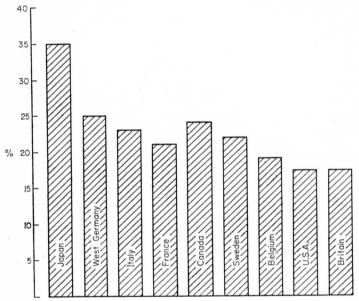

Figure 14.1. *Average Investment Rates* 1956–1963, *percentage of GNP going to capital formations.*
Source: *The Economist*, 27 May 1967.

greater significance. The desirable situation is one where the investment percentage is high and where the quality is maximum, but this is interpreting matters only in terms of economic growth; no one has attempted to set an optimum ratio of investment and consumption because this is a moral rather than an economic question. Gross investment in Britain is, on average, about 17 per cent of GNP while the rates in many of the advanced countries are much higher. The quality of investment in Britain is therefore very important.

There is a link here between what has been said about the need of British industry, in the light of its past development, to keep one step ahead and the quality of investment. It is possible that British industry as a whole still maintains a proclivity for the past. Professor Barna, in 1963, in comparing Britain's export performance with that of the USA and Germany (for the National Institute of Economic and Social

Table 14.3

Trade balances (surplus of exports over imports) 1954, 1960 and 1961 (in billion dollars)

	United Kingdom			United States			West Germany		
	1954	1960	1961	1954	1960	1961	1954	1960	1961
Fast-growing machinery and chemicals	0·4	0·5	0·6	1·1	2·2	2·3	0·7	1·5	2·0
Motor and aircraft	0·9	1·4	1·5	1·9	1·9	2·0	0·5	1·3	1·4
Other engineering and chemical products	1·5	1·8	1·9	2·6	2·6	2·8	1·3	2·4	2.5
Other manufactures	1·6	0·8	1·0	0·8	−1·1	−1·2	0·7	0·4	0·4
Total manufactures	4·4	4·5	5·0	6·4	5·6	5·9	3·2	5·6	6·3
Food and raw materials	−6·4	−7·4	−7·0	−2·9	−1·8	−1·4	−2·5	−4·3	−4·5
Total trade balance	−2·0	−2·9	−2·0	3·5	3·8	4·5	0·7	1·3	1·8

Britain has the largest import surplus of food and raw materials but the smallest export surplus of manufactures to pay for it.

Source: Prof. Barna. See text p. 219.

Research) demonstrated that Britain's exports were at their relatively best position in those goods that were less sophisticated and more orthodox, such as bicycles, electric batteries, the older vintage plastics rather than the latest ones, non-electric typewriters rather than electric ones, and so on.[87] This implies a concentration on goods whose production requires too little capital or too unsophisticated a technology. If that is the case, at least some of the blame for Britain's poor performance in comparison with other advanced economies must be attributed to economic evolution. Not only are the consequences of an early industrialization involved here, but so also is a concentration on the markets of the underdeveloped Commonwealth countries. Providing goods for these areas has helped to expand Britain's economy in the past, but the greatest export potential now lies in Europe itself. Britain's competitors have been taking full advantage of European expansion while Britain has still been devoting effort to selling to the Commonwealth countries where incomes are not so high and demand is for the less sophisticated goods. Britain's serious efforts to enter the Common Market indicate that the need for expansion in European markets is understood and that the Commonwealth markets will not receive the same priority.

It is sometimes said that the British defence programme affects her ability to make fast economic growth, the implication being that Britain devotes more investment (percentage of GNP) to defence than her economic rivals. Certainly Britain's political and economic past has left a commitment that seems well beyond the country's size. The debate over Britain's rôle East of Suez has economic connotations as well as political ones. The cuts in the defence programme made early in 1968 were intended to ease Britain's economic difficulties in this way, by drastically curtailing military commitments overseas. Countries such as Sweden and Switzerland have shown what economic advantage can be reaped from a disengagement from international power politics. Yet it can be argued that France devotes a greater percentage to her defence budget and still boasts a more impressive growth rate, while the USA through investment in defence projects greatly stimulates the scientific and technological research and development which is necessary for the sophisticated industries. Britain is, perhaps, at the transitional stage, as illustrated by the aircraft industry, where there is insufficient investment capacity to promote independent defence projects (e.g. the cancellation of the TSR 2), whereas the defence commitments that Britain has acquired, and the need to keep industries one step ahead, demand that the results of these projects should be available. The solution seems to lie once again in Britain's entry into Europe where both of these requirements could be met.

Planning

One other factor needs to be mentioned in the context of economic growth. How necessary is planning? We have considered the increasing rôle of government control in Britain's economy. The French economy has been subject to 'Le Plan' since shortly after the last war and the French record of growth is a good one. But France is not the only advanced economy to have experienced a 'miracle' since the war. West Germany and Japan have done the same thing without any similar overall government supervision. Nonetheless French planning must take credit for economic expansion and everything points to the French example being emulated in Britain because Britain has reached the appropriate stage of economic evolution. French planning, after all, has been based upon planning by consent rather than strict government control, and this is the aim of the latest developments in British policy.

The influence of geography

The economic activities of the British people (economic history) have been of tremendous importance in founding Britain's present wealth, while the economic combination of the physical environment and the available resources (economic geography) has been a vital contributory factor; both history and geography go a long way to explain not only the nature of Britain's economy but its difficulties.

Britain's geographical situation between east and west trade has served her well in the past and played a leading part in her economic evolution. As a maritime nation her merchants were able to take great advantage of their skilled seamanship in establishing trade routes along the sea lanes which were the most effective lines of communication before the nineteenth century. In the days when the national economic unit was small and economic rivalry was growing, an insular situation close to Europe proved to be a trump card. A good system of rivers navigable a long way inland, subsequently supplemented by a canal network, facilitated trade. Also, as we have seen, a plentiful supply of the two vitally important natural resources of iron ore and coal helped to promote the transition to an industrialized economy. These geographical advantages are now not nearly so important. The advent of new means of communication and the greatly diminished rôle played by Britain's own natural resources in her manufacturing industries have compelled Britain to alter the course of her economic development in deference to the changes that have ensued. Insularity has become from the point of view of economic expansion something of an embarrassment, and the need to import so many raw materials has greatly aggravated the problems concerned with the balance of payments. Britain is thus in the process of acquiring new geographical advantages by close association, if not unification with, the continent of Europe. The essential economic advantages of close association with Europe have already been mentioned, but the effects of the earlier geographical advantages that Britain enjoyed should not be forgotten. They were in no small measure responsible for Britain's present position as one of the advanced economies of the world. While they were pertinent to economic change they contributed to the conversion of Britain from an agricultural to an industrial economy where a mere 4 per cent of the working force are engaged in agriculture.

The impact of geographical factors that last for so many centuries must leave their mark on a nation, even if those factors diminish ultimately in their importance. The beneficial effects are plain to see in the high standard of living that Britain enjoys and the sophistication of her industries, but there are disadvantages too. They are to be found partly in the early industrial towns and cities as a physical reminder bequeathed to us of what was once of much greater significance. Although much has been done in recent years to remove the worst of the industrial slums that originated in the last century there is still evidence of the unsightliness caused by the pursuit of coal and iron ore in the earlier days of capitalism.

Of greater effect is the impact made by the trends of economic geography on the attitudes of mind of the people of this country. Here again, there is resistance to change. Comment has already been made on the reluctance to accept the declining importance of the major natural resource of coal, not only to the detriment of the industry itself but also to the disadvantage of the substitute industries; mention must also be made of the attachment of the British people to their insularity. Several hundred years of economic and political independence made possible by a sea barrier have produced an aloofness with regard to the Continent which the British are finding hard to lose and which has made close association with Europe difficult. Perfidious Albion is an epithet with geographical causes even if the connotations are political. The movement towards European economic unity, to which Britain is now anxious to commit herself, has been held back largely by reluctance to accept that the economic geography of centuries has changed its emphasis and requires a similar change in attitude of mind. Since 1945 the movement has gathered impetus. While the continental countries have taken active steps towards unification, Britain has hung back; the issue has been treated to a protracted national debate (but not a referendum) which has ultimately produced a majority opinion in favour of the Common Market. The success of the Common Market with Britain as a member would depend very much upon the genuineness of Britain's change of attitude, and this has yet to be put to the test. The French reluctance to accept Britain into the Common Market in the 1960s was made possible only because of British reluctance to enter in the 1950s.

The attitude of mind of a nation of people is a somewhat nebulous concept and because it cannot in any way be measured statistically the economist fights shy of it, but it is nonetheless a very important psychological factor in determining economic activity. Economists have recognized the importance of the psychological factor in economic growth and, indeed, an attempt is regularly made to measure business confidence at a national level; in the same way the attitudes of worker to employer, manager to union, citizen to government control all affect the efficiency and enthusiasm of the individual and, hence, the nation itself. It has been a major purpose of this book to demonstrate that the attitude of mind of the British nation (and in this it differs in no way from other nations) is greatly influenced by its past. The long period of economic evolution from the days of laissez-faire to the present mixed economy has created attitudes that have become an enduring part of the economic life of this country. The relationship between the three authorities that control economic production – the government, the owners/managers and the unions – are dominated by attitudes of mind dictated by the past; an understanding of these attitudes helps to make resistance to change more explicable and for that reason to make the change itself more acceptable. Von Neumann once wrote 'there is no cure for change', and since there is something in each one of us which militates against change an understanding of the factors of change is helpful.

The British economy is now enormously complex and the need for its proper and efficient control is publicly recognized. It is a feature of our time that economics has come to be regarded by the public as a modern essential to good business and good government. The study of economics has taken its place as a necessary part of education in a technological age. The success of economic management can be measured by the increase in the standard of living that is observable now because of the rapid pace of change.

The comparison of the performance of this country with that of its rivals in the rest of the world has led to a self-criticism in Britain in the 1960s because the economic growth of this country, fast though it has been, has not been as fast as elsewhere. The point of greatest interest in what has turned into almost a welter of self-reproach, is that on all sides it has been accepted that Britain still clings to her past. It is felt that the image of Britain is of a nation steeped in the past (the Beefeater image abroad), not of a forward-looking country devoted to rapid economic growth by investment in the most modern techniques.

This period of self-criticism has, perhaps, been carried too far. Critical appraisal of one's faults can be healthy, but persistence in such a practice for too long can be very damaging to self-confidence. This book, it is hoped, will place the matter in a reasonable perspective. Certain features of Britain's economy, for example the international nature of its currency, are a direct result of the past and cannot readily be avoided even if it were desirable to do so; other features such as the condition of industrial relations in Britain stem from the past and an understanding of their evolution will help to make change possible. In the midst of all the criticism and analysis of change, it must not be forgotten that Britain is an affluent nation with every prospect of increasing her standard of living at an ever increasing pace. The only argument is how fast ought that pace to be?

References

1. W. W. ROSTOW, *Stages of Economic Growth*, Cambridge University Press, 1960.
2. J. CLAPHAM, *An Economic History of Britain*, 3 vols, Cambridge University Press, 1930–38.
3. W. ASHWORTH, *An Economic History of England 1870–1939*, new edn, Methuen, 1960.
4. *Ibid*, p. 34.
5. W. S. CHURCHILL, *The World Crisis: The Aftermath*, Butterworth, 1929, p. 32.
6. ASHWORTH, *op. cit.*, p. 288.
7. Report of the Committee of Industry and Trade, Survey of Overseas Markets, 1925, p. 10, quoted in P. Gregg, *A Social and Economic History of Britain 1760–1960*, 3rd edn, Harrap, 1962, p. 422.
8. G. C. ALLEN, *British Industries and Their Organization*, 3rd edn, Longmans 1952, p. 195.
9. A. J. YOUNGSON, *Britain's Economic Growth, 1920–66*, Allen & Unwin, 1967, p. 199.
10. J. H. DUNNING and C. J. THOMAS, *British Industry*, Hutchinson, 1961, p. 23.
11. Quoted in S. POLLARD, *The Development of the British Economy 1914–1950*, Arnold, 1962, p. 100.
12. POLLARD, *op. cit.*, p. 238.
13. POLLARD, *op. cit.*, p. 127.
14. P.E.P. Report, *Location of Industry in Great Britain*, 1939, p. 294.
15. *Ibid*.
16. Quoted by GREGG, *op. cit.*, p. 430.
17. A. SILBERSTON, 'The Motor Industry', in *The Structure of British Industry*, ed. D. Burn, Cambridge University Press, 1958, vol. 2, p. 3.
18. The three volumes that have been particularly useful for this chapter and are recommended for further reading are GREGG, YOUNGSON and POLLARD, see nos. 7, 9, 11 above.
19. J. K. GALBRAITH, *The Affluent Society*, Hamish Hamilton, 1958, p. 3.
20. A. SHONFIELD, *Modern Capitalism*, Oxford University Press for R.I.I.A., 1965.
21. E. COOPER-WILLIS, *Towards Equality*, Fabian Society, 1950.
22. I have drawn freely on CHARLES FURTH's excellent book, *Life Since 1900*, Allen & Unwin, 1956, for the relevant facts in this paragraph.
23. Treasury Report, *Committee on Turnover Taxation* (Richardson Report), HMSO, 1964.
24. R. M. TITMUSS, *Income Distribution and Social Change*, Allen & Unwin, 1962.
25. COOPER-WILLIS, *op. cit.*
26. DUNNING and THOMAS, *op. cit.*,
27. *Ibid*.
28. *Ibid*.
29. KEITH RICHARDSON, in *The Sunday Times*, 16 April 1967.
30. The *Stage One Report* of the Development Co-ordinating Committee of the British Iron and Steel Federation, p. 10.
31. O.E.C.D., quoted in *Steel Review*, April 1963.
32. *The Economist*, 7 May 1966.

33. Steel Review and the *Stage One Report* noted above have proved invaluable for the information included in this chapter.
34. Professor P. M. S. BLACKETT, Fawley Foundation Lecture, 1966, published by University of Southampton. Summary in *Esso Magazine*, vol. 16, no. 2, 1967.
35. EDWARD FENNESSY, Director, The Plessey Electronics Group, in *The Financial Times Review of British Industry*, 1967.
36. C. M. CUNDALL in *The Times Review of Industry*, 1966, vol. 4, no. 5.
37. Source: The Radio and Electronics Component Manufacturers Federation.
38. See R. J. BALL, J. R. EATON and M. D. STEUER, 'The Relationship between U.K. export performance in Manufactures and the internal pressure of demand', *The Economic Journal*, September 1966, pp. 501–18.
39. T. A. B. CORLEY, *Domestic Electrical Appliances*, Cape, 1966, p. 66.
40. *Ibid*, p. 68.
41. See M. E. BEESLEY and G. W. TROUP, 'The Machine Tool Industry' in *The Structure of British Industry*, ed. D. Burn, vol. 1, p. 361.
42. Survey of Machine Tools in *Financial Times*, 18 Sept. 1967.
43. Board of Trade Report by Machine Tool Advisory Council, *The Machine Tool Industry*, HMSO, 1960.
44. GRAHAM TURNER, *The Car Makers*, Eyre & Spottiswoode, 1963; Penguin, p. 67.
45. *Ibid*.
46. G. MAXCY and A. SILBERSTON, *The Motor Industry*, Allen & Unwin 1959, p. 79.
47. *Ibid*, p. 80.
48. GRAHAM TURNER, *op. cit.*
49. MAXCY and SILBERSTON, *op. cit.*
50. GRAHAM TURNER, *op. cit.*, p. 69.
51. Department of Economic Affairs, *Progress Report*, no. 13, January 1966.
52. GRAHAM TURNER, *op. cit.*, p. 133.
53. I am greatly indebted to two sources in particular for this chapter, GRAHAM TURNER (no. 44 above) and MAXCY and SILBERSTON (no. 46).
54. A. K. CAIRNCROSS and J. R. PARKINSON, 'The Shipbuilding Industry', in *The Structure of British Industry*, op. cit., Vol. 2.
55. POLLARD, *op. cit.*, p. 313.
56. CAIRNCROSS and PARKINSON, *op. cit.*
57. Sir STEWART MCTIER, in *British Shipping*, no. 29, 1965, p. 8.
58. B. ROBERT JOHNSTON, Chairman of Cammell Laird, in *Liverpool Daily Post Industrial Review*, 1967.
59. Report of Shipbuilding Advisory Committee, HMSO, 1961.
60. See Royal Institute of Naval Architects, *Transactions*, vol. 104, 1962.
61. M. A. SINCLAIR SCOTT, *Shipbuilding*, January 1967.
62. R.I.N.A. *Transactions*, vol. 104, 1962.
63. Association of Chemical Manufacturers, *Report on the Chemical Industry*, 1949.
64. W. B. REDDAWAY, 'The Chemical Industry', in *The Structure of British Industry*, ed. D. Burn, vol. 1, p. 224.
65. *Report on the Chemical Industry*, 1949.
66. Chemical Industries Association Report, *The Chemical Industry*, 1953.
67. DUNNING and THOMAS, *op. cit.*, p. 145.
68. Chemical Industries Association, *The Chemical Industry and North Sea Gas*, 1966.
69. DUNNING and THOMAS, *op. cit.*, p. 145.
70. *The Financial Times Review of British Industry*, 1966.
71. J. N. BARLOW, in *The Times Review of Industry*, 1966, vol. 4, no. 6.
72. Association of the British Pharmaceutical Industry.
73. D. C. HAGUE, 'The Man-made Fibres Industry', in *The Structure of British Industry*, ed. D. Burn, vol. 2.

74. S. WEBB and B. WEBB, *The Story of the King's Highway*, Longmans, 1913.
75. A very useful volume among many on transport is K. M. GWILLIAM, *Transport and Public Policy*, Allen & Unwin, 1964.
76. CLIVE JENKINS and J. T. MORTIMER, *British Trade Unions Today*, Pergamon, 1965.
77. Trades Union Congress, *84th Annual Report*, 1952.
78. BLACKETT, *op. cit.*
79. J. K. GALBRAITH, 'The New Industrial State', Reith Lectures 1966, *The Listener*, 17 November–22 December 1966.
80. *Fortune Magazine*, Time Inc., 1966, quoted by CHRISTOPHER LAYTON in *Encounter*, April 1967.
81. CHRISTOPHER LAYTON in *Encounter*, April 1967.
82. *The Economist*, 8 April 1967.
83. GALBRAITH, *op. cit.*
84. See C. P. SNOW, 'Education and Sacrifice', Richmond Lecture, Downing College, Cambridge, 1 May 1963, reported in *New Statesman*, 17 May 1963.
85. P. GREGG, *Social and Economic History of Britain, 1760–1960*, 3rd edn, Harrap, 1962, p. 573.
86. EDWARD HEATH, speech at Milton, 29 May 1967, reported in *Daily Telegraph*, 30 May 1967.
87. Figures published in *The Times*, 3 April 1963.

Further reading

G. C. ALLEN, *British Industries and their Organization*, Longmans, 1959.

G. C. ALLEN, *The Structure of Industry in Britain*, Longmans, 1961.

W. ASHWORTH, *An Economic History of England 1870–1939*, Methuen, 1960.

W. ASHWORTH, *A Short History of the International Economy 1850–1950*, Longmans, 1951.

A. BIRNIE, *An Economic History of the British Isles*, 3rd edn, Methuen, 1955.

N. BRANTON, *Economic Organization of Britain*, English Universities Press, 1966.

D. BURN, ed., *The Structure of British Industry*, 2 vols, Cambridge University Press, 1958.

P. DEANE and W. A. COLE, *British Economic Growth, 1688–1959*, Cambridge University Press, 1962.

P. DONALDSON, *Guide to the British Economy*, Penguin, 1965.

J. H. DUNNING and C. J. THOMAS, *British Industry: Change and Development in the 20th Century*, Hutchinson, 1961.

M. W. FLINN, *Readings in Economic and Social History*, Macmillan, 1964.

C. FURTH, *Life Since 1900*, Allen & Unwin, 1956.

P. GREGG, *A Social and Economic History of Britain 1760–1960*, 3rd edn, Harrap, 1962.

W. JOHNSON, J. WHYMAN, and G. WYKES, *A Short Economic and Social History of 20th Century Britain*, Allen & Unwin, 1967.

J. M. LIVINGSTONE, *Britain & the World Economy*, Penguin, 1966.

S. POLLARD, *The Development of the British Economy 1914–1950*, Arnold, 1962.

H. W. RICHARDSON, *Economic Recovery in Britain 1932–39*, Weidenfeld & Nicolson, 1967.

A. SHONFIELD, *British Economic Policy since the War*, Penguin, 1959.

A. SHONFIELD, *Modern Capitalism*, Oxford University Press for R.I.I.A. 1965.

L. D. STAMP and S. H. BEAVER, *The British Isles*, 4th edn, Longmans, 1954.

W. M. STERN, *Britain Yesterday and Today*, Longmans, 1962.

A. J. YOUNGSON, *Britain's Economic Growth 1920–1966*, Allen & Unwin, 1967.

Index